South Asia at Gunpoint Small Arms, Nuclear Weapons Proliferation

SOUTH ASIA AT GUNPOINT

SMALL ARMS, NUCLEAR WEAPONS PROLIFERATION

V. Sahay. Comdt. (Retd.)

NEHA PUBLISHERS & DISTRIBUTORS
DELHI

Publisher
NEHA PUBLISHERS & DISTRIBUTORS
4832/24,Prahlad Lane,S-207 Ansari
Road, Daryaganj, Delhi-110002
Ph.: 43570976, 23278261
Email: nehapubdistributors@gmail.com

Edition: 2018

ISBN: 978-93-80318-70-7

Laser Typesetting
JEE-VEE Graphics, Delhi

Price: 1195/-

Printed
Vikas Computers, Delhi

Contents

Preface

The terms 'small arms' and 'light weapons' - often used co-terminously - have come into common use in recent years. The definition of the light arms and light weapons used by the Small Arms Survey covers both military-styled weapons and commercial firearms (handguns and long guns). Small guns include weapons like revolvers and self-loading pistols, rifles and carbines, assault rifles, sub-machine guns and light machine guns. Light weapons are heavy machine guns, hand–held under barrel and mounted grenade launchers, portable and anti aircraft guns, recoilless rifles, portable launchers of anti-tank and anti-aircraft missile system and mortars of less than 100-meter calibre.

During the Cold War, arms control negotiations have focused on major weapons systems like nuclear bombs, ballistic missiles, and aircraft. This was partly because the devastation that a nuclear war could cause. However, these are not the weapons that are being used in many of today's conflicts. Today's conflicts now depend almost entirely on small arms and light weapons. Therefore to reduce armed conflict and global insecurity, there is need to focus attention on these weapons. The lethal nature of these weapons together with their ready availability and ease of handling is at the root of the small arms problem. Consequently the problem has acquired greater international attention.

This book is also reflects briefly on ongoing global arms race, arms trade and increasing military expenditures and defence budgets of world nations.

—Editor

1

Arms Production, Exports and Control

Arms production and arms trade should be addressed within the political and security pillar of the ASEM process. Three of the EU ASEM countries are among the most prominent arms exporters - France, the UK and Germany. Of the top importers three countries are from East Asia: China, South Korea and Taiwan. Only China is itself a significant arms exporter. However, the flow of arms trade is like a river going one direction - towards Asia. Despite the fact that some recipient states embarked long ago on the creation of a domestic defence industry, they are still dependent on importing supplies.

There is an Asian as well as a European side to arms exports and production of the countries participating in the ASEM process, but this only tells a partial story. Significant differences exist both within and between regions. Europe is home to three of the ten biggest arms manufacturers worldwide. The Japanese Mitsubishi Heavy Industries with a military turnover of US$ 3.6 billion lies just behind the military industries from the US, the UK and France/Germany, making it by far the biggest arms manufacturer of Asia. Arms production within both Europe and Asia is too diverse to be analysed as one single region. For instance, weapons production in South Korea cannot be compared with Cambodia and Greece (a top ten arms importer) and Germany are playing a very different role in the arms market. Furthermore, the provision in the Japanese constitution against arms trade is not matched in any of the EU countries. These differences indicate the need for further research in establishing the significance of the arms trade and arms production in the ASEM process and for identifying the arms trade connections between the European Union and Asia ASEM countries.

ENHANCED PARTNERSHIPS

In the European Commission Framework document for 'Enhanced Partnerships between Asia and Europe' the latest outline of Europe's Asia policy is given. One of the few remarks on arms trade in the document identifies arms trafficking as a common concern on the level of Ministries of Justice and Home Affairs. Arms traffickers are working across boundaries and co-operation in this field is essential to tackle the illegal flow of arms. One example from 1999 illustrates how an Israeli businessman transported 40 armoured personnel carriers from Germany to Iran. The arms followed a route through the Netherlands, Britain and Singapore before reaching Iran. The Israeli businessman was in close contact with a South Korean arms dealer known to sell arms to Iran. To tackle this kind of flows concerted action between law enforcement bodies of all involved countries is essential.

The Framework document also states that co-operation should exist "for the early and comprehensive ratification of major international Instruments such as the Comprehensive Test Ban Treaty or the Conventions on small arms and anti-personnel mines." Regional and global security is certainly helped by an orchestrated implementation of those conventions. Landmines are a hidden killer and the removal of those weapons from the stocks of armies is essential for the security of those wanting to use the land for productive purposes such as agriculture, leisure and transport. Illegal small arms are causing death and destruction in all parts of the world and their wide distribution leads to killings by criminals, gangs and paramilitaries. The small arms convention is also addressing those used by resistance groups.

The killings by armies, democratically controlled or not, are outside this Convention and so its implementation is limited to law enforcement and control by the government. The scope of arms control is too limited when it stops at the level of law enforcement and nuclear testing. Such an approach uses a narrow concept of security - that is military security.

Arms trade is a way of beefing-up allies, with consequences for regional balances of power and relations between nations and as such part of the conservative security debate. Moreover, major arms deals involving hundreds of millions or even billions of dollars of government expenditure cannot be left out of a genuine people's oriented security debate. Arms trade and acquisitions are part of such a security debate and for this reason should be part of the Framework document.

Finance Packages and Debt

When the EU adopted a strategy on Asia in 1994, it clearly identified the increase in the ambitious armament programmes in the Asian region as one of the factors "which could disrupt world equilibrium and thereby impinging on Europe's Common Foreign and Security Policy objectives." In the 2001 update of the Asia Strategy however, there is less attention to the security dimension of the relationship, with the exception of the issue of small arms trade and nuclear testing.

There can hardly be any justification for this omission. Although the impression exists that arms trade to the ASEM countries declined due to the economic crisis of 1997, this is not yet reflected in the figures given by SIPRI for 1999 . Because the negotiations for arms deliveries in general take a long time it is possible that there will be a significant decrease visible in the near future. Another reason the economic crisis is not yet reflected in the figures, is that Arms companies made financial arrangements with governments and banks, such as low interest loans and favourable re-payment schedules to back up ongoing arms deals and negotiations.

'Buy now, Pay later' became the modus operandi of both arms exporters and importers. An official of the British Ministry of Defence explained it in this way: "In the United Kingdom, we view innovative financing packages as a key factor in any likely success". The Defence business was not willing to let existing deals collapse and used financial flexibility to secure additional new deals. Sales did not stop and some were merely postponed. This of course has led to further public debt. Conveniently, the international attention on the burden of debt on state budgets was put aside in order to continue arms trade.

Growing Demand

Besides, the long term effects of the crisis will be downplayed by new developments. Analysts see a growing demand for arms in South East Asia. The Malaysian Defence Minister Najib Razak told the well attended Defence Services Asia (DSA) arms fair: "With the economy of most of these countries back on track there will be a projected increase in the defence expenditure to procure platforms, weapon systems and solutions to meet national requirements." Defence companies likewise felt rewarded for participating in the DSA 2002. Malaysia alone ordered weapons valued US$ 958 million in April 2002. According to an Australian analyst, the process will go more rapidly in Southeast Asia than in the nineties: "Those that haven't started to move with new fighters, new surface combatants, new subs, are very quickly going to."

Issues raised in the nineties are very much back in the debates on arms trade in Asia. Is an arms race ongoing or not?. Do the acquisitions find their logic in modernisation, overhaul or refurbishment? Is it old shopping lists which now materialise? All these questions which had been set aside for five years are once again on the agenda.

However, there are also new issues with the turmoil in Indonesia being an important new factor. What is not yet very much back in the discussion is the ASEAN Regional Forum (ARF) or any other initiative on genuine regional security co-operation. Military exercises with the US and Australia are the most developed forms of regional military co-operation at present. The absence of a multilateral framework for regional security co-operation seriously hampers confidence among the countries in the region and arms acquisitions of one country are followed by similar acquisitions by neighbouring countries.

9/11 Becomes a New Sales Pitch

According to Malaysia's Defense Minister Razak when he defended the Malaysian arms acquisitions during the DSA arms fair "The 9/11 attack drastically changed the outlook toward national security". By invoking the 9/11 terrorist attacks, he was joining those government leaders who have used the 9/11 events to popularize a new sales pitch for arms acquisitions. The strike on the World Trade Center and Pentagon is a weak rationale for placing submarines and fighter aircraft on the shopping list of many East and Southeast Asian countries. These are not the best weapons in the fight against terrorism. The current weapons acquisitions are high-tech buys demonstrated during the Second Gulf War on Iraq (1990-91). Furthermore, the latest orders and wish lists follow the images of US technology shown on the Afghan battlefield: the integration of remote operation, new observation techniques, state of the art Information Technology, improved precision guided munitions, and lasers. According to an Australian expert, "we will see increasing sophistication, not only of the platforms, the ships, tanks and aircraft, but of the weapon systems that go with them."

The 9/11 attacks and the creation of US led coalition against terrorism provided the rationale for lifting arms embargoes and relaxing arms export policies on more advanced weapon systems as a reward to countries for their participation. This applied to the Middle East, South Asia, and also in Southeast Asia e.g. Indonesia. The restrictions on military co-operation between Jakarta and Washington (developed between 1994 and 2000) have been under pressure ever since. Likewise the Philippines has received 100 million US$ in military assistance, and has allowed the intervention of US Special Forces in Mindanao.

An additional factor for further militarisation in the region is Missile proliferation and the re-emergence of the US Star Wars programme - pushing military budgets ever higher. According to John Chipman, Director of the International Institute for Strategic Studies in London, " The nature of missile proliferation in the region holds in prospect the kind of arms race that was not seen in the first half of the 1990s"

Defence Industry in East and Southeast Asia

The economic crisis of 1997 did change the picture of the defence industry in Asia. Domestic defence industries in Southeast Asia are opening their firms to foreign investment to build equity and market links with Western nations for capital, technology and markets. Malaysia recently indicated that it wants to become a regional hub to help international defence firms to penetrate Asian markets and most of the ASEAN defence industries are eager to find a foreign partner to attract market access as well as capital. This path is also followed by South Korea.

The French Thales company has a joint venture with Samsung. Taiwan wants to build the submarines offered by the US in 2001 at the China Shipbuilding Corp. as well as import the technology from abroad. All this is underlining dependence on Western funds and weapon technology, developed with large sums on Research & Development programmes (R&D) -estimated at US$ 39.3 billion in the US and at US$ 9.1 billion in Europe annually.

Singapore Technologies follows another route similar to what Western firms do - buying what it needs mainly in the US. This excludes the real state-of-the-art technology because this is prevented from foreign participation even by key allies. Of the six ASEAN countries which are producing small arms at home, only Singapore Technologies has a sound economic policy and export record. It exported ordnance, machine guns and assault rifles to a wide range of regions of tension. Other countries produce arms against higher market prices - which has more to do with national pride than with sound economics and the rule of the market.

The Chinese defence industry still produces obsolete weapon systems. It is not yet able to start the reorganisation process demanded to generate the capacity needed for the technological advanced weapon systems which the Chinese military want to possess. There has been little change in the Japanese weapons industry. However, as a result of the economic recession the Japanese car industry was opened up to foreign investment. Renault took this opportunity and its investment in Nissan resulted in the sale of the military division of Nissan Motor Corp. to Ishikawajima-

Harima Heavy Industries. This reflects the imperative to keep arms production in Japanese hands.

INDIA'S UNENDING DEFENCE EXPENDITURE

Despite criticism from various circles that India is not investing more to tackle development issues as millions remain mired in poverty; the Indian government's ambitious modernisation plan for its military is in full swing. In February this year, Indian military procurement units descended on the DefExpo 2010 trade fair in New Delhi. Inaugurating the Indian Defence Exhibition, Defence Minister A.K. Antony said that India's defence expenditure, which is 2.5 percent of its gross domestic product (GDP), is going to increase.

He pointed out, "our defence industry is open up to 100 percent for Indian private sector, while foreign direct investment is allowed up to 26 percent." Antony further indicated that our government is committed to rapid modernisation of armed forces. Over the next 12 years, India is set to spend a whopping US$200 billion on defence acquisitions to replace its outdated inventory. In this regard, on February 15, 2010, a report of the Indian strategic defence magazine (India Strategic's DefExpo) revealed that 70 per cent of the inventory of the Indian armed forces is 20-plus years old, and needs to be replaced with the modern technology.

It explained that nearly half of this funding ($100b) will go to the Indian Air Force (IAF), which would need to replace more than half of its combat jet fleet as well as the entire transport aircraft and helicopter fleet.

The army needs new guns, tanks, rocket launchers, multi-terrain vehicles, while the navy needs ships, aircraft carriers and new range of nuclear submarines.

In three from 1994 to 1997 India's defence budget was increased from 20 percent to 24.4 percent. For the financial year 2001-2002 defence has been allocated Rs 620,000.00 million. This amount shows an increase of Rs 75,000 million as compared to previous year's revised estimates of Rs 544,610 million. In 2009, India increased its defence budget by a whopping 28.2 percent or Rs 130,000.00 million. Some experts estimate that military spending will increase further, totalling as much as 200 billion dollars over the period to 2022.

India's military has planned a massive upgrade of its mainly 1990s-era weapons systems which is mostly from the former Russia. The plans include the purchase of 126 new combat aircraft to replace an ageing fleet of MiG-21s..The US has emerged as a potential military supplier to India since the two countries signed a deal of civil energy technology in 2008, which lifted sanctions on New Delhi in order to import nuclear technology. India is likely to become a major customer for the US military-industrial complex over the next few years. During the recent visit of the US Secretary of State Robert Gates to New Delhi, American Defence officials, however, have said that US weapons sales to India would not be a focus of the trip. Regardless of such denials, the key reason for the Gates' visit can be found in the fact that India is planning to raise its military budget by 50% to almost $40 billion, making military expenditure 3% of the annual GDP. In contrast to India's planned defence expenditures, Pakistan's entire 2009-10 budget amounts to little over $30 billion.

India, the largest arms buyer among emerging nations, accounted for 7.5 per cent of all international arms sales between 2000 and 2007. It has spent billions of dollars in the past few years on purchases of planes, radars and ships from Britain, France, Germany and Russia and Israel.

In recent years, India has bought reconnaissance aircraft from US aerospace major Boeing worth 2.1 billion-dollars, medium range missiles for 1.4 billion dollars from Israeli Aerospace Industries, and signed an upgrade service contract with the Russian Aircraft Corporation to upgrade its MiG 29 squadrons for 965 million dollars. Several deals are planned for the near future including one of the largest arms contracts of recent times—a 11-billion-dollar project to acquire 126 multi-role combat aircraft.

It is mentionable that after 9/11, both India and Israel which had openly jumped on Bush's anti-terrorism enterprise are acting upon a secret diplomacy, targeting Pakistan China, Iran and Syria. In this context, Indo-Israeli secret diplomacy could be assessed from the interview of Israel's ambassador to India, Mark Sofer published in the Indian weekly Outlook on February 18, 2008. Regarding India's defence arrangements with Tel Aviv, Sofer had surprisingly disclosed "We do have a defence relationship with India, which is no secret" and "with all due respect, the secret part will remain a secret." As regards joint exercises, Sofer replied, "Certain issues need to remain under wraps for whatever reason."

Notably, India's 'The Tribune' wrote on September 10, 2003, "India and Israel took giant leaps forward in bolstering the existing strategic ties", and Tel Aviv has "agreed to share its expertise with India in various fields such as anti-fidayeen operations, surveillance satellites, intelligence sharing and space exploration." With the support of Israel, New Delhi has been acquiring an element of strategic depth by setting up logistical bases in the Indian Ocean for its navy. In fact, India wants to become a mini-superpower of the region and hence it uses the pretext of deterrence against Pakistan and China. In this context, New Delhi with the support of US and Israel has presumed peace-loving Pakistan and China as their arch enemies, but it does not admit officially.

In May, 1998, when India detonated five nuclear tests, Islamabad was compelled to follow the suit through its own atomic experiments. But Pakistan which so far relied upon the minimum nuclear deterrence has again been forced by India's unending spending on arms purchases to counterbalance the former. In this regard, Pakistan has signed a number of agreements with China. Nevertheless, currently, more than half of India's budget is allocated for military, paramilitary, various security forces and debt servicing. That leaves less than half for everything else including infrastructure development projects, education, healthcare, poverty alleviation, and various human services. New Delhi' s latest arms buildup will leave even less for what India needs most to lift hundreds of millions of its citizens from abject poverty, hunger illiteracy and disease.

Indian civil society organisations, while complaining of excessive defence spending indicated that the government spends 2.35 per cent of GDP on defence, but only 1.72 per cent on the social sector. The defence budget for 2009-2010 is 29 billion dollars, up 34 percent over the previous one. Indian defence analyst

Ravinder Pal Singh, while calling New Delhi's unending defence spending at the cost of poverty-alleviation—with security requirements competing with socioeconomic concerns for money calls it guns-versus-butter question.

Even some of Indian officials are surprised in relation to Indian defence expenditure which has no bounds. For example, an official of the country's finance ministry remarked, "There is a dilemma…poverty needs to be eradicated to prevent men from taking to the guns…but more funds for security means less money for poverty alleviation." Meanwhile, a report of United Nations pointed out that India ranks 134th of 182 countries on the United Nations Development Programme's Human Development Index. It estimated that 50 per cent of the world's undernourished population lives in India. Nearly 31 per cent of the billion-plus Indians earn less than a dollar a day.

Secretary General of the Control Arms Foundation of India Binalakshmi Nepram said, "When people are dying of poverty and bad sanitation, what protection will arms provide them?" On the one hand, international community has been making strenuous efforts for world peace in wake of global financial crisis and war against terrorism, on the other, India has initiated deadly nuclear arms in South Asia where people are already facing multiple problems of grave nature. Majority of South Asian people are living below the poverty level, lacking basic facilities like fresh food and clean water. While yielding to acute poverty, every day, some persons commit suicide in India, Pakistan, Sri Lanka etc.

Setting aside regional problems, and resolution of Indo-Pak issues-especially thorny dispute of Kashmir, Indian rulers state that they don't have any aggressive designs. But it becomes a big joke of the 21st century, reminding a maxim, "armed to the teeth, but no enemy", if we take cognisance of India's unending defence expenditure.

MILITARY EXPENDITURE AND ARMS TRANSFERS

Although the term 'globalization' did not appear until recently, the notion of globalization has existed for a long time. The concept is being used for a wide variety of phenomena and trends and the descriptions of current trends in globalization and the conclusions as regards its impact differ accordingly. There exists not one discourse of globalization but several. In a recent survey of the debate and the literature, five major discourses on globalization are identified, basically falling into the areas of economics, sociology, political science, culture and ecology. All these aspects of globalization, together with the globalization of technology, have an impact of the trends and patterns in military expenditure and arms transfers, directly or indirectly by their impact on the causes of military expenditure, arms production and arms transfers.

The process of globalization has gone through several phases during which the various aspects have assumed different importance. During the cold war period, the political aspects were predominant. The impact of this phase of globalization on trends and pattern of military expenditures and arms transfers was significant and is well documented. During the subsequent, current, phase of globalization, the politico-military dynamic of the cold war has been overtaken by a mainly financial phase. It began in the second half of the 1980s, with the enormous expansion of trading in foreign currency after the breakdown in the 1970s of the international Bretton Woods currency system, and has resulted in the abolishing of state controls of capital markets and opening up of new financial world markets, in privatizations of public enterprises and services, in a break-up of national champion monopolies, and in a general encouragement of global competition. Simultaneously with the globalization of financial and economic activities, the end of the cold war has meant a deglobalization of political action.

These factors, around the existence of which there is fairly broad consensus, have an impact on military expenditure and arms transfers in several ways, perhaps primarily through its effect on the arms industry. While the military sector has been the sector most resistant to privatization, commercialization and reduced political control, all these trends are currently affecting the production, procurement and international transfers of arms. The arms industry is increasingly being privatized and commercialized. The European arms industry is going through a process of internationalization, until now relatively limited and primarily through cross-border joint ventures, but more recently (during 1999) also through cross-border mergers of arms producing companies. European companies are also acquiring armsproducing companies in other continents, recent examples include Australia, South Africa and South Korea, while transatlantic military-industrial links are still rare in spite of the lively debate on both sides of the Atlantic about their potential.

The increasing privatization, commercialization, competition and internationalization of arms production, have resulted in an increased pressure from the arms industry to export their excess supply of weapons, and thus to increased commercialization also of the arms trade, in which marketing and generous sales terms play an increasing role. At the same time, increased internationalization means reduced possibilities for national governments to implement national arms export regulations, since companies can choose to export their products from a business unit in another country with more liberal export regulations. For this reason, national export laws are becoming increasingly irrelevant. This points to the need for common or international export rules.

However, globalization may render also international control more difficult. The globalization of technology in general, and in the context of a gradual closing of the gap between military and civil technology, will make it increasingly difficult to control the international transfer of militarily relevant technologies in the future. The challenge is to achieve international limitations in the transfer of military technology without resorting to controls which will inhibit international transfers of all types of advanced technology, that is, also civil technologies which would benefit economic growth in the recipient countries.

A relatively new development is the impact of globalization on armed conflict and the financing of these. The fragmentation and decentralization of the state has produced a new type of wars and with it increasingly financing of wars outside traditional government defence budgets. As described by Mary Kaldor, these new wars take place in the context of extreme globalization, under which territorially-based production has more or less collapsed and production continues only of a few valuable commodities (diamonds, emeralds, drugs), which provide a source of income for whoever can provide 'protection'. These wars are fought by various types of fighting units, public and private, state and non-state, including regular armed forces or remnants thereof, paramilitary groups, self-defence units, foreign mercenaries, and regular foreign troops, usually under international auspices. During these conditions governments, like privatized military groups, need alternative sources of funding for their military activities, many of which involve criminal activities. These fall into the following categories: 1) 'Asset transfer', i.e. the redistribution of existing assets to benefit the fighting units (such as loot, robbery, hostage-taking, and deriving profits from control over market prices); 2) 'war taxes' or 'protection' money from the production of primary commodities and various forms of illegal trading; and 3) external assistance, in particular for imports, such as (a) remittances from abroad to individual families, b) direct assistance from the Diaspora living abroad; (c) assistance from foreign governments; and 4) humanitarian assistance diverted by governments and warring factions for their own use. For countries involved in such new wars, data on government military expenditure are irrelevant for measuring military expenditure. What is more important is that the set of social relationships which are formed by these systems for financing wars constitute strongly resisting factors for the ending of war.

Privatization of security is an increasing trend also in countries which are not involved in regular armed conflict but where there is a demand for more security services than the government can offer. There is an emerging group of private security companies whose main task is the provision of security in many Third World countries, especially in Africa. The demand for private security services has emerged from a combination of factors, including from western governments seeking to reduce defence budgets, African governments in search of security, international mining corporations and rebel movements. They provide a variety of services, ranging from guarding installations, protecting convoys, supporting humanitarian assistance operations to performing reconnaissance and intelligence services, providing logistical and transport support, military training, strategic planning, and engaging in combat. These companies have developed to fill the need for security in the current context of conflict in Africa, in weak states with limited government legitimacy and with limited economic resources, and in which the international community is increasingly reluctant to intervene.

MILITARY SPENDING AND ARMS SALES

Despite their being locked into this poverty trap, poorer nations are still regarded as legitimate and profitable arms customers for Western states which helped create their situation. According to a report for the US congress, arms sales to developing countries together far outweigh arms sales to developed countries. According to their definition, countries of the South accounted for 66 per cent of the value of all international arms deliveries in 2000.

Social Impacts of Conflict

The servicing of debt for arms sales obviously affects health and education, and has other social impacts in the developing world. Money spent on arms, or money spent servicing debts, means less money is spent in social and developmental programs within the country. Countries are prevented by international trade rules from unfairly supporting their own industries above the industries of other nations. Caribbean countries are not allowed to give financial aid to their banana industry on which the region depends, because it is unfair competition for the American-owned banana industry in Central and South America. The Global Agreement on Trade and Services (GATS), which is currently being pushed through the WTO, intends to extend these kinds of rules to other areas such as water, healthcare and education provision.

But at the WTO, and in all other global agreements, the military is specifically excluded from the rules governing global trade. The main WTO governing document, the General Agreement on Tariffs and Trade (GATT), states that a country cannot be prevented from taking any action 'it considers necessary for the protection of its essential security interests... relating to the traffic in arms, ammunition and implements of war and such traffic in other goods and materials as is carried on directly for the purpose of supplying a military establishment.'

In other words, the WTO GATT and other trade agreements do not apply to the arms trade. There are no international restrictions on what munitions a country can buy or sell, how much these should cost, how much a country can spend, who they buy weapons from or to what extent they subsidize their own arms industry. This process has contributed to the pattern of rich countries becoming richer, and poorer nations staying poor, or becoming poorer. Western nations are not prevented by WTO rules from subsidizing their own arms industries, and so are able to acquire military equipment at artificially low knock-down prices, while keeping the finance within the country. Moreover, the exclusion from WTO regulations means they can buy arms domestically, even when other countries are offering better products more cheaply.

Developing nations rarely have established arms industries and so buy their weaponry from abroad at a cost often way above what the equipment is worth, draining yet more money out of the country. Even when there is a local arms industry, this is usually so small that buying abroad remains cheaper. Developing nations pump cash into their own arms industries too, in attempts to improve their economies, because it is the only industry they can legally support in this way.

When seeing how trade rules benefit the rich countries, especially in the arms arena, it is not surprising that airplane and arms manufacturer Boeing was the prime sponsor of the WTO meeting in Seattle in 1999. Global agreements to break down barriers to trade are having the effect of preventing developing and middle income countries from exploiting the resources they do have to trade on the world market, keeping those countries financially subordinate to the rich West.

The argument that the arms trade creates or sustains jobs, or brings money into the national economy, is one of the most difficult arguments campaigners face. These arguments have strong political currency-people don't vote for governments that threaten their livelihood-but they are based on a fallacy which is only now becoming fully apparent.

The arms trade is an immoral business that cause death, maiming, human rights abuses and suffering around the world. It is also a business that does not bring huge economic or employment benefits to the biggest arms-exporting countries. In many cases, high government subsidies, tax breaks, insurance schemes and promotion for arms manufacturers cost governments more money than weapons producers generate for them. Countries are artificially propping up their arms industries while refusing to explore fully the potential for diversification into areas that are not only more productive and socially positive but also economically viable.

The Extent of Government Subsidies

Governments subsidize their arms sector in a number of ways. The difficult job for campaigners and academics is to show by how much, and why it is a bad thing. Information, such as how much a government spends on its own armed forces, what procurement decisions it makes, how much it spends on military research and development and how much export credit insurance it provides for arms companies, is usually secret or difficult to obtain.

Strong, well-informed estimates based on obtainable information are usually the best that campaigners can muster before issuing the challenge to governments: if we are wrong, it falls to you to prove how wrong. After all, if arms exports are big earners for state economies, wouldn't politicians be shouting it from the roof tops?

With that proviso in mind, valiant attempts to look at this issue have been made. In the US, the defence and foreign aid budgets are the largest single source of federal funding to private corporations. According to the World Policy Institute, more than half of all US weapons sales are financed by taxpayers instead of by foreign arms purchasers. During the fiscal year of 1996 (the last year for which figures were available) the US Government spent more than $7.9 billion to help companies secure just over $12 billion in agreements for new international arms sales.

Direct Subsidies

Governments' direct financial support for their arms exports can be roughly placed into a few distinct categories. Each of these subsidies results in taxpayers' money being spent, or risked, helping foreign governments to buy arms.

Export promotion-The major arms-exporting countries each year spend huge amounts of money all over the world promoting and marketing their domestic arms companies' products. Export promotion ranges from diplomatic visits by politicians to the provision of advice and support for companies marketing their systems, to regular attendance and promotion at arms exhibitions and conferences. At the US Pentagon, nearly 6,000 people were employed in 1996 to promote, broker, administer and finance arms sales abroad, at a cost of $378.2 million. In the State Department a further 75 personnel were employed, part of a defence export promotion budget of $3.7 million. And the US commerce department also plays a role, publishing 'defence market assessments' such as How to do business in Indonesia, and mounting US presence at foreign arms exhibitions. During 1996, the US Government sent equipment and personnel to 19 overseas weapons shows, at a cost of more than $5.1 million.

Export credits-Government insurance schemes to compensate arms companies when their foreign clients default on payment generally make up the bulk of the government direct subsidies. They also provide financing support for deals. Governments then attempt to recoup the cost from the defaulting nations, with usually only limited success. Often the companies insist on some kind of insurance or guarantee from their home government before embarking on large weaponry export deals. Arms sales make up, large proportions of the export credits extended in many major arms exporting countries.

The US Export-Import Credit Bank, which could be seen as the equivalent of an export credit organization, is usually prohibited from guaranteeing arms deals (though not always-Congress occasionally makes exceptions). However the US more than makes up for it in other loans and funding programs which subsidize US arms exporters.

The US Foreign Military Financing Program (FMF) received $3.35 billion in 1999 to support grants and loans for the provision of US military equipment and services to more than 24 countries. Recipients of FMF grants in recent years have included Egypt, Israel, Jordan, Turkey and the Ukraine. More funds were allocated for Africa. Another $16 million of subsidy is granted through the US Defence Export Loan Guarantee fund.

Spending distortions-governments also artificially support their arms industries by distorting their own spending on domestic military purchases. They buy more arms from domestic suppliers than really needed, they pay more than these ought to cost, and they choose domestic arms suppliers even if foreign-made equipment is cheaper and better. In any other industry, World Trade Organization rules and other free-trade legislation would prevent such spending distortions as unfair competition. But as we have seen earlier, the military is exempt from international agreements on trade. In a report by the World Policy Institute, William Hartung decries this kind of spending in the US, which he calls 'defence pork'. He argues that politicians add unnecessary and expensive military equipment purchases to the Pentagon's budget in order to please arms companies, secure or create jobs and so gain campaign donations and votes. In 1998, $3.8 billion was added by senators and officials to the amount that the Pentagon had said it needed to meet its own defence plans. While most 'defence pork' is US-bought-so not an arms export subsidy-the example shows how political pressure distorts procurement decisions.

Other Subsidies

The above are just three direct financial subsidies which governments provide for their arms industries. But there are many different ways that governments indirectly financially support their arms industries, and while it is more difficult to quantify this kind of support in concrete terms, the benefits to arms companies can be quite considerable.

Research and development (R&D)-Governments spend large portions of their defence budgets on research and development of new weapons systems, which they contract arms companies to carry out on their behalf. In 1998/99, the three big US weapons manufacturers received over $8 billion in R&D funding. Commissions and bribes-According to one World l Bank estimate, the sums distributed worldwide each year as pay-offs and bribes total $80 billion. Campaign group Transparency International (TI) has surveyed attitudes to corruption in business, and found that arms and construction companies were perceived to be the most likely to pay bribes.

Jobs in the Arms Industry

Off-set deals and joint procurement aside, a further argument-that the weapons business is a thriving employer-is also false.... the global arms industry has been gradually shrinking since the end of the Cold War.

Linked to this, the number of people employed in the sector has also fallen. Moreover, the argument that a government should spend huge amounts of money propping up an industry to safeguard a relatively small number jobs is one that only has so much credibility. Governments should no more subsidize their arms business than any other industry to safeguard jobs. Sir Samuel Brittan, the British economist and journalist, has written extensively on the weakness of the employment argument.

He says the argument is based on the myth that there is a 'lump of labour' that is engaged in making specific products, that cannot be deployed elsewhere. If defence orders are lost, those people become unemployed and unemployable, runs the line. Brittan points out that millions of people change jobs, find jobs or leave jobs every year. 'Indeed, it is almost certainly easier for arms workers, many of whom have a wide range of valued skills, to find new jobs... Where will the new jobs come from to replace those lost in exporting weapons? Other jobs, on a much greater scale, arose to take the place of handloom weavers [and] drivers of horse-drawn carts. A report by the British Ministry of Defence and York University, published in 2001, revealed that 40,000 arms export jobs would be replaced by 67,000 civilian posts if arms exports were cut in half, albeit at a lower average salary per job.

Mercenaries: The Dogs of War

Selling arms is one side; purchasing people to use them is another. The use of privately hired might is nothing new. The Romans used mercenaries, and the practice probably went back even before them. Italian merchants in the 16th century hired muscle to protect their assets and control trade routes. Colonial explorers were accompanied by hired fighters. From the mid-20th century, Western firms setting up mines and oil exploration in Africa, Asia and Latin America protected their assets by hiring armed heavies.

Mercenaries come under a number of guises, but all include the provision of military might or advice for a profit. Under the guise of 'security' for example, private military companies, consultants, advisors or training outfits, all manner of services to both governments and companies are supplied, including full participation in conflicts, the provision of arms, and armed protection of royal families and industrial plants.

Former members of security services often run modern mercenary companies, exploiting their contacts in the arms and political world. They hire disaffected, unemployed former soldiers wherever they win contracts, and source second-hand weapons and equipment for them to fight with. They will often provide whatever services are required, in exchange for hard currency or interests in mining and oil exploration. UN Special Rapporteur Bernales Ballesteros was appointed by the UN General Assembly in 1996 to report on 'the use of mercenaries as a means of violating human rights and impeding the exercise of the rights of peoples to self-determination'.

Child Soldiers

At least mercenaries can usually make their own l choices; it is different for children. There are more than half a million children (under 18s) serving in armed forces, in more than 87 countries. At least 300,000 children are actively fighting in 41 countries, including Colombia, Sri Lanka, Sierra Leone, Uganda and Chechnya.; In some countries, very young children are used as messengers, spies and equipment carriers, but by the age of 10 they are given rifles, or rapid repeating machine-guns and set to fight in conflicts they cannot possibly understand. As members of armed forces, children become lawful targets for attack, but the use of child soldiers also increases the danger faced by civilian children who come under suspicion from warring parties. Within armed forces, children are often treated brutally, suffering physical, emotional and even sexual abuse. But it is not only faraway nations mired in internal conflicts that use child soldiers. The US is the country most opposed to setting 18 as the minimum age limit for recruiting and participation in armed forces. One in every 200 of its armed personnel is 17, while many more become temporary members as part of youth military training programs.

The UK continues to recruit 16-year-olds leaving school, and the recruitment process begins even while they are still at school. British soldiers under the age of 18 fought-and died-in both the Falklands/Malvinas conflict and the Gulf War. Other countries that recruit under-18s to the armed forces, via conscription or voluntary enlistment include: Australia, Bangladesh, Belgium, Brazil, Burundi, Canada, Chile, Croatia, Cuba, Denmark, El Salvador, Estonia, Finland, France, Germany, Honduras, India, Indonesia, Iran, Iraq, Ireland, Israel, Italy, Japan, Jordan, Libya, Luxembourg, Mexico, Namibia, Netherlands, Aotearoa/New Zealand, Norway, Pakistan, Peru, Portugal, Republic of Korea, Sudan, Switzerland, Uganda and Yugoslavia.

A number of factors lead to the use of children as soldiers. Technological advances have made semi-automatic rifles light enough to be used and simple enough to be operated by a child, while rabid proliferation has made them cheap and easily obtainable. The longer a conflict goes on, the more likely children are to be 'recruited' as manpower becomes short-both young girls and boys are recruited-and new soldiers are needed to replaced the killed and injured.

Children are perceived to make obedient soldiers, they are cheap and are easy to manipulate. Children 'volunteer' or are coerced to join-up in order to survive, to prove their 'adulthood' or because it is a natural step in a culture of violence. In the Revolutionary United Front in Sierra Leone, children are held and trained for two or three months, threatened with death if they disobey orders or attempt to escape. In the Kamajors militias, they are initiated into secret societies and told they will gain magical powers and be immune to bullets if they join military forces.

Prevailing international law at the United Nations sets 15 as the minimum age for military recruitment and participation in armed conflict, though there is widespread agreement that this age is too low.

The Coalition to Stop the Use of Child Soldiers is an international movement of organizations seeking the adoption and implementation of an Optional Protocol to the Convention on the Rights of the Child (CRC) setting the minimum age for all forms of military recruitment and use in hostilities at 18 years of age.

By the end of 2001, a total of 92 countries had signed or ratified the Optional Protocol, but implementation will take many years and a great deal of effort. Programs to prevent child recruitment, including monitoring, providing alternatives, and establishing proper procedures, as well as programs to ensure safe demobilization and integration of former child soldiers are particularly needed.

Landmines: The Legacy

Children, whether child soldiers or not, are often the main victims of landmines, perhaps the most vicious weapons brokered by the arms dealers. In the words of the International Campaign to Ban landmines, Put simply, anything that landmines can do to an enemy's army, they can do to a civilian population. What they cannot do is discriminate between the soldier and the civilian. Their impact cannot be confined to the duration of the battle. Thus, under the laws of war, they are an illegal weapon.'

More than any other weapon of war, landmines have received much public and legislative attention over recent decades. They are horrific because their effects on civilian communities, after battles have ended, are so long-term and devastating. Under internationally recognized definitions, landmines fall into two broad categories:

* Anti-personnel (AP) landmine-'A mine designed to be exploded by the presence, proximity or contact of a person and that will incapacitate, injure or kill one or more persons'.
* Anti-tank (AT) landmine-A device designed to detonate by more than 100 kilograms of pressure.

Whether anti-tank or anti-personnel, the effect of landmines on civilian communities is the same. They kill and maim indiscriminately, taking children just as easily as heads of households. Families are devastated not only because of the loss of a loved one, but also because their means of income or a future generation is destroyed. In the same way, those who are not killed when a landmine explodes are maimed or permanently disabled, becoming a long-term financial and emotional burden on families. Some landmines are designed to scatter thousands of shards of metal up to 50 meters, specifically to injure rather than kill.

Landmines also have devastating effects when they don't kill or maim, rendering thousands of acres of land unusable for farming or livestock. Families are forced to make a terrible choice between starvation or risking their lives on mined fields. In Cambodia alone there are over 35,000 amputees as a result of landmines, and they are just the survivors. Mine deaths and injuries in the past few decades amount to hundreds of thousands. They are a daily threat in Afghanistan, Angola, Bosnia, Cambodia, Chechnya, Croatia, Iraq, Mozambique, Nicaragua, Somalia and dozens of other countries. In December 1997, following decades of pressure from campaigners, a total of 122 governments signed the Ottawa convention, officially titled 'The Convention on the Prohibition of the Use, Stockpiling, Production and Transfer of AntiPersonnel Mines and on their Destruction'. Less than one year later the treaty became international law when Burkina Faso became the 40th country to ratify.

It is the most comprehensive international treaty of its kind, and became law quicker than any other treaty of its kind in history. But despite worldwide support, and condemnation of the use, sale and stockpiling of anti-personnel landmines, a total of 53 countries still refuse to sign including China, Egypt, Finland, India, Israel,

Pakistan, Russia and the US. The US's refusal has a devastating political influence, giving credence to other countries' refusal. The campaign continues to demand that these countries drop their opposition to the treaty, and to expand it to cover anti-tank mines and other 'area denial weapons'-a euphemism meaning they blow you up if you stray where you 'should not'-like cluster munitions and unexploded ordnance.

The 'trade' in landmines, as traditionally defined at least, is all but non-existent. Cuba, the United States, Russia, Egypt, Iran, Iraq, Burma, China, India, North Korea, South Korea, Pakistan, Singapore and Vietnam are still classified as producers of the weapons by the International Campaign to Ban Landmines, though some of them have only failed to prove written attestation to the contrary.

Military monitor Jane's Mines and Mine Clearance 2000-2001 revealed there has been a 'virtual absence of mines-legitimate or otherwise-at arms shows and military equipment exhibitions this year'. Thirty-four countries are known to have exported anti-personnel landmines in the past. All but Iraq have attested that they no longer do so. The trade in anti-personnel landmines has been confirmed to exist only in a relatively small amount of illicit trafficking.

For a book on the arms trade, it could be argued the issue should stop there-the trade in anti-personnel landmines no longer exists, and the manufacture is nominal. Unfortunately, the step is not so easily taken. The Ottawa treaty covers only certain types of antipersonnel landmines, leaving vast loopholes where area denial weapons, including anti-tank weapons, remain available and traded.

The campaign against landmines concentrates now on encouraging the states who have so far failed to sign and ratify the Ottawa treaty to do so, but it has also broadened its outlook to the new and next generations of landmines and weapons that are landmines by any other name. The weapon causing most concern for campaigners is the cluster bomb. Usually dropped from a plane, it explodes just above the ground, scattering hundreds of miniature 'bomblets' over a wide area. Many of these bomblets fail to explode, remaining in the ground, just like anti-personnel landmines, until disturbed.

Like landmines, unexploded ordnance (UXO) poses a serious threat to lives and livelihoods. Between 1964 and 1973 the US dropped a huge number of cluster bombs over Laos. It is estimated that millions of unexploded bomblets remain. Cluster munitions were used in Kosovo and Vietnam, during the Gulf War, in the Falklands/Malvinas conflict, and during the recent attacks on Afghanistan. NATO admits to a failure rate of between 8 and 12 per cent in Kosovo, leaving as many as 35,000 live bomblets on the ground. The campaign against landmines is far from won. Many countries, having signed Ottawa, pour money and research into mine clearance programs-an expensive and time-consuming business. But while taking mines away with one hand, the landmines of the future are being created and delivered across war zones all over the world. The arms companies which are earning millions from developing mine clearance equipment are also at the forefront of developing new generations of weapons, laying the foundation of devastation in the future. The International Campaign to Ban Landmines is calling for a moratorium, banning the use of cluster weapons because of their devastating and long-lasting effects.... government ministers, advisers and senior members of the armed forces frequently move into the employment of arms companies and vice versa. The supposed wall between government and the industry has a huge gaping hole in it, in which a constantly revolving door has been established.

In Frank Vogl's Earth Times article on bribery and corruption in the arms trade, he outlines how the George W Bush regime in the US takes 'this game of political pressure to an unprecedented new level'. 'Rarely before has US business taken such total charge of the Pentagon. Not only does the Secretary of Defence [Donald Rumsfeld] come from big business, but so too do the new heads of the Army, Navy and Air Force... President Bush has nominated James Roche a vice president at military aircraft seller Northrop Grumman, to become Secretary of the Air Force; Gordon England from arms and naval vessel manufacturer General Dynamics to become Secretary of the Navy.

For good measure, US Vice President Dick Cheney's wife, Lynne, serves on Lockheed Martin's board, a company which is a major contractor to the US Government and its allies.

Purchasing Power

Donations from private companies to political parties and candidates are nothing new, and have been the foundation of many scandals for governments across the Western world. Not surprisingly, because there are lucrative domestic contracts to be won, and restrictive legislation to be challenged, the arms business is a major player in the cash-for-influence money-go-round. As Lumpe and Donarski note in The Arms Trade Revealed, 'Whenever and wherever arms export policy is being made, financially self-interested representatives of the arms corporations are present. Generous campaign contributions from the weaponeer's political action committees (PACs) open doors, providing access and influence on the policy making process.

According to the World Policy Institute, the 25 leading weapons-exporting companies contributed a record \$10.8 million during the 1995-96 general election cycle in the US. Of this, \$6.6 million came in regulated PAC donations and \$4.2 million in unregulated 'soft' money-donations theoretically targeted for party-building activities, but often used to benefit specific candidates. Lockheed Martin was the leading arms corporate donor during this time. The Republican Party, more military-minded than the Democrats, received the bulk of donations.

A US Code of Conduct?

Although the US has relatively strict legislation governing the involvement of its citizens in arms brokering the world's largest arms-exporting country has comprehensively stalled on drawing up its own code of conduct on arms exports. Progressive Congress representatives have been attempting for nearly a decade to introduce a Code of Conduct on arms exports into US legislation. In 1995 International Relations Committee member Cynthia McKinney (Democrat) introduced the 'Code of Conduct on Arms Transfers Act' into the 104th Congress.

Campaign for an International Code I Finally, the US President has now been instructed by Congress to pursue multilateral steps for controlling and monitoring the arms trade. There is a real possibility that within a generation, perhaps even before, an International Code of Conduct on Arms Transfers could be introduced, building on the EU Code. In 2000 the US and the EU signed a declaration to work towards a common vision on the question of arms export controls. In May 1997, 14 Nobel Laureates met in New York to launch their own International Code as a first step to persuade arms exporting countries to adopt standards: 'Today, we speak as one to voice our common concern regarding the destructive effects of the unregulated arms trade. Together, we have written an International Code of Conduct on Arms Transfers, which, once adopted by all arms-selling nations, will benefit all humanity, nationalities, ethnicity, and religions.

Their proposed Code requires that arms transfers are only granted if transfer would complement and comply with international human rights standards, international humanitarian law, respect for international arms embargoes and military sanctions, promotes peace, security and stability, promotes human development and opposes terrorism. It calls too for public accounting of the Code's implementation, and transparent international co-operation through the UN and other bodies to improve and adjust the code as appropriate. While the proposal needs updating to account for recent changes in the international arms trade, it is a bold attempt to set in motion some international moves to curb the arms export business. It is perhaps the best tool arms trade campaigners currently have to effect change on a global scale.

A Broader View of Campaigning

From Seattle onwards, politicians and executives of the biggest and richest transnational corporations realized that wherever they went, and whatever they did, an inspired, passionate group of united people was watching, criticizing and acting for social justice and equality. Also for the first time, campaigners on widely diverse issues, from gay rights to third-world poverty, from peace and nuclear disarmament to environmental activists, joined together.

They realized their concerns overlapped in many different and complex ways. They discovered that united campaigning, using the concerns they shared as a foundation, was more effective than disparate, isolationist campaigns along strictly issue-based lines. The campaign against arms trading cannot, and should not, be considered in isolation from other concerns of social justice, except perhaps for convenience' sake.

In almost every area of global injustice, the arms trade plays its deadly role. It was revealed how the trade exacerbates conflict, promotes human rights abuses and worsens poverty in developing countries. The trade is also intimately connected to environmental destruction, inequality, immigration and asylum, gender and cultural rights, privatization and worker exploitation-in fact, most of the world's evils have their roots in the fighters, tanks, mines, guns and bullets that corrupt individuals and destroy lives.

TRADE CONTROL EFFORTS

At present, UN Security Council arms embargoes are the only global, legally binding prohibitions on arms transfers. Since 1990, the United Nations has imposed 28 arms embargoes against targets in 17 countries and one nonstate entity (Osama bin Laden and al Qaeda).

The most recent new arms embargo was introduced against Eritrea on December 23, 2009. Recent UN arms embargo resolutions recognize that nonstate actors play an important role in the contemporary arms trade and in the facilitation of arms transfers to "undesirable" end-users. States retain primary responsibility for enforcing arms embargoes and controlling the activities of arms brokers and dealers operating from their national territory or registered with their national authorities.

Sanctions committees and panels of experts charged with monitoring arms embargoes have documented the role different states have played in violating arms embargoes, such as in the case of Eritrea's involvement in transfers to Somalia. Also, states have been accused of giving shelter to individuals and entities accused of violating embargoes and of failing to investigate alleged violations but in such instances have not been sanctioned themselves. Stronger transfer control policies and increased political will are of central importance for preventing violations of UN arms embargoes.

States have long been reluctant to give up any element of national control in the field of arms transfer controls. Yet, the Iraqi invasion of Kuwait in 1990 and the scandals involving Western states and companies in the arming of Iraq prompted the development of the guidelines for conventional arms transfers, under which the permanent members of the UN Security Council agreed to exercise restraint in exports of conventional arms transfers.

Suppliers were required to ensure that exports met only the "legitimate self-defence" needs of the recipient and did not contribute to conflict or regional instability or introduce "destabilizing military capabilities in a region." There is no international agreement on what constitutes legitimate self-defence or "destabilizing military capabilities."

Efforts to improve controls on international arms transfers have primarily been driven and directed by suppliers in North America and Europe. Motivations have included protecting national industries by preventing the spread of technologies and limiting potential adversaries' access to key technologies. The prevention of conflict and human rights abuses also has long been at the heart of efforts to control the arms trade.

States, export control regimes such as the Wassenaar Arrangement, and regional organizations (e.g., the Economic Community of West African States, the EU, the Organization for Security and Cooperation in Europe, and the Organization of American States) have developed various sets of best-practice guidelines and model legislation to help ensure that arms exports do not provoke or exacerbate conflict and are not used to commit violations of human rights and humanitarian law. In addition, efforts have been undertaken to prevent the diversion of arms to terrorists, criminals, and armed groups.

Experience with existing regional mechanisms and export control regimes demonstrates some of the problems that an ATT is likely to face when it comes to ensuring harmonized interpretations of the criteria it puts in place. Despite developing agreed export criteria and mechanisms of consultation and information exchange, members of the Wassenaar Arrangement have demonstrated contrasting attitudes toward exports of arms and military equipment to a range of destinations.

Although the EU and the United States have arms embargoes against Iran, Myanmar (Burma), Sudan, and Zimbabwe, Russia continues to supply weapons systems to these states. Meanwhile, Russia has repeatedly called for restraint on arms transfers to Georgia, but Wassenaar Arrangement members the Czech Republic, Turkey, and Ukraine have continued to supply arms to Georgia. It appears that bilateral pressure on nonmembers Bosnia and Herzegovina, Israel, and Serbia led to some deals to Georgia being canceled.

Even within the EU, where states have agreed that their export license decision-making should be guided by eight criteria relating to issues such as conflict prevention, human rights, and economic development, there appear to have been differences of opinion among members regarding exports to Georgia.

EU member states reported issuing licenses worth more than $180 million between 2004 and 2007 for exports of arms and military equipment to Georgia and making exports worth almost $96 million during that period. Also during this period, EU member states denied 41 export licenses for arms and military equipment for Georgia because of concerns about the potential impact of the transfer on the possibility of conflict within Georgia. In several cases, EU member states denied an export license for the export of a particular type of military equipment that other EU member states had exported.

Researchers have found evidence of a correlation between the introduction of the politically binding EU Code of Conduct on Arms Exports in 1998 and a decline in arms exports from EU member states to countries in conflict or considered violators of international human rights and humanitarian law, but differences in decision-making on "responsible" recipients continue within the EU.

In this regard, the impact of the EU arms exports code and the legally binding Council Common Position 2008/944/CFSP, defining common rules governing the control of exports of military technology and equipment, which replaced the EU arms exports code, continues to illustrate the challenges of reaching agreement on how to interpret and implement a set of agreed common standards among (supposedly) like-minded states. Disagreements in the Wassenaar Arrangement show the difficulties in achieving similar objectives when the group is composed of states that hold very different opinions on what constitutes a responsible end-user.

2

Small Arms Development

New production methods for weapons such as stamping, riveting, and welding came into being to produce the number of arms needed. While this had been tried before, during World War I, it had resulted in quite possibly the worst firearm ever adopted by any military for use: the French Chauchat light machine gun. Design and production methods had advanced enough to manufacture weapons of reasonable reliability such as the PPSh-41, PPS-42, Sten, MP 40, M3 *Grease Gun*, Gewehr 43, Thompson submachine gun and the M1 Garand rifle.

Other Weapons commonly found During World War II include the American, Browning Automatic Rifle (BAR), M1 Carbine Rifle, as well as the Colt M1911; The Japanese Type 100 submachine gun, the Type 99 machine gun, and the Arisaka bolt action rifle all were significant weapons used during the war.

World War II saw the birth of the reliable semi-automatic rifle, such as the American M1 Garand and, more importantly, that of the first real assault rifles. The Germans essentially created and pioneered the idea of an "assault rifle" or sturmgewehr, coining the name for the species in the process. Earlier renditions that hinted at this idea were that of the employment of the Browning Automatic Rifle and 1916 Fedorov Avtomat in a *walking fire* tactic in which men would advance on the enemy position showering it with a hail of lead. The Germans first developed the FG 42 for its paratroopers in the assault and later the Sturmgewehr 44 (StG 44), the world's first true assault rifle. The FG 42 would probably hold this place but for its use of a full powered rifle cartridge making it hard to control by an unskilled operator.

Developments in machine gun technology culminated in the Maschinengewehr 42 (MG42) which was of an advanced design unmatched at the time. It spurred post-war development on both sides of the upcoming Cold War and is still used by some armies to this day including the German Bundeswehr's MG 3. The Heckler & Koch G3, and many other Heckler & Koch designs, came from its system of operation. The United States military meshed the operating system of the FG 42 with the belt feed system of the MG42 to create the M60 machine gun used in the Vietnam War.

Despite being overshadowed by self-loading/automatic rifles and sub-machine guns, bolt-action rifles remained the mainstay infantry weapon of many nations during World War II. When the United States entered World War II, there were not enough M1 Garand rifles available to American forces which forced the US to start producing more M1903 rifles in order to act as a "stop gap" measure until sufficient quantities of M1 Garands were produced.

During the conflict, many new models of bolt-action rifles were produced as a result of lessons learned from the First World War with the designs of a number of bolt-action infantry rifles being modified in order to speed up production as well as to make the rifles more compact and easier to handle. Examples of bolt-action rifles that were used during World War II include the German Mauser Kar98k, the British Lee-Enfield No.4, and the Springfield M1903A3. During the course of World War II, bolt-action rifles and carbines were modified even further to meet new forms of warfare the armies of certain nations faced e.g. urban warfare and jungle warfare. Examples include the Soviet Mosin-Nagant M1944 carbine, which were developed by the Soviets as a result of the Red Army's experiences with urban warfare e.g. the Battle of Stalingrad, and the British Lee-Enfield No.5 carbine, that were developed for British and Commonwealth forces fighting the Japanese in South-East Asia and the Pacific.

When World War II ended in 1945, the small arms that were used in the conflict still saw action in the hands of the armed forces of various nations and guerrilla movements during and after the

Cold War era. Nations like the Soviet Union and the United States provided many surplus, World War II-era small arms to a number of nations and political movements during the Cold War era as a pretext to providing more modern infantry weapons. Besides seeing conflict long after World War II ended, the small arms of World War II are now considered collector's items with many civilian firearm owners and collectors around the world due to their historical nature, low cost (due to many of these firearms now appearing on the firearms market in large numbers over the past decade), and their durability.

The Atomic Bomb

The massive research and development demands of the war included the Manhattan Project, the effort to quickly develop an atomic bomb, or nuclear fission warhead. It was perhaps the most profound military development of the war, and had a great impact on the scientific community, among other things creating a network of national laboratories in the United States.

Development was completed too late for use in the European Theater of World War II. Its invention meant that a single bomber aircraft could carry a weapon sufficiently powerful to devastate entire cities, making conventional warfare against a nation with an arsenal of them suicidal. The strategic importance of the bomb, and its even more powerful fusion-based successors, did not become fully apparent until the United States lost its monopoly on the weapon in the post-war era. The Soviet Union developed and tested their first nuclear weapon in 1949, based partially on information obtained from Soviet espionage in the United States. The competition between the two superpowers would lead to the Cold War. The strategic implications of such a massively destructive weapon still reverberate in the 21st century.

There was also a German project to develop an atomic weapon. This failed for a variety of reasons, most notably German Antisemitism. The first tier of continental high energy physicists (Einstein, Bohr, Fermi, and Oppenheimer) who did much of their early study and research in Germany, were either Jewish or, in the case of Enrico Fermi, married to a Jew. Oppenheimer, who was an American Jew, was also a Socialist by conviction, and associated with the Communist Party. When they left Germany, the only significant atomic physicist left in Germany was Heisenberg, who dragged his feet on the project. He made some faulty calculations suggesting that the Germans would need significantly more heavy water than was necessary. The project was then doomed due to insufficient resources.

The Empire of Japan was also developing an Atomic Bomb, however, it floundered due to lack of resources despite gaining interest from the government.

SMALL ARMS

The problem, however, is not confined to officially supported exports of high technology equipment such as aircraft and missiles. It is most often small arms that have been used for domestic repression in armed conflict in the last decade – the vast majority of them civilians and most of them killed by small arms. Clare Short's 2000 White Paper on International Development stated: 'Of the 40 poorest countries in the world, 24 are either in the midst of armed conflict or have only recently emerged from it. This problem is particularly acute in Africa… An estimated five million people have died.' Sophisticated defenders of arms sales agree that there is a case for banning exports of small arms altogether except for the armed forces of western democratic states. For instance Philip Towle argues that the profits Britain makes from this trade are very small despite the benefits to some specialised manufacturers.

The Scott Report of 1996 advocated legislation to put control on arms exports and arms brokering on a permanent non-emergency basis. In the spring of 2001 the Labour government undertook to introduce such legislation in the next parliament and published a draft bill with explanatory memoranda. This will introduce a licensing requirement for trafficking and brokering in arms between overseas countries. It will also introduce licensing requirements for export of military technology by electronic means. Nevertheless the government is still likely to be inhibited by two factors: its reluctance to move too far ahead of competitor countries and its belief that small arms can legitimately be sent to official governments as distinct from so called rebels.

Al Yammamah

There is a further category which is not overtly a subsidy, but is certainly a special arrangement. This is the obscure Al Yammamah deal with Saudi Arabia under which weapons were exchanged for oil. Full details have never been published, but a great deal of information has been collected in *The Arabian Connection*, published by the Campaign against the Arms Trade, which is a useful source even for those who might not agree with all the objectives of the Campaign.

The first Yammamah deal was negotiated in the middle to late 1980s and has its origin in the reluctance of the US Congress to sanction weapons exports to Saudi Arabia. American policies have fluctuated since then; but a second Yammamah agreement was negotiated in the late 1980s; and despite may difficulties it became operational in the early 1990s. Its biggest 'achievement' was to produce a market for the Tornado aircraft, which was said at one time to have saved 19,000 jobs.

The Blair government shows no sign of wanting to banish this kind of agreement, despite the distortions that the heavy investment in arms is producing in Saudi Arabia, the horrific human rights record of the regime there, and the basic instability of that regime. As for the argument about oil supplies, the US, Britain and France cannot – like other western countries – buy their oil on the international market, remembering that Middle Eastern countries often need to sell the oil even more urgently than we need to buy it. It is interesting that this so-called argument of economic strategy usually comes from foreign ministries rather than ministries of finance or economics.

The UK Record

The recent UK record is not all bad. In July 1997 the then new British Foreign Secretary Robin Cook stated that the new Labour government would not permit the sale of arms to regimes that might use them for internal repression. It is the least he could have said after the *Arms for Iraq* scandal. The government has fulfilled an election pledge to publish annual reports on UK's strategic export controls. These have gradually improved in quality; and the third one, issued in July 2000, has been described by Saferworld as 'the most transparent report published by any European country and one which offers a potential template for best practice through the EU.' But even this latest report is criticised for failure to provide information on ultimate end users, the absence of summary information on licences refused and lack of detailed information on actual deliveries, as distinct from licences.

The Blair government inherited various international obligations such as membership of the Australia Group of 30 countries aiming to discourage the proliferation of chemical and biological weapons. An international convention was reached in December 1997 banning the production and transfer of anti-personnel mines. This came too early to be attributed to the Labour government elected in the same year. But the new government indeed took a lead in pressing for a European Union Code of Conduct on Arms Exports which was agreed in June 1998. The Chancellor of the Exchequer, Gordon Brown, began the millennium by adding 22 new poor countries over and above the previous 41 covered by the ban on export credits 'for unproductive expenditure'.

Indonesia, however, remains off the banned list. And because the Chancellor's action was in the context of debt relief for poor countries, it did not affect Saudi Arabia, which has accounted for about one third of British arms sales. It is thus fair to say that there is still a long way to go. Amnesty International's view has been that the Department of Trade and Industry 'is not meeting its responsibility to promote trade in a manner which is not harmful to human rights.' It was also worried that this same department is responsible both for the licensing of arms sales and for their promotion. A joint report of four House of Commons committees reiterated that a serious error of judgement was made in late 1998 and early 1999 in granting several open export licences for military equipment to the government of Zimbabwe, despite that government's heavy involvement in the fighting in the Congo and its domestic infringements of human rights. The same report urged considering a stricter interpretation of the arms embargo on China and also raised issues about licences for arms to other countries.

At the height of the East Timor crisis in early 1999 there appeared a telling *Times* cartoon. On one side of the cartoon a buoyant Tony Blair was shown exclaiming: 'We need a hawk' – meaning a more determined military effort to put pressure on the government of Indonesia. On the other side he was shown piloting one of the Hawk aircraft that the UK had been delivering to Indonesia for many years for the use of the country's former military dictator, General Suharto.

Export Promotion

A popular view is that some arms sales may be undesirable, but that they help promote jobs, growth and employment. Therefore a balance has to be drawn between these two considerations – a compromise always appeals to the so-called practical man. We will thus never really stop dubious arms sales until the myth of the export drive is nailed once and for all. The root of the matter is the belief throughout the political and business establishment that exports are worthwhile for their own sake, irrespective of the terms on which they are sold and how much they have to be subsidised. It is for this reason that prime ministers, whether Thatcher, Major or Blair, time and again come down against the Treasury in favour of controversial arms deals or dubious overseas capital projects. These attitudes are a hangover from the siege economy days of Stafford Cripps (Labour Chancellor in the late 1940s) and have no place in a global market economy.

The balance of payments preoccupation goes back many centuries. Mercantilist writers in the 16th, 17th and 18th century, campaigned for a favourable balance of trade and for an inflow of gold and silver. These writers were refuted as conclusively as anything can be in political economy by 18th century members of the Scottish Enlightenment such as David Hume and Adam Smith. During the subsequent period of rapid world economic growth towards the end of the 19th century huge current account surpluses and deficits built up, far greater than any of the imbalances which commentators have bemoaned in recent decades.

The origin of both the export drive and the reinvention of so-called balance of payments problem was in the immediate post-war years when sterling was on a fixed exchange rate and was also inconvertible. The financial policy regime was then one of suppressed inflation, which tended to spill over into the balance of payments, and which was held down by a mixture of controls and exchange rate overvaluation. It was, moreover, a world with strict controls over capital flows.

These controls could not be severe enough to protect determined speculators from launching an attack on a suspect currency, but they were enough of a deterrent to the regular flows of capital across borders which normally finance imbalances on current account. The post-World War Two generation of political and economic leaders was brought up on slogans and posters such as 'export or die', the 'dollar drive' and even on one occasion 'exporting is fun'. By contrast we are now back in a world of relatively free capital flows. There are bound to be large imbalances between countries with high savings ratios and relatively few investment outlets and other countries, such as the United States, which have had low savings but many investment opportunities. Moreover we now have floating exchange rates.

Advanced industrial countries with floating exchange rates need never have balance of payments problems. They may suffer from unwelcome downward pressure on their exchange rate due to financial market's distrust of their policies or of fears about domestic inflation. If so, such fears should be tackled directly. In today's circumstances export drives really amount to the diversion of public resources towards special interest groups under the guise of patriotic slogans.

The basic political and business fallacy is not to realise that exports, like investment, are a cost and not a benefit. If we could finance the imports that British citizens want to buy without any exports – say by interest-free loans from overseas on indefinite repayment terms – we would be better off. Of course this would require a period of adjustment. But such adjustments are necessary after any kind of economic or industrial change. In the world as it is, exports are a waste of resources and serve no purpose if they are not paid for, or are paid for very late and on a heavily subsidised credit basis and with a strong political risk factor.

The Jobs Argument

The most popular argument for subsidising exports is the effect on jobs. We should be on our guard when politicians defend dubious policies by declaring 'jobs are at stake'. This is so whether it is an 'Old Labour' supporter wanting to protect manufacturing, a Tory spokesman talking about the employment provided by hunting, or a business lobbyist pushing for arms sales to dubious regimes. The argument that jobs derived from exporting weapons cannot be replaced is akin to the argument for keeping open uneconomic coalmines for the sake of employment. Yet it is often just those people who lecture us on the need for workers to change jobs, and who say that full employment cannot the same employment, who are most keen to promote the sale of arms.

Such arguments are based on the myth that there is a lump of labour that is engaged in making specific products. Then, it is supposed, if orders or output are lost in one area they cannot be regained anywhere else. But people change jobs constantly. Well over three million people leave the unemployment register each year even in recession periods, over half of them for new jobs or training. Indeed, it is almost certainly easier for arms workers, many of whom have a wide range of valued skills, to find new jobs than it was for miners, whose training was more specific There are those who ask, 'Where will the new jobs come from to replace those lost in exporting weapons?' The onus is on them to explain how it is that other jobs, on a much greater scale, arose to take the place of handloom weavers or the drivers of horse-drawn carts – or for that matter the owners of pack-asses replaced by wheeled traffic at the dawn of history. The multiplication of population and the multiple rise of productivity in the last two centuries, so far from these having caused mass unemployment, have been accompanied by a multiple increase in the number of jobs.

One of the key ideas of economics is that of the circular flow of income. The point is that there is a continuing flow between purchasers who desire to buy products, the incomes received from supplying their needs, and still further purchases. The idea is so basic that economists regard it as too obvious to mention and take it for granted rather than discuss it explicitly. The smoothness of this flow can be helped by sensible policies, such as efforts by the Bank of England Monetary Policy Committee to maintain an adequate, but not excessive, flow of total spending, and by sensible exchange rate policies. The interested citizen needs to know mainly that there is or can be such a circular flow, and that there therefore need be no fear of one country being undercut in everything by another.

Terms of Trade

A slightly more respectable argument is that relating to the terms of trade. A royal visit or a small amount of official publicity, or arm-twisting by the Foreign Office, might enable a company to sell more overseas at a given price or to sell a given amount of goods at a higher price. This enables the home country to exchange exports for imports on slightly more profitable terms. The argument has very little application in a highly competitive world where a country of the size of Britain has little monopoly power. If e-commerce means anything at all this should vanish completely as buyers are able to find the most competitive offer unaided by royal visits.

A further argument relates to small exporters, who might not have the resources to engage in the required market research and export promotion. But surely this kind of thing is the job of market research and advertising agencies, chambers of commerce and industry associations. If it does not pay them to engage in such promotion, it is because government support agencies are providing these services on a free or subsidised basis.

Spillover Benefits

The last resort of any sector or industry whose subsidies are challenged is to say that it brings spillover benefits to the rest of the economy. Concorde was virtually launched on such arguments. Weapons producers argue that the government should continue to support exports because the proceeds contribute to the overhead costs of firms supplying the British military. These considerations cut both ways. The drive for arms sales itself distorts the design and production plans of British manufacturers and, in the view of some defence economists, offsets the savings in overheads. In any case, only some arms exports would be affected by a ban in the spirit of our supposedly ethical foreign policy. The posited economies of scale could readily be achieved by greater specialisation among Nato counties – a process inhibited by the desire of so many governments to protect domestic firms.

The NERA Report

A report on export credit by the National Economic Research Associates (NERA). There has been some misguided celebration of the fact that NERA did not recommend that ECGD should be privatised. But the more important question is whether the provision of insurance cover should be subsidised. Until 1991, the Department showed heavy cash flow losses. It was then instructed to break even in cash flow terms in line with Berne procedures. But the ECGD is still, not required to show the positive return of 6% in real terms normally required on public sector investment projects. NERA could not find any justification for the subsidy – a most important finding which the vested interests involved have contrived to bury.

NERA's first preference is for an internationally negotiated phasing out. We must also face the question of whether there is a case for the UK moving further ahead on its own. But much more important than any of these details is the fact that reports such as NERA's are based on a mutually convenient misunderstanding. Economic research organisations, trying to unearth a case for intervention and subsidy, tend to focus on lapses from perfection inherent in almost all markets: matters such as informational barriers facing potential new exporters, and which governments might be able to help overcome by activities such as trade fairs or start-up credits. NERA indeed found such imperfections.

Politicians and opinion leaders take such reports, however, as confirmation that, without export promotion, the balance of payments would go haywire, the country become bankrupt and thousands of jobs would be lost. They conveniently overlook the fact that these bankruptcy and job fears are dismissed in polite terms as fallacies not worth serious consideration. NERA for instance remarked that the last thing the overheated British economy needed was extra demand for labour. Even in the year 2001 when there was a risk of recession, selective aid to a few heavy goods or arms manufacturers would have been an extremely inefficient way of stimulating demand.

SMALL ARMS TRADE

In the age of nuclear and other weapons of mass destruction, the vast majority of all warfare continues to be conducted using conventional weapons: machine rifles, grenades, landmines, explosives, and light rockets. These small arms, and the ability to obtain them, are the operational means of warfare. The much-touted efficiency of "high-tech" warfare based on computer-guided rockets and remote-controlled war machinery has been generally successful only as bombardment in advance of ground-based attack which ultimately depends on soldiers wielding hand-held weapons. Thus, even when blessed with unlimited war capability and unlimited weaponry options, militaries such as those of the United States and Russia depend on small arms to subdue populations and control territory. So do guerilla revolutionaries and those defending themselves against their own violently abusive governments. This essay will consider the issue of the global trade in small arms, examining its scope, its global economic underpinnings, its relationships to the economies of conflict-plagued countries, its particular connections to the current war in Sudan, and finally possible initiatives for reform of the global small arms trade.

The Scope of the Problem

As recently as World War II, the ability to prosecute war depended on developing the industrial capacity to produce these "small arms." During the Cold War, the United States and the Soviet Union provided conventional weapons for their respective client states fighting "proxy" wars. The high-geared military-industrial economies of the two leviathans have stimulated France, China, Germany, the UK, Italy, Ukraine, and Israel to compete in the lucrative worldwide business of weapons export. In 2002 these nine weapons-selling countries exported $14.8 billion in conventional weapons to the rest of the world. Forty percent of this staggering volume of weapons flows from Russia; 27% is shipped from the USA. The USA, UK, and France earned more in small arms sales to developing countries in 1998-2001 than they gave in aid.

The gigantism of this industry renders it a force in national economic policies. It is in the national interest of these nations, to some degree, to promote violent conflict and war around the world. As is apparent in the case of Sudan, the economic leverage of the weapons industry, including the small arms industry, may determine whether major first-world nations support or impede peace processes in war-torn countries. This positive self-interest that weapons-supplying first-world nations have in the negative interest — the active destruction and resulting impoverishment — of third-world nations is a very dark side of the economic colonialism that typifies neo-liberal economic globalization.

Classic game-theory analyses of arms race determinants assume arms development and production to come at the expense of a nation's economic well-being. While that may actually be true in terms of benefit to an entire nation's economy, it is *always* true that war yields positive economic benefit to national military industries, and that military industries hold disproportionate power over their governments' decision-making processes. In result, the world is flooded with weapons, and the potential to pursue violence is immediately and endlessly available to all. As Mary Kaldor notes, "violence is increasingly privatized both as a result of growing organized crime and the emergence of paramilitary groups." There are reported to be more than 639 million small arms in the world today; in the case of South Asia, 80% are in civilian (non-governmental) hands.

The availability of small arms is further assured through the worldwide financial deregulation that is a cornerstone of neo-liberal economic globalization. The deregulation of financial transactions has effectively rendered the financing of war exempt from national or international governance. Arms merchants and, significantly, diaspora supporters of civil conflicts are easily able to move funds instantly and covertly behind the screens of small states specializing in such banking services, thanks to the blessings of deregulated economic globalization. Weapons procurers are similarly enabled to operate with impunity, even when supplying arms illegally to the perpetrators of humanitarian crimes and genocides.

Even when legal "controls" are in effect, sales and movement of small weapons to parties in conflict can proceed unabated. The illegal arms trade is estimated at more than (perhaps much more than) $1 billion per year. Conflict entrepreneurs – weapons manufacturers, gun-runners, merchant middle-men, and the weapons users themselves, profit both from the supply of weapons and from their use in protracted conflict.

During the Cold War massive supplies of conventional and more sophisticated weapons systems were pumped into client states by the Cold War powers, providing vast stores of machinery for ensuing post-Cold War wars. Weapons fed into the Afghanistan and Cambodian conflicts have been the foundation of supply for current South Asian violence. Massive supplies of weapons supplied to the Congo and Angola wars provided the stockpile for succeeding West African wars. The killing lives of such weapons may last many years. During the Cold War, the Coordinating Committee for Multilateral Export Controls (CoCom) operated as the Western self-regulation of which weapons and technologies were to be restricted. By 1989, however, the appeal of economic gains effectively overwhelmed security concerns. CoCom was disbanded in 1994, and first-world weapons producers have since fed arms to parties in conflict with unrestricted, free-market eagerness.

SOURCES OF SMALL ARMS

China and North Korea are the countries reported to be sources of small arms proliferation in the region. In the post-Communist era, there is practically no official control over small arms production and trade. The strict ban on the owning and trade of small arms that existed before 1991 has been lifted. But even during the last decade of the Communist rule, the law banning small arms ownership was not fully enforced for all social groups. Obtaining a license to own and carry small weapons was no longer a complicated process after 1992. Now, many Russian companies and organizations have their own arsenals of small weapons without any license. Millions of private citizens of the Russian Federation are also purchasing firearms in order to protect themselves and their families from the social chaos of crime expansion in contemporary Russia.

Small Arms and the Russian Defence Industry

East Siberia and the Russian Far East have been traditionally reported as areas of increased concentration of unlicensed firearms among private citizens. Since the end of the 1970s most of the families and individuals residing in the underpopulated northern sector of the area owned from one to several rifles, revolvers, pistols or even automatic rifles. Even the Communist authorities tended to tolerate that situation keeping in mind the isolation of rural communities and individual settlements, the vital necessity of hunting and self-defence (including self-defence from wild animals), and finally restricted capability of law enforcement structures to control sparse population scattered across the vast mountainous and forested territory.

The Russian state military industry has been in crisis since the end of the Cold War. Budget cuts, in combination with gradual reduction of federal military forces, led to the degradation of its traditional internal constituency. Trying to improve their financial situation, many state enterprises are looking for new markets to sell their production. Current legal regulations make the legal, large-scale sales of Russian-made firearms to Russian consumers a difficult task, so the military industry looks to the development of small arms exports. In East Asia, Russian military industry still remains a traditional supplier of the armed forces of China, Vietnam and Cambodia. China mainly concentrates on purchasing heavy weapons, aircraft and submarines. Nevertheless, small amounts of Russian small arms are regularly purchased by China. During the last two years Russian arms dealers have been repeatedly visiting other countries of the region (among them Indonesia, Malaysia, Singapore and Thailand) trying to explore and develop new markets.

The state military industry in Russia is backed by government and parliamentary circles, making it easy for the industry to boost small arms exports to traditional partners, as well as to search for new markets. Widespread corruption and corporate protectionism in modern Russian society make it difficult to draw a distinct line between legal and illegal export of arms produced by Russian military industry (in spite of the government declarations about its "strict adherence to norms of international law"). It is also worth mentioning that human rights violations in such countries of Asia such as the PRC or Vietnam never influence the delivery of Russian arms to those countries.

All arms trading in Russia is formally controlled by the federal arms export agency, or "Rosvooruzhenije" (from the Russian: Rus[sian]/Arms). The head of Rosvooruzhenije is Yevgenij Ananev. The second main figure is Rear Admiral Oleg Belavintsev who serves as its deputy general director. Since December 1997, one of Ananev's chief advisors has been former Russian Defence Minister Pavel Grachev, who is reportedly involved in corruption scandals. (Grachev and Belavintsev are reported to be close personal friends.)

Reorganization of the Defence Industry

In February 1998, a new government commission for the financial recovery of the defence industry was formed in Moscow. On 23 February, in accordance with the resolution signed by Prime Minister Chernomyrdin, First Deputy Prime Minister Anatolij Chubais was appointed as its chairman with Deputy Prime Minister and Economics Minister Yakov Urinson appointed as deputy chairman. Chubais announced on 20 February that the government was aiming at revision of its procedure for concluding contracts with defence enterprises, as well as at reduction of the number of such enterprises receiving state orders from 1,700 to 600.

Several powerful Russian opposition leaders, holding a majority in Russian Parliament (among them Vladimir Zhirinovski), have declared the arms trade one of Russia's economic goals. They strongly believe, and try to convince the Russian public, that the arms trade is a good and reliable business which should be developed to bring cash to the country, as well as to keep military industry jobs. A number of former state enterprises in Russia specializing in small arms production (exact data not available) have sold some of their shares to private structures and citizens. As a result of this, many of them fell into the sphere of the activity of "Russian Mafia" and became sources of totally uncontrolled production and trade of small arms both for Russian and foreign markets.

The Russian Mafia

Well organized criminal groups started forming in Russia (USSR) at the end of the Civil War (1918-1922). After more than fifty years of evolution and transformation, they have managed to preserve their viability and coordination, have accumulated significant funds and have found ways to integrate themselves with the power structures of the Soviet Empire including high-ranking officials of the Communist Party of the USSR and the KGB. The processes of disintegration of the Soviet State during the period of "Perestroyka" and "Glasnost" (1986-1991) further reinforced the above-mentioned alliance between "professional mobsters" and a part of communist "Nomenclatura," thus creating a special form of organized crime which is often called "Russian Mafia." Modern structures of "Russian Mafia" operating in the sphere of arms production and sales are represented by several powerful groups consisting of criminal syndicates (sometimes called "brotherhoods") working in close cooperation with certain industrial, financial and political groups, recruiting agents in law enforcement structures and involving foreign companies and individual citizens in their network. Severe discipline, conspiracy, excellent equipment, well developed "intelligence" and "counter-intelligence" and relatively professional approach towards marketing and business — all make modern criminal groups of Russia strong and dangerous, as well as, to a greater or lesser extent, unknown and invisible to Western countries (including Canadian and American observers).

Organized criminal "syndicates" and "brotherhoods" of the Russian Federation with their headquarters in the cities of Moscow, St. Petersburg, Yekaterinburg, Chelyabinsk, Khabarovsk and Vladivostok (the latter two in the Russian Far East), were reported to be involved in small arms exports to other countries of East Asia.

By "involvement" is meant various degrees of control over the above sphere of business mainly resulting in accumulating considerable commissions from international arms deals. Smaller criminal groups operating between East Siberia and the Urals tend to control the trafficking of small arms through the provinces of Tyumen, Omsk, and Kemerovo, and through Krasnoyarsk territory, in order to obtain small commissions from the deals. The local transport police (GAI) is often involved in controlling small arms trafficking for the benefit of criminal groups.

The process of rapid decay of the Soviet Army (now Russian Federal Army) started at least at the end of the 1970s with the period of 1993-98 as its culmination. Openly corrupt top brass, an underpaid officer corps, starving soldiers, undermanned and under-equipped regiments — all these factors have resulted in massive thefts of military property, including firearms, which can be easily sold on the black market or used for private purposes such as self-defence or work in private security structures. (Many sergeants and officers combine military service with part-time or freelance work in commercial companies, often as security officers. Strictly banned until 1992, this practice is nowadays widely tolerated).

Defining the Region

The area of current research includes the territory of Transbaykal Military District embracing Chita and Irkutsk provinces and ethnic republics of Sakha-Yakutia and Buryat-Mongolia (approximately 80,000 military personnel at present) and Maritime (Primorskij) Military District embracing the provinces of Magadan, Kamchatka, and Sakhalin Island, territories of Maritim and Amur, and Chukotka (Chukchi) Autonomous District (approximately 77,000 military personnel at present).

The two Military Districts officially contain at least 60 divisions, which were originally supposed to be manned with at least 300,000 military personnel) However most of those divisions are 25 to 75% undermanned leaving thousands of small arms in stores and subject to regular misappropriation by officers, sergeants and private soldiers. The Russian Far East is also the area of Russian Pacific Fleet basing (Magadan, Petropavlovsk-Kamchatsky, Yuzhno-Sakhalinsk, Vanino, Nakhodka, Vladivostok). The above-mentioned problems of the two military districts are typical for the Pacific Fleet as well. Chinese and to some extent North Korean state-owned military industries also serve as sources of both legal and semi-illegal small arms proliferation in the area of research. In China, military industry is not controlled by organized criminal groups to the extent to which it has become in Russia (at least for the reason that in modern China there do not seem to exist well organized criminal structures similar to "Russian Mafia").73 However, corruption is well-developed in the Chinese military industry, which in combination with insufficient control over resources and production makes it possible to produce thousands of firearms for further sale, bypassing official export channels.

GATHERING THE FACTS ON THE SMALL ARMS TRADE

In late 1997, following the Oslo conference that drafted the treaty against anti-personnel landmines, many NGOs and governments began pressing for more public attention to the devastation wrought by the worldwide sale and distribution of light arms–weapons that can be carried by a person–such as assault rifles, mortars, and grenades. Such arms are believed to be responsible for the vast majority of combat deaths, including many tens of thousands of civilian deaths annually. Even after conflicts end, demobilization and reconciliation efforts are frustrated by the over-supply of these inexpensive weapons, which often flow into criminal hands.

Among the governmental and non-governmental initiatives at the time, in late December 1997, on the first anniversary of the murder of Red Cross/Red Crescent workers in Chechnya, PRIO and three other organizations in Oslo–Norwegian Red Cross, Norwegian Church Aid and the Norwegian Institute of International Affairs–banded together to form the Norwegian Initiative on Small Arms Transfers (NISAT). The database proposal here is a central part of NISAT's activities.

Need for the Project

In the past few years, the European Union, OSCE, Organization of American States, Organization of African Unity, Economic Community of West African States, and the South African Development Community all took up some aspect of small arms control.

Almost every part of the UN engaged the topic, including—increasingly—the Security Council. Modeled on a 1997 OAS treaty, the UN in Vienna began negotiation of a global protocol against firearms trafficking in 1999. In addition, the UN General Assembly voted in 1999 to hold a United Nations conference in 2001 on the illicit arms trade "in all its dimensions."

Despite this high level of engagement by governments and NGOs, the knowledge base on which these efforts rest is extremely thin. There are enormous gaps in the factual record on arms production and transfers. The lack of focused research in this area leaves open fundamental questions such as whether the legal or the illegal arms trade is the leading source of supply, and which states are the largest legal exporters of small arms.

Approximately 70 states produce small arms and/or ammunition. Some production enterprises are state-owned (usually military armories), and some are private companies. From the existing reference works,

- it is not difficult to know what types of small arms the major producer states manufacture;
- it is much harder to determine production quantities; and
- it is nearly impossible to know where weapons are being exported.

The standard sources of data on the international arms trade–SIPRI, the UN Register of Conventional Arms, *World Military*

Expenditures and Arms Transfers–do not include information on small arms shipments.

Few governments provide information to their parliaments on major weapons exports they have approved, and even fewer on their small arms trade. An exception to the prevailing pattern of secrecy is the US government. Since 1997, the United States openly reports in a highly specific manner all of its small arms shipments and export license approvals (with the notable exception of covert government-run arms supply, like the Iran-contra operation). Other states that have recently begun to provide more detailed public reports on their arms exports (including small arms shipments) are Belgium, Canada, the Netherlands, Norway, South Africa, Sweden and the United Kingdom. These are the eight leaders in transparency, on which the database will first concentrate in 2000-2001.

Despite this improvement in transparency, there is a need to organize the newly available data. In the above eight and other countries, the relevant information is scattered across many agencies and departments–in shipping documents at customs offices, judicial records, police records, and documents in the foreign, defense and trade ministries. No one is currently pulling this information together systematically, translating it, or presenting it to the international community in a readily useable format. That is what the database project will do.

The Need for Transparency

The information included in the database will serve as a template for the kind of governmental transparency that we will encourage the Norwegian Foreign Ministry to press for through its diplomatic contacts and on the international stage. In addition, we hope the database itself will encourage greater openness on the part of some governments, when they see the amount and types of information that the United States and – to a lesser degree – some others already make public without adverse effect.

Increased transparency and organization of the available data will also improve the ability of governments to verify the appropriate end-uses and end-users of weapons exports they are authorizing. It will allow the non-governmental community, as well as national legislatures, to play an important role in aiding governments' efforts to curb diversion of these arms by providing oversight through research, questioning and reporting. Such information is also important for the safety of aid and relief workers operating in a region where a sudden influx of guns has occurred or is anticipated.

Increased openness about weapons shipments could serve as a confidence building measure among forces within a state, or states in a region, potentially heading off some purchases spurred by 'fear of the unknown'.

Finally, such information will greatly facilitate formal disarmament activities, by providing some baseline information about arms stocks and supply in the state or region.

How the Project Addresses These Needs

The centerpiece of this proposal is an on-line database of small arms production and transfers. The database addresses the need for better information on three levels:

- it provides a composite picture of the small arms trade by collecting, translating and organizing the hard-to-find data;
- it interlinks policy-relevant information so as to provide both governments and activist organizations a stronger base for argumentation, strategy and agreement on common norms; and
- it demonstrates the positive aspects of transparency.

The database will eventually contain information on virtually every country of the world. It will be a public resource, accessible to all Internet users.

We believe that the database will yield substantial results within one year of full funding, and if so we are committed to further developing and sustaining the initiative for as long as small arms control measures are required. As more governments provide public information about their light weapons shipments, the resource will grow in value (in terms of providing a fuller picture of the dynamics of the arms market).

GLOBAL DISARMAMENT AND ARMS CONTROL

Global, verifiable and non-discriminatory nuclear disarmament is a national security objective. India shall continue its efforts to achieve the goal of a nuclear weapon-free world at an early date. Since no-first use of nuclear weapons is India's basic commitment, every effort shall be made to persuade other States possessing nuclear weapons to join an international treaty banning first use. Having provided unqualified negative security assurances, India shall work for internationally binding unconditional negative security assurances by nuclear weapon states to non-nuclear weapon states.

Nuclear arms control measures shall be sought as part of national security policy to reduce potential threats and to protect our own capability and its effectiveness. In view of the very high destructive potential of nuclear weapons, appropriate nuclear risk reduction and confidence building measures shall be sought, negotiated and instituted.

Physics and Politics in the 1930s

In the first decades of the twentieth century, physics was revolutionized with developments in the understanding of the nature of atoms. In 1898, French physicist Pierre Curie and his Polish wife Maria Sklodowska-Curie had discovered that present in pitchblende, an ore of uranium, was a substance which emitted large amounts of radioactivity, which they named radium. This raised the hopes of both scientists and lay people that the elements around us could contain tremendous amounts of unseen energy, waiting to be tapped.

Experiments by Ernest Rutherford in 1911 indicated that the vast majority of an atom's mass was contained in a very small nucleus at its core, made up of protons, surrounded by a web of whirring electrons. In 1932, James Chadwick discovered that the nucleus contained another fundamental particle, the neutron, and in the same year John Cockcroft and Ernest Walton "split the atom" for the first time, the first occasion on which an atomic nucleus of one element had been successfully changed to a different nucleus by artificial means.

In 1934 the idea of chain reaction via neutron was proposed by Leó Szilárd, who patented the idea of the atomic bomb. The patent was transferred in secret to Britain's Royal Navy in 1936. In a very real sense, Szilárd was the father of the atomic bomb academically. In 1934, French physicists Irène and Frédéric Joliot-Curie discovered that artificial radioactivity could be induced in stable elements by bombarding them with alpha particles, and in the same year Italian physicist Enrico Fermi reported similar results when bombarding uranium with neutrons. In December 1938, the German chemists Otto Hahn and Fritz Strassmann sent a manuscript to *Naturwissenschaften* reporting they had detected the element barium after bombarding uranium with neutrons; simultaneously, they communicated these results to Lise Meitner. Meitner, and her nephew Otto Robert Frisch, correctly interpreted these results as being nuclear fission. Frisch confirmed this experimentally on 13 January 1939. Even before it was published, Meitner's and Frisch's interpretation of the work of Hahn and Strassmann crossed the Atlantic Ocean with Niels Bohr, who was to lecture at Princeton University. Isidor Isaac Rabi and Willis Lamb, two Columbia University physicists working at Princeton, heard the news and carried it back to Columbia. Rabi said he told Fermi; Fermi gave credit to Lamb. Bohr soon thereafter went from Princeton to Columbia to see Fermi. Not finding Fermi in his office, Bohr went down to the cyclotron area and found Herbert Anderson. Bohr grabbed him by the shoulder and said: "Young man, let me explain to you about something new and exciting in physics."

It was clear to a number of scientists at Columbia that they should try to detect the energy released in the nuclear fission of uranium from neutron bombardment. On 25 January 1939, an experimental team at Columbia University conducted the first nuclear fission experiment in the United States, which was done in the basement of Pupin Hall; the members of the team were Herbert L. Anderson, Eugene T. Booth, John R. Dunning, Enrico Fermi, G. Norris Glasoe, and Francis G. Slack. As the Nazi army marched into first Czechoslovakia in 1938, and then Poland in 1939, beginning World War II, many of Europe's top physicists had already begun to flee from the imminent conflict. Scientists on both sides of the conflict were well aware of the possibility of utilizing nuclear fission as a weapon, but at the time no one was quite sure how it could be done. In the early years of the Second World War, physicists abruptly stopped publishing on the topic of fission, an act of self-censorship to keep the opposing side from gaining any advantages.

From Los Alamos to Hiroshima

By the beginning of World War II, there was concern among scientists in the Allied nations that Nazi Germany might have its own project to develop fission-based weapons. Organized research first began in Britain as part of the "Tube Alloys" project, and in the United States a small amount of funding was given for research into uranium weapons starting in 1939 with the Uranium Committee under Lyman James Briggs. At the urging of British scientists, though, who had made crucial calculations indicating that a fission weapon could be completed within only a few years, by 1941 the project had been wrested into better bureaucratic hands, and in 1942 came under the auspices of a Military Policy Committee led by General Leslie Groves as the Manhattan Project.

Scientifically led by the American physicist Robert Oppenheimer, the project brought together the top scientific minds of the day (many exiles from Europe) with the production power of American industry for the goal of producing fission-based explosive devices before Germany could. Britain and the U.S. agreed to pool their resources and information for the project, but the other Allied power—the Soviet Union under Joseph Stalin—was not informed. A massive industrial and scientific undertaking, the Manhattan Project involved many of the world's great physicists in the scientific and development aspects. The United States made an unprecedented investment into wartime research for the project, which was spread across more than 30 sites in the U.S. and Canada. Scientific knowledge was centralized at a secret laboratory known as Los Alamos, previously a small ranch school near Santa Fe, New Mexico.

Uranium appears in nature primarily in two isotopes: uranium-238 and uranium-235. When the nucleus of uranium-235 absorbs a neutron, it undergoes nuclear fission, splitting into two "fission products" and releasing energy and 2.5 neutrons on average. Uranium-238, on the other hand, absorbs neutrons but does not split, effectively putting a stop to any ongoing fission reaction. It was discovered that an atomic bomb based on uranium would need to be made of almost completely pure uranium-235 (at least 80% pure), or else the presence of uranium-238 would quickly curtail the nuclear chain reaction. The team of scientists working on the Manhattan Project immediately realized that one of the largest problems they would have to solve was how to remove uranium-235 from natural uranium, which was composed of 99.3% uranium-238. Two methods were developed during the wartime project, both of which took advantage of the fact that uranium-238 has a slightly greater atomic mass than uranium-235: electromagnetic separation and gaseous diffusion—methods which separated isotopes based on their differing weights. Another secret site was erected at rural Oak Ridge, Tennessee, for the large-scale production and purification of the rare isotope. It was a massive investment: at the time, one of the Oak Ridge facilities (K-25) was the largest factory under one roof. The Oak Ridge site employed tens of thousands of employees at its peak, most of whom had no idea what they were working on. Though uranium-238 cannot be used for the initial stage of an atomic bomb, when U-238 absorbs a neutron, it transforms first into an unstable element, uranium-239, and then decays into neptunium-239, and finally the relatively stable plutonium-239, an element which does not exist in nature. Plutonium is also fissile and can be used to create a fission reaction, and after Enrico Fermi achieved the world's first sustained and controlled nuclear chain reaction in the creation of the first "atomic pile"—a primitive nuclear reactor—in a basement at the University of Chicago, massive reactors were secretly created at what is now known as Hanford Site in the state of Washington, using the Columbia River as cooling water, to transform uranium-238 into plutonium for a bomb.

For a fission weapon to operate, there must be a critical mass—the amount needed for a self-sustaining nuclear chain reaction—of fissile material bombarded with neutrons at any one time. The simplest form of nuclear weapon is a gun-type fission weapon, where a sub-critical mass of fissile material (such as uranium-235) would be shot at another sub-critical mass of fissile material. The result would be a super-critical mass which, when bombarded with neutrons, would undergo fission at a rapid rate and create the desired explosion. The weapons envisaged in 1942 were the two gun-type weapons, Little Boy (uranium) and Thin Man (plutonium), and the Fat Man plutonium implosion bomb. In early 1943 Oppenheimer determined that two projects should proceed forwards: the "Thin Man" project (plutonium gun) and the "Fat Man" project (plutonium implosion). The plutonium gun was to receive the bulk of the research effort, as it was the project with the most uncertainty involved. It was assumed that the uranium gun-type bomb could then be adapted from it.

But in April 1944 it was found by Emilio Segrè that plutonium produced by the Hanford reactors had too high a level of background neutron radiation, and underwent spontaneous fission to a very small extent, due to the presence of impurities of the Pu-240 isotope. If such plutonium were used in a "gun assembly," the chain reaction would start in the split seconds before the critical mass was assembled, blowing the weapon apart before it would have any great effect (this is known as a fizzle). So development of Fat Man, the implosion bomb, was given high priority. Chemical explosives were used to implode a sub-critical sphere of plutonium, thus increasing its density and making it into a critical mass. The difficulties with implosion were in the problem of making the chemical explosives deliver a perfectly uniform shock wave upon the plutonium sphere— if it were even slightly asymmetric, the weapon would fizzle (which would be expensive, messy, and not a very effective military device). This problem was circumvented by the use of hydrodynamic "lenses"—explosive materials of differing densities—which would focus the blast waves inside the imploding sphere, akin to the way in which an optical lens focuses light rays.

After D-Day, General Groves had ordered a team of scientists—Project Alsos—to follow eastward-moving victorious Allied troops into Europe in order to assess the status of the German nuclear program (and to prevent the westward-moving Russians from gaining any materials or scientific manpower). It was concluded that while Nazi Germany had also had an atomic bomb program, headed by Werner Heisenberg, the government had not made a significant investment in the project, and had been nowhere near success. Historians claim to have found a rough schematic showing a Nazi nuclear bomb. Research was conducted in the German nuclear energy project. In March 1945, a Nazi scientific team was directed by the physicist Kurt Diebner to develop a primitive nuclear device in Ohrdruf, Thuringia.

By the unconditional surrender of Germany on May 8, 1945, the Manhattan Project was still months away from a working weapon. That April, after the death of American President Franklin D. Roosevelt, former Vice-President Harry S. Truman was told about the secret wartime project for the first time. Because of the difficulties in making a working plutonium bomb, it was decided that there should be a test of the weapon, and Truman wanted to know for sure if it would work before his meeting with Joseph Stalin at an upcoming conference on the future of postwar Europe. On July 16, 1945, in the desert north of Alamogordo, New Mexico, the first nuclear test took place, code-named "Trinity," using a device nicknamed "the Gadget." The test, a plutonium implosion type device, released the equivalent of 19 kilotons of TNT, far mightier than any weapon ever used before. The news of the test's success was rushed to Truman, who used it as leverage at the upcoming Potsdam Conference, held near Berlin.

After hearing arguments from scientists and military officers over the possible uses of the weapons against Japan (though some recommended using them as "demonstrations" in unpopulated areas, most recommended using them against "built up" targets, a euphemistic term for populated cities), Truman ordered the use of the weapons on Japanese cities, hoping it would send a strong message which would end in the capitulation of the Japanese leadership and avoid a lengthy invasion of the island. There were suggestions to drop the atomic bomb on Tokyo, the capital of Japan, but concerns about Tokyo's cultural heritage changed the plan. On May 10–11, 1945 The Target Committee at Los Alamos, led by J. Robert Oppenheimer, recommended Kyoto, Hiroshima, Yokohama, and the arsenal at Kokura as possible targets. On August 6, 1945, a uranium-based weapon, "Little Boy", was let loose on the Japanese city of Hiroshima. Three days later, a plutonium-based weapon, "Fat Man", was dropped onto the city of Nagasaki. The atomic bombs killed at least one hundred thousand Japanese outright, most of them civilians, with the heat, radiation, and blast effects.

Many tens of thousands would die later of radiation sickness and related cancers. Truman promised a "rain of ruin" if Japan did not surrender immediately, threatening to eliminate Japanese cities, one by one; Japan surrendered on August 15. Truman's threat was in fact a bluff, since the US had but one remaining uranium-gun type bomb completed.

Soviet Atomic Bomb Project

The Soviet Union was not invited to share in the new weapons developed by the United States and the other Allies. During the war, information had been pouring in from a number of volunteer spies involved with the Manhattan Project (known in Soviet cables under the code-name of *Enormoz*), and the Soviet nuclear physicist Igor Kurchatov was carefully watching the Allied weapons development. It came as no surprise to Stalin when Truman had informed him at the Potsdam conference that he had a "powerful new weapon."

Truman was shocked at Stalin's lack of interest. The Soviet spies in the U.S. project were all volunteers and none were Russians. One of the most valuable, Klaus Fuchs, was a German émigré theoretical physicist who had been a part in the early British nuclear efforts and had been part of the UK mission to Los Alamos during the war. Fuchs had been intimately involved in the development of the implosion weapon, and passed on detailed cross-sections of the "Trinity" device to his Soviet contacts. Other Los Alamos spies—none of whom knew each other—included Theodore Hall and David Greenglass. The information was kept but not acted upon, as Russia was still too busy fighting the war in Europe to devote resources to this new project.

In the years immediately after World War II, the issue of who should control atomic weapons became a major international point of contention. Many of the Los Alamos scientists who had built the bomb began to call for "international control of atomic energy," often calling for either control by transnational organizations or the purposeful distribution of weapons information to all superpowers, but due to a deep distrust of the intentions of the Soviet Union, both in postwar Europe and in general, the policy-makers of the United States worked to attempt to secure an American nuclear monopoly. A half-hearted plan for international control was proposed at the newly formed United Nations by Bernard Baruch ("The Baruch Plan"), but it was clear both to American commentators—and to the Soviets—that it was an attempt primarily to stymie Russian nuclear efforts. The Soviets vetoed the plan, effectively ending any immediate postwar negotiations on atomic energy, and made overtures towards banning the use of atomic weapons in general.

All the while, the Soviets had put their full industrial and manpower might into the development of their own atomic weapons. The initial problem for the Soviets was primarily one of resources—they had not scouted out uranium resources in the Soviet Union and the U.S. had made deals to monopolise the largest known (and high purity) reserves in the Belgian Congo. The USSR used penal labour to mine the old deposits in Czechoslovakia—now an area under their control—and searched for other domestic deposits (which were eventually found). Two days after the bombing of Nagasaki, the U.S. government released an official technical history of the Manhattan Project, authored by Princeton physicist Henry DeWolf Smyth, known colloquially as the Smyth Report. The sanitized summary of the wartime effort focused primarily on the production facilities and scale of investment, written in part to justify the wartime expenditure to the American public.

The Soviet program, under the suspicious watch of former NKVD chief Lavrenty Beria (a participant and victor in Stalin's Great Purge of the 1930s), would use the Report as a blueprint, seeking to duplicate as much as possible the American effort. The "secret cities" used for the Soviet equivalents of Hanford and Oak Ridge literally vanished from the maps for decades to come. At the Soviet equivalent of Los Alamos, Arzamas-16, physicist Yuli Khariton led the scientific effort to develop the weapon. Beria distrusted his scientists, however, and he distrusted the carefully collected espionage information. As such, Beria assigned multiple teams of scientists to the same task without informing each team of the other's existence. If they arrived at different conclusions, Beria would bring them together for the first time and have them debate with their newfound counterparts. Beria used the espionage information as a way to double-check the progress of his scientists, and in his effort for duplication of the American project even rejected more efficient bomb designs in favour of ones which more closely mimicked the tried-and-true "Fat Man" bomb used by the U.S. against Nagasaki.

Working under a stubborn and scientifically ignorant administrator, the Soviet scientists struggled on. On August 29, 1949, the effort brought its results, when the USSR tested its first fission bomb, dubbed "Joe-1" by the U.S., years ahead of American predictions. The news of the first Soviet bomb was announced to the world first by the United States, which had detected the nuclear fallout it generated from its test site in Kazakhstan. The loss of the American monopoly on nuclear weapons marked the first tit-for-tat of the nuclear arms race. The response in the U.S. was one of apprehension, fear, and scapegoating, which would lead eventually into the Red-baiting tactics of McCarthyism. Yet recent information from unclassified Venona intercepts and the opening of the KGB archives after the fall of the Soviet Union show that the USSR had useful spies that helped their program, although none were identified by the McCarthy. Before this, though, President Truman would announce his decision to begin a crash program to develop a far more powerful weapon than those which were used against Japan: the hydrogen bomb.

The First Thermonuclear Weapons

The notion of using a fission weapon to ignite a process of nuclear fusion can be dated back to 1942. At the first major theoretical conference on the development of an atomic bomb hosted by J. Robert Oppenheimer at the University of California, Berkeley, participant Edward Teller directed the majority of the discussion towards Enrico Fermi's idea of a "Super" bomb which would utilize the same reactions which powered the Sun itself. It was thought at the time that a fission weapon would be quite simple to develop and that perhaps work on a hydrogen bomb would be possible to complete before the end of the Second World War. However, in reality the problem of a "regular" atomic bomb was large enough to preoccupy the scientists for the next few years, much less the more speculative "Super." Only Teller continued working on the project—against the will of project leaders Oppenheimer and Hans Bethe.

After the atomic bombings of Japan, many scientists at Los Alamos rebelled against the notion of creating a weapon thousands of times more powerful than the first atomic bombs. For the scientists the question was in part technical—the weapon design was still quite uncertain and unworkable—and in part moral: such a weapon, they argued, could only be used against large civilian populations, and could thus only be used as a weapon of genocide. Many scientists, such as Bethe, urged that the United States should not develop such weapons and set an example towards the Soviet Union. Promoters of the weapon, including Teller, Ernest Lawrence, and Luis Alvarez, argued that such a development was inevitable, and to deny such protection to the people of the United States—especially when the Soviet Union was likely to create such a weapon themselves—was itself an immoral and unwise act.

Oppenheimer, who was now head of the General Advisory Committee of the successor to the Manhattan Project, the Atomic Energy Commission, presided over a recommendation against the development of the weapon. The reasons were in part because the success of the technology seemed limited at the time (and not worth the investment of resources to confirm whether this was so), and because Oppenheimer believed that the atomic forces of the United States would be more effective if they consisted of many large fission weapons (of which multiple bombs could be dropped on the same targets) rather than the large and unwieldy predictions of massive super bombs, for which there were a relatively limited amounts of targets of the size to warrant such a development. Furthermore, were such weapons developed by both the U.S. and the USSR, they would be more effectively used against the U.S. than by it, as the U.S. had far more regions of dense industrial and civilian activity which would serve as ideal targets for the large weapons than the Soviet Union did.

In the end, President Truman made the final decision, looking for a proper response to the first Soviet atomic bomb test in 1949. On January 31, 1950, Truman announced a crash program to develop the hydrogen (fusion) bomb. At this point, however, the exact mechanism was still not known: the "classical" hydrogen bomb, whereby the *heat* of the fission bomb would be used to ignite the fusion material, seemed highly unworkable. However, an insight by Los Alamos mathematician Stanislaw Ulam showed that the fission bomb and the fusion fuel could be in separate parts of the bomb, and that *radiation* of the fission bomb could first work in a way to *compress* the fusion material before igniting it.

Teller pushed the notion further, and used the results of the boosted-fission "George" test (a boosted-fission device using a small amount of fusion fuel to boost the yield of a fission bomb) to confirm the fusion of heavy hydrogen elements before preparing for their first true multi-stage, Teller-Ulam hydrogen bomb test. Many scientists initially against the weapon, such as Oppenheimer and Bethe, changed their previous opinions, seeing the development as being unstoppable. The first fusion bomb was tested by the United States in *Operation Ivy* on November 1, 1952, on Elugelab Island in the Enewetak (or Eniwetok) Atoll of the Marshall Islands, code-named "Mike". "Mike" used liquid deuterium as its fusion fuel and a large fission weapon as its trigger. The device was a prototype design and not a deliverable weapon: standing over 20 ft (6 m) high and weighing at least 140,000 lb (64 t) (its refrigeration equipment added an additional 24,000 lb as well), it could not have been dropped from even the largest planes.

Its explosion yielded 10.4 megatons of energy—over 450 times the power of the bomb dropped onto Nagasaki— and obliterated Elugelab, leaving an underwater crater 6240 ft (1.9 km) wide and

164 ft (50 m) deep where the island had once been. Truman had initially tried to create a media blackout about the test—hoping it would not become an issue in the upcoming presidential election—but on January 7, 1953, Truman announced the development of the hydrogen bomb to the world as hints and speculations of it were already beginning to emerge in the press. Not to be outdone, the Soviet Union exploded its first thermonuclear device, designed by the physicist Andrei Sakharov, on August 12, 1953, labeled "Joe-4" by the West. This created concern within the U.S. government and military, because, unlike "Mike," the Soviet device was a deliverable weapon, which the U.S. did not yet have. This first device though was arguably not a "true" hydrogen bomb, and could only reach explosive yields in the hundreds of kilotons (never reaching the megaton range of a "staged" weapon). Still, it was a powerful propaganda tool for the Soviet Union, and the technical differences were fairly oblique to the American public and politicians.

Following the "Mike" blast by less than a year, "Joe-4" seemed to validate claims that the bombs were inevitable and vindicate those who had supported the development of the fusion program. Coming during the height of McCarthyism, the effect was most pronounced by the security hearings in early 1954 which revoked former Los Alamos director Robert Oppenheimer of his security clearance, on the grounds that he was unreliable, had not supported the American hydrogen bomb program, and had made long-standing, left-wing ties in the 1930s.

Edward Teller participated in the hearing as the only major scientist to testify against Oppenheimer, a role which resulted in his virtual expulsion from the physics community. On February 28, 1954, the U.S. detonated its first deliverable thermonuclear weapon (which used isotopes of lithium as its fusion fuel), known as the "Shrimp" device of the "Castle Bravo" test, at Bikini Atoll, Marshall Islands. The device yielded 15 megatons of energy, over twice its expected yield, and became the worst radiological disaster in U.S. history. The combination of the unexpectedly large blast and poor weather conditions caused a cloud of radioactive nuclear fallout to contaminate over 7,000 square miles, including Marshall

Island natives and the crew of a Japanese fishing boat, as a snow-like mist. The contaminated islands were evacuated (and are still uninhabitable), but the natives received enough of a radioactive dose that they suffered far elevated levels of cancer and birth defects in the years to come.

The crew of the Japanese fishing boat, *Lucky Dragon 5*, returned to port suffering from radiation sickness and skin burns. Their cargo, many tons of contaminated fish, managed to enter into the market before the cause of their illness was determined. When a crew member died from the sickness and the full results of the contamination were made public by the U.S., Japanese concerns were reignited about the hazards of radiation and resulted in a boycott on eating fish (a main staple of the island country) for some weeks.

The hydrogen bomb age had a profound effect on the thoughts of nuclear war in the popular and military mind. With only fission bombs, nuclear war could be considered something which could easily be "limited." Dropped by planes and only able to destroy the most built up areas of major cities, it was possible to consider fission bombs simply a technological extension of previous wartime bombing (such as the extensive firebombing which took place against Japan and Germany during World War II), and claims that such weapons could lead to worldwide death or harm were easily brushed aside as grave exaggeration.

Even the decades before the development of fission weapons there had been speculation about the possibility for human beings to end all life on the planet by either accident or purposeful maliciousness, but technology had never allowed for such a capacity. The far greater power of hydrogen bombs made this seem ever closer.

The "Castle Bravo" incident itself raised a number of questions about the survivability of a nuclear war. Government scientists in both the U.S. and the USSR had insisted that fusion weapons, unlike fission weapons, were "cleaner" as fusion reactions did not result in the dangerously radioactive by-products as did fission reactions. While technically true, this hid a more gruesome point: the last stage of a multi-staged hydrogen bomb often used the neutrons produced by the fusion reactions to induce fissioning in a jacket of natural uranium, and provided around half of the yield of the device itself.

This fission stage made fusion weapons considerably more "dirty" than they were made out to be, a fact made evident by the towering cloud of deadly fallout which followed the "Bravo" test. When the Soviet Union tested its first megaton device in 1955, the possibility of a limited nuclear war seemed even more remote in the public and political mind: even if a city or country was not the direct target of a nuclear attack, the clouds of fallout and harmful fission products would disperse along with normal weather patterns and embed themselves in the soil and water of non-targeted areas of the planet as well. Speculation began to look towards what would happen as the fallout and dust created by a full-scale nuclear exchange would affect the world as a whole, rather than just the cities and countries which had been directly involved. In this way, the fate of the world was now tied to the fate of the bomb-wielding superpowers.

THE GLOBAL SMALL ARMS MARKET

Small arms require a special mention in any assessment of the global trade in armaments, simply because they are so prolific, the trade in them is so difficult to control and the devastation caused by them is so severe. Taking the definition of the UN panel of government experts on small arms, the category includes all of the following military, police and domestic weapons: revolvers and self-loading pistols, rifles and carbines, assault rifles, sub-machine guns and light machine guns, heavy machine guns, hand-held under-barrel and mounted grenade launchers, portable anti-tank and anti-aircraft guns, recoilless rifles, portable launchers of anti-tank and antiaircraft systems, and mortars of less than 100 mm caliber.

So there are plenty of them, and they are everywhere. They are used by police and security patrols, by national armies and by guerrilla and revolutionary groups, they are carried by civilians legally in a number of countries, for sport in many more, and illegally in every country. They feature in practically every armed conflict between nation-states, in internal and civil wars, in gang fighting and as status symbols.

They are so prolific because they are small and relatively cheap, easy to pass on, smuggle, hide, steal, capture from an enemy or buy over the counter. But, they are ubiquitous because of the sheer numbers they are produced in: millions of them, every day, all over the world. It is a myth that the trade in small arms is only one of recycling second-and third-hand weapons. New production merely creates more second-and third-hand guns. In 1999, 45 different countries reported to the UN that firearms, components and ammunition were legally produced in their territories for domestic or export markets.

Many more countries didn't respond to the requests for information. The main producers of these little killers are China, Russia and the US. Another 20 or so countries, mainly in Europe and Asia, produce most of the rest of the world's supply. A further 29 countries produce nominal quantities mainly to meet their domestic never be accurate data on which countries have the most of them. Even if there were, accurate figures for exactly which of these were legal, illegal, military or civilian would be impossible to determine.

'The total number and global distribution of small arms remains one of the greatest enigmas in the field of international peace and security', says the Small Arms Survey. The Survey is a project of the Graduate Institute of International Studies in Geneva, which has attempted to profile and estimate the proliferation of firearms (hand-held guns and rifles, rather than hand-held missile launchers and the like), based on rough estimates and incomplete reporting by countries.

Their research estimates that there are at least 550 million legally-held firearms in the world today-at least one gun for every 11 of the world's people. Over half of all of these are privately owned. The group was unable, not surprisingly, to estimate the number of illegally-held arms in the world. The 20th century was the most violent one in human history. Not only did it witness two world wars, and 30 years of major arms-fuelled tension between the world's superpowers, it also featured hundreds of localized conflicts, armed border disputes, civil wars, military coups and counter coups, revolutionary struggles and armed invasions.

According to the Armed Conflicts Report 2000 and the State of the World Report 1999, there were 40 armed conflicts underway in 36 different countries as the 21st century was born. Even in the short time since the millennium, the world has witnessed a new 'war on terror' waged by the US and its allies against Afghanistan, with the threat of extension to Somalia, and the possibility of intensified attacks on Iraq.

Earth is a planet at war, and to a large extent this is a consequence of the legal and illicit sale of arms. In crude but plain terms, without weaponry, combat would be more limited in scale. In most conflict zones in the world, war is a way of life.

Waging war is a means of generating money, exerting political power, and providing employment. In some areas of the developing world, children grow up knowing nothing else but bloodshed, dead, injured or maimed relatives, the daily risk of landmines; even bearing arms themselves. If they survive long enough to procreate, their own children will know only the same.

War Today

Despite tension between India and Pakistan, the future stability of the world is probably now less at risk from an all-out nuclear catastrophe-as was thought during the Cold War era-than from a slow, insidious, systematic proliferation of small wars and local strife in mainly smaller nations, many of them in Africa. In 1998, Africa suffered 11 major armed conflicts. It is now the most war-torn region in the world.

Those small wars are created and sustained in a constant battle to control territory, plunder resources and wield power. William Hartung, of the World Policy Institute, illustrates the problem. When the current Liberian president Charles Taylor invaded Liberia on Christmas Eve in 1989, he did so with just 100 irregular soldiers, armed with AK47 rifles. Within months they had seized mineral and timber resources and used the profits to purchase more light weapons: the first few turns in an ongoing vicious cycle.

According to Hartung: 'This pattern of war as plunder has been repeated with local variations in Sierra Leone, where the Liberian-backed Revolutionary United Front (RUF) has used diamond sales to fuel its campaign of terror; in Colombia, where government forces, right-wing paramilitaries and anti-government rebels have skimmed off profits, fees and bribes from the cocaine trade; in Angola, where UNITA rebel forces have raised billions of dollars through diamond sales and the Angolan Government has countered by stocking its arsenal with revenues drawn from its large offshore oil deposits."

The seizure or trafficking of drugs, diamonds and other valuable commodities produces profits for warring factions. Profits are spent not on peace, reconciliation or education, but on more weapons-bought on the illicit market, and through more 'legitimate' channels. The weapons suppliers to the perpetrators of the 1994 genocide in Rwanda included brokers and shippers in Britain, South Africa and France, working with collaborators in Albania, Belgium, Bulgaria, Egypt, Italy, the Seychelles and the former Zaire (now DR Congo/DRC). Arms and military training are also supplied to warring or revolutionary factions, both openly and secretly, by Western nations to serve their own political ambitions.

Bigger Picture

But the arms trade also has a role in sustaining larger, more 'official' tensions and conflicts between states. The deadly dealing increases strains and thereby fuels wars between established nations. Here are some examples. From 1989 to 1998, the US provided over $227 million in weapons and training to African military forces. Of this, over $111 million went to governments that have been directly or indirectly involved in the war in the Democratic Republic of Congo (DRC): Angola, Burundi, Chad Namibia, Rwanda, Sudan, Uganda and Zimbabwe. The big seven arms-selling countries in the world-the US, France, Germany, Britain, Russia, China and Italy have all sold arms to states currently involved in conflict including Sri Lanka, Indonesia, Israel, China, Taiwan, India and Pakistan. And they usually show their deadly wares at arms fairs.

Military Training

Military training Military training is an aspect of the industry often overlooked by campaigners and politicians working towards arms control. Yet the provision of training to foreign armies, or warring factions, is commonplace and was clearly illustrated with the allied forces' training and assistance given to the Afghan United Front forces during their reclaiming of Afghanistan at the end of 2001. Just as with the hardware, military training is used by governments to further their strategic and political objectives, as well as being a tool in international relations. But like arms sales, military training of foreign fighters can also bounce back. Since the US armed forces are among the most highly trained and best financially supported in the world, it is no surprise that the US is a major provider of military training. Here's an example. Towards the end of his presidency, Bill Clinton took a special interest in Africa. His proposed 'new partnership' was not to supply aid or help build civil society as was hoped, but apparently to establish a wide program of troop training. In 1998, the US provided $45.8 million in international military education training (IMET) for over 400 African soldiers.

THE GLOBAL SMALL ARMS CAMPAIGN

The humanitarian, political-economic and security dimensions of excessive and destabilizing accumulations of small arms confront civil and political society with the need for immediate action. With political awareness aroused by the human toll of illicit small arms in Africa, Asia, Europe and the Western Hemisphere, denoting the issue's global dimension, the UN is embarking on the important task to convene, by 2001, an international conference on the illicit trade in small arms in all its aspects. A nascent global campaign is to be commended for successfully pushing small arms onto the agenda of multilateral arms control. Unlike the international campaign to ban landmines, however, the emerging "movement" is lacking in focus and direction. A plethora of initiatives notwithstanding, concerns persist that economic and political interests of the few may hinder tangible humanitarian results for the many.

The potential for diversion is immense as even basic agreement on how to define the issue remains wanting. Is it, for example, an arms control, disarmament or crime prevention issue; is one to address oneself on the supply or the demand side, the precipitating versus root causes of small arms violence? Too overwhelming, then, the dualism which connects illicit arms to the licit trade, where a majority of them originate, too daunting the interaction between the licit and illicit trade, too challenging the interconnectedness between the root and precipitating causes of civil conflict and small arms violence.

Small arms violence poses as much an arms control challenge as a humanitarian challenge. It can also be said, since a majority of weapons producers are located in the developed world and a majority of weapons recipients in the developing world, the small arms issue is, at its core, a North-South issue. In the North, the global campaign on small arms must be put in the framework of development, demilitarization and peace building. In the South, such a campaign must be put in the context of a broader justice-oriented community and human rights.

Reducing the number of small arms requires a multisectoral and comprehensive approach, encompassing a whole range of measures, both operative and normative, which must be dealt with both within the context of conflict prevention and conflict resolution. Small arms action must address both security, humanitarian and developmental concerns.

Economic development is dependent on a secure and stable political environment. Some refer to this as the "Security First" approach. But the opposite is also true: without economic development, many of the root causes of grievance cannot be properly addressed and there will be no political stability. A more appropriate-nonetheless more daunting-approach instead of "Security First" is "a proportional and integrated approach to security and development." In areas of conflict, both security and development aspects must be integrated into national programs as well as into international cooperation efforts. Whereas, however, taking a narrow approach "Security First" advances security at the expense of development, the proportional-integrated approach takes too broad a venue with respect both, to the supply of and demand for small arms, existent and future stockpiles and inherent linkages between security and development. It would appear that it strives to achieve too much in too short a period of time.

Recognizing security and development as corollaries in reducing supply the EPG compromise cooperative regulatory approach advances a constructive parallelism between both input functions without establishing ipso facto linkages which, from a bargaining point of view, should lend itself to tangible results within a reasonable time frame. The compromise approach built around a universal, comprehensive and non-discriminatory Small Arms Control Regime which centres on transparency and accountability should not be seen as an alternative, but as a minimalist position concomitant to the integrated-proportional approach.

An independent international commission the Eminent Persons Group strives to make a specific contribution to the emerging global small arms effort. While fully acknowledging the need for a broad approach, EPG pursues a cooperative regulatory approach to the international trade in small arms. As a sub-campaign and integral to the larger small arms campaign being led by the International Action Network on Small Arms (IANSA), EPG undertakes to confront the supply side of the illicit trade by making cross-border arms sales subject to arms control, export and transparency regimes.

Moreover, governments will be encouraged to limit the number of small arms approved for export, to combat illicit transfers of weapons and to assist in extracting surplus weapons which are circulating the global market. In this complex situation, a sincere abhorrence of covert wars and civilian destruction would prove conducive to putting in place the norms that would regulate state behaviour. The attainment of the goal requires an integrated proportional approach between governments and civil society to advance elements of a realistic plan of action for the 2001 UN conference on small arms trafficking in all its aspects. Within the preparatory process for the conference, this approach consists of two tracks: first, the involvement of EPG on the inter-governmental level and secondly, the participation of EPG within the NGO community. For the two levels of action, the governmental and non-governmental, are co-dependent and mutually enhancing in building momentum for regulatory controls and micro-disarmament.

EPG's ability to remain highly visible at both, the non-governmental and inter-governmental levels of small arms action, defines the Commission's juxtaposition within the global small arms effort. The Commission's uniqueness lies in the special blending of incumbent and former officials at the highest levels of government from around the world. Members of the Commission represent both, weapons-exporting and weapons-importing countries.

This active involvement of decision-makers in the early stages of and throughout the preparatory process is essential to political advances towards curtailing small arms proliferation. It is the high caliber of members of the commission, which provides for the level of credibility and political prestige to assure serious deliberations. With respect to the governmental level, EPG is in exploratory talks with UN member States, within the Group of Interested States (GIS), to provide for a consultative framework, affiliated with but independent of the eminent persons group. GIS is comprised of foreign ministers of those UN member States which are taking the lead on the small arms issue and which find themselves in conceptual agreement on the cooperative regulatory approach inherent in SACR. Without prejudice to national bargaining positions, GIS facilitates consultations on a multilateral approach to small arms proliferation both, throughout the preparatory process and at the conference itself. With respect to the non-governmental level EPG is actively cooperating with and working through IANSA. At the same time, as part of its commitment to help raise the profile of small arms proliferation globally, EPG is pursuing a vigorous public diplomacy schedule.

In close consultation with UN member States, the UN Secretariat and other NGOs the group will, within the preparatory committee, advance elements of an action agenda aimed at curtailing illicit small arms by confronting the illicit trade. To be successful such an action agenda must centre on increased transparency and raised common standards and provide concrete and practical measures on the global and regional level. The group will submit to the UN conference a report on the scope and magnitude of the illicit arms trade, ways to curb it and the United Nations role in collecting and disseminating information in this area, prevention and enforcement.

SMALL ARMS VIOLENCE: THE HUMANITARIAN CHALLENGE

The destabilizing accumulation of small arms outside of formal regulatory controls and the resulting toll inflicted on civilian populations in countries around the world poses one of the great humanitarian challenges of our time. Small arms violence undermines good governance and, in so doing, jeopardizes fundamental human rights, economic development, political stability, social justice and peace. The overabundance of small arms has come to affect nearly all parts of the UN system.

In exacerbating armed conflict, violence, crime, social disruption, displacement of peoples and human suffering, and threatening UN peace and relief missions, curtailing the proliferation of small arms will be "one of the key challenges in preventing conflict in the next century."

The qualitative and quantitative nature of post-modern warfare has changed and greatly increased its impact on civilians.

There has been a complete elimination of the well-recognized distinction between combatants on the one hand and the civilian population on the other. In many wars, the primary strategy seems to effect maximum civilian casualties by either maiming or outright killing. Indeed, decimation of the opponent's civilian population has become an essential part of the strategy of modern warfare.

Small arms are the weapon of choice in most conflicts and responsible for 90% of casualties; they are the weapons that kill most people in most wars. A majority of the 200,000 deaths annually are civilian, most notably children, with only a minimal decline of casualties (less than 30%) in the post-conflict phase. For these weapons are inexpensive, readily available and easy to operate.

In Uganda, for example, an AK-47 automatic rifle, of which there are around 55 million in circulation, and which can be easily carried, maintained and assembled by a ten year old child, can be bought for the price of a chicken and in Northern Kenya for the price of a goat. In many conflicts, children are forced to engage in open hostilities. UNICEF estimates that a quarter million have ended up as "child combatants" in some 30 recent conflicts. A whole generation of children the world over is being inducted into a culture of violence marked by violent death and injury, with dire psychological consequences. This mental militarization, de-humanisation and transformation of societal values, which lead to the quest of some to solve social problems in a violent manner will, over time, tear apart the last remnants of civil society. In developing countries around the world, ever-expanding small arms and light weapons expenditures aggravate deteriorating domestic conditions. Civil wars disrupt trade, tourism and investment. With more and more resources diverted to maintaining internal order, human rights abuses increase, basic human needs are neglected and democracy and development are put at risk.

The growing control of crime over civil society poses additional dangers to political and economic reform by threatening democratic structures. In many countries, precious natural resources, rather than being means for economic and political empowerment for the many, end up fueling the engines of war and annihilation to enrich the few. The trade in diamonds, oil and precious metals increasingly provides funds for illicit arms purchases and has led to the creation of a dangerous strategic triad of political, criminal and commercial interests.

A 1996 World Bank report explains the connection between war and poverty. During the past decade, fifteen of the twenty poorest countries in the world have experienced major conflict. Virtually every low-income country in the world has either undergone major conflict, or borders on one or more countries in conflict. The inability of increasing numbers of governments to redress social iniquities worsens the conditions of the disenfranchised and greatly contributes to frustration and sudden explosions of violence.

The world has seen more conflict in the last twenty years than at any time that century. As a result, about 35 million people are currently displaced, either outside or within their country.

While the mere presence of small arms in large numbers and outside formal security structures may not in and of itself generate conflict, it nonetheless increases the likelihood of violent eruptions and increases their scale and lethality. At the same time, their continued presence or improper management during a peace process may prolong conflict. Moreover, increasingly, these weapons are being turned against relief workers, who provide desperately needed social services throughout the world.

Beyond threatening intra-state political and economic stability, the ready supply of inexpensive small arms through the illicit arms trade proves conducive to heightening inter-state conflict. Weapons routes crisscross the entire continent and it is no longer necessary to be a neighbor to a conflict area to feel its ill effects. Weapons from Afghanistan, for example, travel eastward to reach China's coastal cities and southwards to feed conflict in Sri Lanka.

With cross-border guerilla groups proliferating and dividing into warring factions capable of outgunning government forces, internal instabilities increasingly tend to evolve into larger regional wars, putting the nation-state system itself in jeopardy. The conflict in Congo-Kinshasa involves the armed forces of eight countries and several militia groups. As a result, of the 22 million refugees globally, 8.1 million are in Africa.

Around the globe, there are at least 20 locations where an armed conflict could occur or recur due largely to an incomplete process of disarmament either of former combatants or civilians, particularly among societies with fragile or fledgling state structures.

3

Nuclear Weapons and Programme

India should step up efforts in research and development to keep up with technological advances in this field. While India is committed to maintain the deployment of a deterrent which is both minimum and credible, it will not accept any restraints on building its R&D capability.

THE NUCLEAR PROGRAMME

Usually analysts proffer four arguments about proliferation. These are: (i) security concerns, (ii) prestige, (iii) technological imperatives, and (iv) domestic politics. Let us go through each briefly. The security or the realist argument posits that security concerns directly related to a state's physical security and survival ultimately drive a state to acquire nuclear weapons. Thus, a state operating under an anarchic international system and facing serious security pressures might go for the nuclear option. The second position informs us that nuclear weapons are a symbol of prestige. States acquire great power status or international recognition by developing a nuclear arsenal. The third view proposes that a state's decision to go for nuclear weapons is an inevitable outcome of the technological momentum created by nuclear research and development programmes. The final argument is that intra-bureaucratic politics as well as politicians' drive to score domestic political points may lead a state down the nuclear path. In other words, bureaucrats acting on the basis of their own individual policy preferences or bureaucracies carrying out their specific institutional interests may propel a country towards nuclear weapons.

India went for nuclear weapons has followers of all schools vying with each other to explain India's actions. For George Perkovich, domestic factors and prestige issues play the most important role in India's actions. He points out that India's quest for nuclear weapons capabilities began before a Chinese threat emerged and was driven not by military or national security experts but rather by bureaucrats like Homi Bhabha.

It was also a reflection of India's moral norms and post colonial identity manifested through Nehru's recognition that India could gain international power, standing and a measure of security if she went for nuclear weapons. Others like C. Raja Mohan and Bhumitra Chakma argue that it was mainly security concerns that led to India's decision to acquire nuclear weapons.

Chakma convincingly writes that given India's pressing economic problems it is very difficult to imagine that she would invest such huge resources in a nuclear programme merely to satisfy the need for recognition and prestige. Similarly, India's decision to persist with the nuclear programme was not strongly influenced by technological imperatives or domestic pressures. If such were the case, then India would not have abstained from going nuclear in the 1960s and Indira Gandhi and other prime ministers would have chosen to carry out the tests when their domestic popularity was plummeting.

While prestige, technology and domestic factors might have played some role, it was the emergence of China as a nuclear weapon state and later on, the development of the Pakistani nuclear bomb, which led India to acquire a nuclear arsenal. Raja Mohan argues in a similar vein.

He mentions the same reasons as Chakma, but adds that in the 1990s the demise of the Soviet Union and the removal of a security back-up, the emergence of the US as the sole superpower, China's rise and international pressure to adhere to the NPT and CTBT" all aggravated India's security concerns and pushed New Delhi inexorably towards the nuclear option. Sumit Ganguly also places emphasis on the realist rationales while conceding that prestige and technological imperatives also had roles to play.

While the role played by prestige, technological and bureaucratic factors in India's nuclear programme must be acknowledged, the arguments made by Chakma, Raja Mohan and Ganguly – regarding the importance of realism in deciphering India's nuclear posture – appear to be the most convincing. At the same time, this 'realism' is strictly an Indian understanding of realism, and a study of Indian strategic culture is necessary to unearth the peculiar ways in which Indians have viewed security. Some argue that realism and culturalist explanations of international events are two distinct approaches. They then consider whether the culturalist explanations might yield superior insight. Stuart Poore, for his part, sees strategic culture protagonists as posing a direct challenge to the hegemony of realist thinking. However, there are, and can be, no unencultured realists. As argued above, India's approach to nuclear weapons – including the means of their development, the rationale for them, and India's stance on global efforts to stem proliferation – reflects a distinctive Indian way of thinking and acting. The use of *moralpolitik* is a good example of such behaviour.

Indian Strategic Culture and Administering

The Indian strategic culture, even one dealing with nuclear weapons, must start by understanding the role of history in the development of Indian strategic culture. Why is history so important? Because the movers and shakers behind India's nuclear journey were men and women who were conditioned by the way they understood Indian history. Writing about the first atomic bombs, constructed by refugee scientists in the United States, John Lukacs reminds us that the "causes" of the atom bomb are historical (and ultimately, personal); they are scientific and technical only on a secondary level of "causes." The main reasons for the development of the bomb included Hitler, the Second World War and the persecution of Jews in Germany. Lukacs contends that the bomb was made at a particular time and for a specific purpose, not merely because at a certain phase of scientific development a certain stage of technological know-how was attained. He argues that it was actually because at a certain point in history, certain scientists began to fear that other scientists might be building an atom bomb for Hitler. Although important scientific and technological breakthroughs had taken place between 1938 and 1945, these ought not to obscure the principal reasons behind the bomb's creation, which as in every historical act, were formed by personal choices, through historical thinking and historical consciousness, and conditioned by the political, racial, national, religious and ideological inclinations of responsible individuals. In the same way, one can see how Nehru's understanding as well as the general Indian perspective of Indian history influenced opinions about the building of the bomb.

The fact that India has been constantly subjected to foreign invasions and subjugation is ever present in the Indian mind, and Nehru was a serious student of Indian history who knew the feeling of insecurity it generated. This insecurity was premised, in part, on the belief that the Europeans had been able to intervene in India because of Indian divisiveness, and that Britain's ability to play off the Indian powers against one another had been particularly successful. But the overarching feeling was that this conquest was made easier, if not possible, because of superior Western technology. Nehru himself was no exception to this conviction. Speaking on the occasion of the introduction of the Atomic Energy Bill, he noted that in the past few hundred years of human history the world had developed a new source of power, i.e. steam, and that this had subsequently ushered in the industrial age. India, Nehru pointed out, did not develop steam power and it became a backward country for that reason. The message of the speech is that India was colonised because of her lack of technological sophistication. This understanding of technological backwardness and its disastrous consequences for India's security has been a powerful rationale in Indian thinking about the nuclear bomb.

But there is another dimension to this need for countries like India. Technological backwardness not only meant a danger to her security, making her vulnerable to colonial and neo-colonial powers, but also implied social backwardness. Lacking in technological skills, and unable to master elementary, let alone complex, scientific and technological knowledge – this was how the civilisations of India, China and Africa were identified by European conquerors and colonisers and were thus deemed unfit to be counted as equals. Michael Adas writes that underlying all attempts to 'transform' non-Western societies was the assumption that Europeans were best suited to rule African and Asian societies because they represented the most progressive and advanced civilisations ever known. The ultimate proof of this assumption lay in Europe's unrivalled scientific and technological achievements.

European superiority manifested through technological advancements gradually but surely attained racial connotations. But even in the 19th century, when racist theories relating to non-Western people found wide acceptance among the articulate classes of Europe, many thinkers gave credence to scientific and technological proofs of Western superiority while rejecting those based on racist arguments. Racism should therefore be viewed as a subordinate rather than dominant theme in the European intellectual discourse on non-Western peoples.

For newly independent India's leader, the attainment of technological and scientific prowess through the mastery of nuclear science was an objective that would not only ensure security, but also serve as a proof of the ability of Indians to compete with Western powers. Thus, India's strategic culture was influenced by the need to destroy the myth of Western technical (also read military) superiority that has become the symbol of the Western claim to racial superiority. And any attempt to prevent such a policy is seen as perpetuating the inferior status of India and Indians as experienced during colonial rule. The terms India has used to justify her nuclear programme – apartheid, racism, equal treatment, etc. – have been reiterated a number of times. They are wielded either to endorse India's progress in developing a nuclear arsenal, or to explain India's position at various conferences on nuclear proliferation. This characteristic of Indian strategic culture was not limited to people like Nehru, who had spent most of his life under colonial rule, but can also be seen in recent times.

Jaswant Singh's article and his position have already been mentioned. And Perkovich points out that when a Western researcher reported that India had sought material help from China for her nuclear programme, the then IAEC Chairman Raja Ramanna lashed out by saying that Indians are used to "white" people having a low opinion of them and that the researcher's remark indicated envy at India's achievement of total independence in her nuclear requirements. Raja Ramanna's behaviour, according to Perkovich, highlighted the recurrent and vitally important issue of racist colonialism prevalent, as India sees it, in the international nuclear arena.

Given the waves of foreign invaders that came to India, it is only natural that Indians should be concerned about any foreign intervention in South Asia. The Indian desire for nuclear weapons must be seen in this light. It has already been shown how the *Enterprise* exercise of 1971 led India to believe that a superpower's nuclear arsenal could also be used to thwart Indian objectives and threaten India herself. The fear of (Western) intervention with its obvious security connotations for India has been a part of Indian strategic culture due to Western forays and the subsequent conquest by Britain in the eighteenth century, reinforced by the experience of 1971.

The importance of seeking a nuclear capability to ward off the probability of any such event occurring again cannot be emphasised enough. India has always been sensitive to any nuclear threat made by Western powers against non-nuclear states, and Rajiv Gandhi was in tune with this position when he made known that he was very concerned by the nuclear threats implied during the Gulf crisis of 1990-91. A similar concern and uneasiness engulfed Indian policy makers and analysts when the North Atlantic Treaty Organization (NATO) decided to intervene in the crisis surrounding the former Yugoslavia in 1999. Such an act was perceived by Indians, suffering from their own separatist conflicts, as a harbinger of more unilateral actions by the United States and thus justified India's acquisition of nuclear weapons. Indian history, in short, is an important source for understanding Indian strategic culture with regard to nuclear weapons.

The role of religion in understanding the nature of Indian strategic culture is also significant for "religion is a particularly useful device for sacralizing violence and thus legitimizing it." Not only does religion play a cathartic influence on the way societies see war, it also influences the way societies act in times of war and peace and their approach to the use of force. Looking for the traits of a community's strategic culture in religion might not be a common practice in contemporary social sciences, but in a country like India, where the influence of Hinduism is so powerful and pervades all aspects of life, it would be a most serious error to ignore it.

The Indian quest for nuclear weapons has been justified by some analysts as having its roots in Hinduism's sacred texts. In the *Vedas*, the *Epics* and the *Puranas*, citations can be found which might be said to describe ancient weapons of mass destruction, perhaps even nuclear weapons. Indeed some analysts identify the most terrible weapon described in the *Mahabharata* (one of the *Epics*), the *Brahmastra*, as the ultimate weapon, the modern version of which is the nuclear bomb. While the modern mind will rightly find this claim incredible, given the powerful impact such religious texts have on the Indian mind, it would be wise not to ignore them totally. A devoted admirer of science and technology like Nehru identified the tendency to cite the presence of WMD in the ancient texts as nothing more than traditional stories of magical exploits. But elsewhere Nehru quotes Goethe's observation on Roman myths ("if the Romans were great enough to invent things like that, we at least should be great enough to believe them") and suggests that Hindu epics and stories should be believed. It is clear that nuclear weapons were not totally unacceptable to the Indian mind, at least from a religious point of view.

It has already been pointed out that *moralpolitik* has been a significant, if not the most important, characteristic of the Indian strategic culture insofar as the issue of nuclear weapons is concerned. This *moralpolitik* trait also finds its justification and practice in Hindu religious texts. A study of the two epics, *Ramayana* and *Mahabharata*, provides a better understanding of the Indian propensity to take a high moral position publicly but to secretly and deviously act in a completely different manner. This paper proposes that Indian strategic culture has two traits, both derived from the central characters of *Ramayana* and *Mahabharata,* i.e., Rama and Krishna respectively. Both Rama and Krishna's features operate concurrently in the Indian strategic mind.

Let us briefly identify these two features. The central character of the *Ramayana* is Rama, a prince forced into exile through the evil machinations of his stepmother. The *Ramayana* is all about the adventures of Rama as he endures his exile and finally reclaims the throne. Rama is an incarnation of Vishnu (one of the three main gods who rule the Hindu pantheon of gods) and is the very embodiment of goodness. He is virtuous, truthful, and mighty but always on the side of the right, a fierce warrior but seldom moved by anger, kind and helpful. There were only a few minor lapses in his impeccable conduct. Rama displayed a fatalistic nature through his acceptance of suffering. He would not fight for his rights. He accepts his fate or karma and will not struggle against it. The main character of *Mahabharata* is somewhat difficult to pin down as the epic contains quite a few great heroes. The story centres on an apocalyptic battle pitting two sides (kinsmen) and ends with the defeat of Kauravas and the victory of Pandavas. The Pandavas are helped in this titanic battle by Krishna, another incarnation of Vishnu. But unlike Rama, Krishna is not bound by any ethical considerations. It was Krishna's crafty and resourceful ways that led to the extermination of the Kauravas. Deception, subterfuge, a relentlessly offensive posture and the use of cunning methods were Krishna's forte. It is Krishna who urges Arjuna, the great warrior hero of the Pandavas, immobilised by the prospect of fratricidal war, to show no pity or remorse, but to do his duty (*dharma*) and kill his enemies even if they were Arjuna's cousins, teachers, mentors and kinsmen.

Indian strategic culture sees an interaction between both these traits. Thus India talks about morality, virtue and victimhood – the Rama of world politics. At the same time India will resort to whatever means are necessary to attain her objective – the Indian Krishna. Therefore, the *moralpolitik* trait of Indian strategic culture embodies both these values within itself. But it has to be remembered that though the *Ramayana* and the *Mahabharata* are immensely popular epics, it is the *Mahabharata* that really captures the Indian mind. In other words Rama is the Indian ideal, Krishna the Indian reality. India will adhere simultaneously to both postures, as *moralpolitik* stipulates, without any contradiction. After all, are not Krishna and Rama incarnations of one entity, Vishnu?

The importance of religious beliefs influencing Indian strategic culture must also take into account that most familiar feature of Hindu religion – the caste system. In an interesting model developed by Anirudha Gupta, one sees independent India formulating a foreign policy in South Asia based on a "caste" system. Thus, India is the Brahmin of the region and other states fall into various castes according to their capabilities. The same framework can be applied to the world system which is perceived to be rigidly hierarchical. As per the stipulations of the caste system, the Brahmin is at the top of the social hierarchy and India's quest for nuclear weapons can be identified as a means by which a 'Brahmin' India seeks to be in the top rank of the world hierarchy. And as no one can deny the Brahmin his divine right to be at the top, any proliferation measure intended to prevent India from attaining her rightful status is to be ignored. Therefore, the reasoning behind India's nuclear programme and her behaviour with regard to such weapons must be approached with an understanding of the religious beliefs and characteristics of Indian society. Such an understanding will help explain why India's realist, i.e. *moralpolitik*, approach to nuclear weapons is so uniquely Indian. While religious texts and beliefs help shed light on the use of *moralpolitik*, one must also note that India's actions have their origins in the teachings of traditional Indian strategic thinking.

The most important source of such thinking is the *Arthashastra* written by Kautilya. It was with the help of Kautilya that Chandragupta Maurya laid the foundations of a truly great Indian empire in 320 B.C. For understanding India's adherence to *moralpolitik* policies, it should be noted that Kautilya advocated the use of deceit to attain one's objective and such methods as wearing a mask of moral probity, religious righteousness or citing moral righteousness to mask one's intentions, all fall under this category. Nehru was strongly influenced by Kautilya's theories, and it is important to consider how Indian strategic culture has been influenced by Kautilya's teachings. Indian strategic culture and its impact on the nuclear programme must take India's geographical realities into consideration.

George Tanham in his seminal essay on Indian strategic thinking identified geography as having profoundly affected Indian history and culture and therefore her strategic thinking. A history of invasion along India's north-western routes has traditionally oriented defence planners to pay special attention to that region. The arrival of the Europeans from the sea and their naval superiority made India aware of the need for a powerful navy. When one thinks of India's nuclear programme, geography is seldom mentioned.

But it has profound implications. Even though India is placed in the South Asian region by analysts, India's security thinking takes into consideration the fact that China, too, is an actor in the South Asian strategic framework. China and India share a long border and China has a geographical advantage through her control over the Tibetan plateau overlooking the plains of India. There is also the reality of China's military and nuclear connection with Pakistan. Most Western analysts are unable to include an 'outside' country in their neatly compartmentalised artificial geographical units, but the fact is that China is included by the Indians in any nuclear calculation in South Asia.

Expression of Indian Strategic Culture

The exclusion of the armed forces from the nuclear programme decision-making process has been made clear by George Perkovich in his study. The absence of the armed forces from the decision-making loop on the nuclear issue resulted in one army chief, General K. Sundarji, depicting the frustration of the service chiefs through a novel titled *The Blind Men of Hindustan*. On the other hand, various other actors such as the political parties, the Indian Parliament, the bureaucracy and even public opinion, have had little or no impact on decisions relating to the nuclear programme.

The real debate on nuclear weapons has been carried on by followers of Mahatma Gandhi who stressed the principles of nonviolence and morality in India's actions. While this paper has argued that Gandhi himself was not against violence when it came to pursuing India's interests, the truth is that some segments of the Indian population came to adhere rigidly to such a concept, as a result of misreading the subtle nature of the thoughts and actions of Gandhi and Nehru. Nevertheless, in the 1970s the seemingly contradictory approaches were merged through a clever synthesis, resulting in a now widely accepted formula. Known as the Subrahmanyam formula, it reinforced the broad strategic culture under which the nuclear programme is located. It stipulated that India would acquire nuclear weapons in order to pressure the nuclear 'haves' to disarm, and to protect itself against nuclear blackmail. Thus, by combining idealism with self-interest, the thunder of the no-bomb lobby – which had a negligible impact, if at all, on the programme – was taken away.

But while in the previous years the armed services had very little to do with nuclear weapons, this now seems to be changing. Further, Indian strategic culture should not be perceived to be static. With the development of an Indian triad, it is undergoing a slow but substantive change, and this is taking place in the balance between the political and operational aspects of deterrence. The once overwhelming political understanding of nuclear weapons manifested through the total absence of the armed forces from the nuclear arena is slowly giving way to a more operational conception of nuclear weapons.

The development of various delivery systems – including long range missiles and weapons platform systems like nuclear submarines – is pushing the erstwhile practice of deterrence, which remained restricted to broad declarations on doctrine and the development of limited capabilities, towards more pressing operational questions about the quantity and quality of weapons and the infrastructure surrounding them.

The journey India has taken from the writing of the letter in 1944 by Bhabha to the Tata Foundation, to the nuclear tests of 1998, has been a long and arduous one.

As this paper has tried to show, realist security considerations played the most important role in propelling India towards nuclear weapons. But this realist thinking has been Indian in nature. The motivations for such thinking and behaviour are influenced by what India thinks about herself. Thus, one notices how history, religion and geography have all interacted and produced a distinctively Indian approach to nuclear weapons.

While all the nuclear states of the world have travelled more or less the same path towards developing nuclear weapons, the rationales and the way they went about doing it differed. Strategic culture helps explain these different pathways and styles. In India's case a distinctive style, that of *moralpolitik,* epitomises the Indian way of approaching the nuclear issue. This *moralpolitik* has been brought about by India's history, geography, religious and strategic thinking. It is important to recognize that this culture is not transhistorical, either in the sense that it can be traced back to some 'authentic' pre-colonial tradition or that it is timeless, immutable and unchanging. It is a strategic culture influenced by events, experiences past and present and modified as and when thought necessary. As the world awakens to the growing importance of India, an understanding of Indian strategic culture as discerned from her nuclear policy will certainly help make sense of the way India sees the world.

NUCLEAR WEAPONS PROGRAMME

The end of World War II marked a revolution in world affairs - the recasting of nations and relations between nations, and the emergence of a new technology which fundamentally changed the role of warfare. Within the span of two years and two months, from 1945 to 1947, three critical events occurred whose reverberations have brought the threat of nuclear war in South Asia seemingly daily to the front pages of newspapers everywhere. The three events were - in chronological order - the establishment of the United Nations on 26 June 1945; the dramatic demonstration of the destruction of which even crude nuclear weapons are capable in August 1945; and the calamitous partition of British India into the modern states of India and Pakistan at midnight on 14-15 August 1947.

It is clear to everyone that the legacy of partition is a key driving force behind the nuclear standoff that now exists between India and Pakistan. Partition split apart a region that had been united for millenia amid communal massacres on a scale never before seen, leaving in its wake the unresolved issue of contested Kashmir - a Muslim-majority region held by Hindu-majority India. The skirmishing that has continued now for over fifty years, punctuated by outbreaks of full-scale war (in 1947, 1965, and 1971), have given both nations ample motivation to develop potent weapons to gain advantage over — or restore balance with — the other. Another motivation for India's acquisition of nuclear weapons, less often considered in the West, is the potential threat and regional challenge presented by the nuclear-armed state of China, which faces India along much of its northern border. Disputes covering 80,000 square kilometers of this border region exist:

- China currently occupies the Aksai Chin plateau adjacent to Ladakh in Kashmir;
- India occupies the North-East Frontier Agency claimed by China.

These territorial disputes, a legacy of British rule, erupted into the Sino-Indian War on 20 October 1962, when China launched a massive attack on India to which India was powerless to respond. India had relied for years on a warm relationship with the Soviet Union as a counterweight to China, but with the USSR facing down the United States at the same moment in the Cuban Missile Crisis, India was shocked to find the Politburo suddenly switching to support China in an effort to bolster its own position. PM Nehru was forced to appeal to the U.S. for help. U.S. naval air forces arrived off the coast, but before the USAF could deploy to India, China halted its attack on 21 November and partially withdrew. China continues to hold the Aksai Chin region captured in the initial advance. The legacy of this incident was the discovery that the Soviet Union was an unreliable ally, and the deep resolve not to be at a similar disadvantage with respect to China in the future.

Finally, an even less well known factor is a deep-seated drive to achieve international influence commensurate with India's size, and its importance throughout history as one of the world's principle civilizations. At the founding of the United Nations in 1945 the composition of the UN Security Council, the world's most influential and powerful international body, was fixed and has never changed from that time. By an accident of history India was not an independent state at that moment, and its only hope for representation at the conference was the Churchill administration, then in its closing days, which vehemently opposed India's national aspirations. As a result China - with a similar geographic size, population, and state of economic development - was given a seat on Security Council, but India was not. Nuclear weapons did not exist at the time the Security Council composition was debated, but over time the five Council members all acquired nuclear, then thermonuclear, arms. With the signing of the Nuclear Non-Proliferation treaty in 1970, and the replacement on the Council of the non-nuclear Taipei Chinese government with the nuclear armed government in Beijing shortly thereafter, the de facto principle that Security Council permanent members and the "nuclear club" were one and the same was firmly established.

The crucial importance of the desire for recognition of India as a world power in driving forward the nuclear weapons program, even overshadowing considerations of military necessity and deterrence is underscored by remarks by former weapons program leader Raj Ramanna: "There was never a discussion among us over whether we shouldn't make the bomb. How to do it was more important. For us it was a matter of prestige that would justify our ancient past. The question of deterrence came much later. Also, as Indian scientists we were keen to show our Western counterparts, who thought little of us those days, that we too could do it."

Thus it should be no surprise that India, now tied for third place among the world's largest economies (with Germany), and soon to become the most populous nation on Earth, has concluded that to be given its due in world affairs, it must become a member of the nuclear club as well.

What is notable however is how the world's largest democracy developed such capabilities. The decisions were made by a handful of people, with virtually no input or oversight by the public or the legislature. India's nuclear weapons program from its outset has answered only to the Prime Minister's office, and only the Prime Minister and a select few of his or her appointees have ever had any say in its development and acquisition.

Origin of India's Nuclear Weapon Program

India's indigenous efforts in nuclear science and technology were established remarkably early. The first step was taken by Dr. Homi Jehangir Bhabha in March 1944 when he submitted a proposal to the Sir Dorab Tata Trust (established in honor of Bhabha's own uncle, Sir Dorab Tata) to found a nuclear research institute, over three years before independence and a year before the first nuclear weapon test. This led to the creation of the Tata Institute of Fundamental Research (TIFR) on 19 December 1945 with Bhabha as its first Director. The new government of India passed the Atomic Energy Act, on 15 April 1948, leading to the establishment of the Indian Atomic Energy Commission (IAEC) not quite one year after independence. At that time Prime Minister Pandit Jawaharlal Nehru declared: We must develop this atomic energy quite apart from war - indeed I think we must develop it for the purpose of using it for peaceful purposes.... Of course, if we are compelled as a nation to use it for other purposes, possibly no pious sentiments of any of us will stop the nation from using it that way."

This note of ambivalence in Nehru's speech foreshadowed his policies on nuclear research for the next decade. Nehru took a prominent role in international politics, founding the Non-Aligned Movement, and advocating nuclear disarmament. However, he refused to foreclose India's nuclear option while other nations maintained nuclear arsenals and supported programs designed to bolster India's weapons potential. In 1954 the Indian nuclear program began to move in a direction that would eventually lead to establishment of nuclear weapons capability. On 3 January 1954 the IAEC decided to set up a new facility - the Atomic Energy Establishment, Trombay (AEET), later to become the "Indian Los Alamos". On 3 August 1954 the Department of Atomic Energy (DAE) was created with Dr. Bhabha as Secretary. This department answered directly to the Prime Minister and has continued to do so down to the present day.

The program grew swiftly. The atomic energy budget increased 12-fold from 1954 to 1956. By 1958 the DAE consumed one third of India's research budget. By 1959 AEET employed over one thousand scientists and engineers. In 1955 construction began on India's first reactor, the 1 MW Apsara research reactor, with British assistance. And in September 1955, after more than a year of negotiation, Canada agreed to supply India with a powerful research reactor - the 40 MW Canada-India Reactor (CIR). Under the Eisenhower Administration's "Atoms for Peace" program the US agreed to supply 21 tons of heavy water for this reactor in Februrary 1956, and the reactor was dubbed the Canada-India Reactor, U.S. or CIRUS (now commonly written as Cirus).

The acquisition of Cirus was a watershed event in nuclear proliferation. Although the sale was made with the understanding that the reactor would only be used for peaceful purposes (the heavy water contract at least made this explicit), it occurred before any international policies were in place to regulate such technology transfers and no provision for inspections were made. And in fact India was careful to ensure that no effective regulation would accompany the reactor. India refusing to accept fuel from Canada for the reactor and set up a program to manufacture the natural uranium fuel for Cirus indigeneously so as to keep complete control of the plutonium produced there. This program, led by metallurgist Brahm Prakash, succeeded in developing the techniques for producing the precisely manufactured, high purity material demanded by the reactor.

The reactor was a design ideal for producing weapons-grade plutonium, and was also extraordinarily large for research purposes, being capable of manufacturing enough plutonium for one to two bombs a year. The acquisition of Cirus was specifically intended by India to provide herself with a weapons option and this reactor produced the plutonium used in India's first nuclear test in 1974; provided the design prototype for India's more powerful Dhruva plutonium production "research" reactor; and is directly responsible for producing nearly half of the weapons grade plutonium currently believed to be in India's stockpile. The sale further set a precedent for similar technology transfers which greatly assisted Israel in obtaining its own plutonium production reactor from France shortly thereafter. The Atomic Energy Establishment, Trombay was formally inaugurated by PM Nehru on 20 January 1957. It acquired its present name — Bhabha Atomic Research Centre (BARC) — on 12 January 1967 when PM Indira Gandhi renamed it in memory of Dr. Bhabha who died in an airplane crash on 24 January 1966.

Apsara, fueled by enriched uranium from the UK, went critical on 4 August 1957, becoming the first operating reactor in Asia outside of the Soviet Union (though only days ahead of Japan's first reactor). Cirus achieved criticality at BARC on 10 July 1960.

As a nation India has always placed a premium on self-sufficiency. It is, in fact, the most self-sufficient large economy in the world and does not import any nuclear fuel. [The traditionally closed nature of economy though accounts for the import/export based Chinese economy far outstripping its growth from the late seventies to the early nineties.] Due to its vast domestic resources of thorium (a potential fuel for breeder reactors) but limited supplies of uranium, from the start of its nuclear program India has always placed strong emphasis on the development of breeder reactor fuel cycles. Breeder reactors require highly concentrated fissionable material for reactor fuel: either highly enriched uranium or plutonium. This provided a peaceful rationale for developing a plutonium separation capability, but the principal impetus for the India's first fuel reprocessing plant was to obtain a nuclear option.

In July 1958 PM Nehru authorized project Phoenix to build a plant with a capacity of 20 tonnes of fuel a year - sized to match the production capacity of Cirus. The plant was based on the U.S. developed Purex process and an American firm, Vitro International prepared the plans for it. Construction of the plutonium plant began at Trombay on 27 March 1961 and was commissioned in mid-1964.

India's civilian nuclear program was also established during this period. Discussions with American firms to construct India's first nuclear power plants at Tarapur were held in 1960-61. An interesting incident sheds light on Nehru's amd Bhabha's thinking at that time. In 1960 Kenneth Nichols, a former U.S. Army engineer who played significant roles in the Manhattan Project, represented Westinghouse in discussions on power plant construction. In a meeting with Nehru and Bhabha, Nichols relates that Nehru turned to Bhabha and asked:

"Can you develop an atomic bomb?" Bhabha assured him that he could and in reply to Nehru's next question about time, he estimated that he would need about a year to do it.... He concluded by saying to Bhabha "Well, don't do it until I tell you to."

NUCLEAR DOCTRINE

In April 1998, the Indian government had constituted a Task Force to recommend the establishment of a National Security Council (NSC). The Task Force submitted its report in June 1998 and, in November 1998, the government constituted a three-tier NSC with a full time National Security Advisor and a National Security Advisory Board (NSAB).

Although the first task that was planned to be originally entrusted to the NSAB was to conduct a strategic defence review, because of post-Pokhran II compulsions, the NSAB was asked to first formulate India's nuclear doctrine. The NSAB submitted a draft nuclear doctrine paper to the government that was released to the public for wider debate on August 17, 1999. The key features of the proposed nuclear doctrine are reproduced below:

India shall pursue a doctrine of credible minimum deterrence. In this policy of 'retaliation only', the survivability of our arsenal is critical. This is a dynamic concept related to our strategic environment, technological imperatives and the needs of national security. The actual size, components, deployment and employment of nuclear forces will be decided in the light of these factors. India's peacetime posture aims at convincing any potential aggressor that:

- Any threat of use of nuclear weapons against India shall invoke measures to counter the threat; and

- Any nuclear attack on India and its forces shall result in punitive retaliation with nuclear weapons to inflict damage unacceptable to the aggressor.

The fundamental purpose of Indian nuclear weapons is to deter the use and threat of use of nuclear weapons by any state or entity against India and its forces. India will not be the first to initiate a nuclear strike but will respond with punitive retaliation should deterrence fail. India will not resort to the use or threat of use of nuclear weapons against states that do not possess nuclear weapons, or are not aligned with nuclear weapons powers. The draft nuclear doctrine, while generally following the policy guidelines enunciated by the Prime Minister in Parliament, fleshed out his pronouncements and "provides a broad framework for the development, deployment and employment of India's nuclear forces."

The draft paper proposes that India should establish a credible, minimum nuclear deterrent capability comprising sufficient, survivable and operationally ready nuclear forces based on the principle of no first use of nuclear weapons. It emphasises that the level of India's nuclear capability should be consistent with maximum credibility, survivability, effectiveness, safety and security. It provides for the establishment of effective intelligence and early warning systems. It recommends that India's nuclear forces be based on a triad of strategic bombers, land-based ballistic missiles and submarine launched ballistic missiles (SLBMs). Though a sea-based nuclear capability will take many decades to develop, the requirement of SLBMs is considered inescapable due to their relatively lower vulnerability. Nuclear forces that need to survive a first strike have no option but to ensure that at least 50 to 60 per cent of the arsenal is made comparatively invulnerable by being maintained as SLBMs. The draft paper proposes that India's nuclear strike capability be configured to inflict punitive retaliation the consequences of which would be unacceptable to a potential adversary who will therefore be deterred from doing the unthinkable. The doctrine highlights the cardinal supremacy of civilian control over India's nuclear weapons and proposes that the final authority for the release of nuclear weapons must vest with the Prime Minister or his designated successor(s).

The proposed doctrine also rejects the concept of nuclear warfighting and does not, hence, consider it necessary for India to match its nuclear warheads and delivery systems with those of its potential nuclear adversaries. A small number of survivable nuclear warheads and delivery systems that can inflict damage which would be unacceptable to the adversary are considered adequate for the purposes of deterrence. Although the paper has left some ambiguity by not clearly rejecting the need for tactical or battlefield nuclear weapons in India's context, the tenor of the paper and its emphasis on a retaliatory policy appear to rule out any thinking towards tactical nuclear weapons. However, the real distinguishing feature of India's nuclear doctrine is that it is "... anchored in India's continued commitment to global, verifiable and non-discriminating nuclear disarmament..." that has been described as India's national security objective. The use of nuclear weapons is considered "the gravest threat to humanity and to peace and stability in the international system." The doctrine paper clearly points out India's desire to see the world completely rid of nuclear weapons.

As expected, the draft doctrine initiated a major debate in the country about its nuclear policies. Amitabh Mattoo called it "an unapologetic realpolitik articulation of the principal raison d'être of India's nuclear weapons and the requirements needed to lend credibility to the country's deterrent posture." While agreeing with the thrust of India's nuclear policy, he wrote that India's primary quest appeared to be to acquire the strategic autonomy necessary for making independent decisions in an often unfriendly world and to pursue economic and political development without fear of external threats. R. Prasannan called the draft doctrine a wish list attached to the collective speeches of the Prime Minister and his Cabinet colleagues. Bharat Wariavwalla criticised the draft doctrine on the grounds that the definition of minimum deterrence would be very different vis a vis China and Pakistan and, hence, the term is much too loose to pass off as doctrine.

Many analysts and even foreign governments have sought to raise doubts about India's draft nuclear doctrine. It did not help matters that the doctrine was unveiled the week after the Indian

Air Force had shot down a Pakistani Atlantique reconnaissance aircraft that had intruded into Indian territory. The US government rejected the Indian desire to develop a nuclear arsenal." The Indian tests also spurred fears of a new Middle East arms race. However, not all Western powers denounced India's attempts to establish a credible weaponised nuclear deterrent. France welcomed the release of India's draft nuclear doctrine as a "logical and indeed wanted step". The most surprising criticism of the draft doctrine is that it conjures up dark visions of a nuclear arms race in Southern Asia. If all nuclear weapons states were to follow a no first use policy, it would be logical to assume that there would gradually be a net reduction in the size of nuclear arsenals - an arms race in reverse! Jasjit Singh offers the following explanation:

The concerns about a potential arms race reflect a perception arising out of the prism of Cold War mind-sets where first strike (and even "launch on warning") was the order of the day. This necessitated large arsenals and potentially pre-emptive strikes with nuclear weapons. The result was the peak of 67,000 nuclear warheads. But China did not follow the same route and relied on minimum deterrence concept with a no first use commitment. There is no evidence that China's nuclear posture led to any arms race. Even in future, China's nuclear arsenal is likely to be dictated by the size of US/Russian arsenals and issues like ballistic missile defences etc. rather than the defensive doctrine of India.

The worst criticism of the draft doctrine has been that opting for a triad of nuclear forces is not indicative of a minimalist posture but of a maximalist one, particularly as sea-based nuclear weapons have been envisaged to form part of the nuclear force. This criticism fails to take into account the fact that the credibility of a nuclear deterrent that is limited to retaliatory strikes only hinges around the ability of the nuclear force to survive a first strike in sufficient numbers to inflict unacceptable punishment in retaliation. Since submarines offer the best survival potential, India has to rely on a small number of SLBMs for credible deterrence. Raja Menon has also criticised the proposed doctrine: "...There is a serious dysfunction between 'minimum deterrence' and a tri-Service arsenal. The two cannot go together, and is (sic) akin to yoking a horse and camel together." However, surprisingly, he finds no use for aircraft-delivered nuclear bombs and states that "to even consider the role of the army in nuclear deterrence, minimum at that, is truly distressing." His hypothesis is that an arsenal for minimum deterrence requires only second-strike weapons, which can only be based on SSBNs.

Some critics have averred that the nuclear threats have not been enunciated and that the draft document does not define the nuclear force levels that India considers "minimum". Others have protested that the costs of India's nuclear deterrent have not been spelt out. The critics of the draft document forget that doctrine defines only a set of beliefs and guidelines on which policy and strategy is based. In the Preamble of the draft paper it is clearly stated in Para 1.6 that "this document outlines the broad principles for the development, deployment and employment of India's nuclear forces." Details regarding the targeting philosophy, nuclear force structures and the finer nuances of command and control cannot be expected to appear in a paper on nuclear doctrine.

The exception in the draft doctrine that India's non-use of nuclear weapons policy against countries that are not nuclear weapons states does not apply if they are militarily aligned with nuclear weapons states, has also been criticised. This exception would include non-nuclear members of NATO and the military allies of the US such as Japan. Rajesh Rajagopalan explains the reasons behind such exceptions:

Two reasons could be suggested for this exception, one practical and the other strategic. The practical reason is that the Negative Security Assurance (NSA) of various nuclear weapons states, around which this non-use policy is based, makes similar exceptions. In fact, the exceptions there are broader and the NSA does not apply to countries that have refused to sign the NPT or are suspected of nuclear weapons ambitions...

The strategic reason... (is that) a good number of non-nuclear countries still host the nuclear arms of nuclear weapons states and share in the command and control infrastructure of nuclear powers. Theoretically, a nuclear attack on India could be mounted by the nuclear forces hosted in third countries. Excluding these countries would mean that no retaliation could be mounted on the bases from where such attacks are launched...

Rajesh Rajagopalan points out that 'minimum deterrence' is mistakenly characterised as doctrine whereas it actually refers to the nuclear force structure. He states that the Indian doctrine is one of 'assured retaliation' and this is to be given effect by a minimalist nuclear force as "an assured retaliation posture is premised on the belief that no one will start a nuclear war if they are assured of a nuclear retaliation, even if it is a weak retaliation. In other words, for an Indian nuclear deterrent to work effectively against China or Pakistan, it is not necessary to threaten them with complete destruction: even retaliating with a few nuclear warheads will create unacceptable costs to both." While the interpretation is no doubt technically correct, it is also true that a policy of assured retaliation, combined with a small nuclear force built on the principle of sufficiency, could overall be characterised as minimum deterrence. However, it is a finely nuanced distinction that must be noted.

Pakistani government spokesmen and scholars have been particularly critical of India's no first use doctrine on the grounds that it is only a declaratory policy and can be easily changed when the need arises. They have failed to take note of the fact that a country's nuclear force structure, command and control system, alert status and its deployment posture are based on its nuclear doctrine. First use doctrines require hair trigger alerts, launch-on-warning and launch-through-attack strategies and elaborate surveillance, early warning and intelligence systems with nuclear warheads loaded on launchers and ready to fire. Nuclear armed aircraft would need to be ready on runway alert, if not constantly airborne as in the case of the erstwhile US Strategic Air Command. India cannot ever resort to any of these measures without Pakistan learning about them almost immediately. What the Pakistanis also forget, or deliberately ignore, is that India has offered to negotiate a mutual no first use treaty with Pakistan that would be binding and verifiable. India's track record of adherence to international treaties has been exemplary. Unfortunately, the same cannot be said of India's neighbours who have violated numerous treaties with impunity, including the NPT and the MTCR.

The charge that India's nuclear doctrine would initiate an arms race in the Southern Asian region is specious and unjustified. China's gradual moves towards a nuclear triad over a period of three and a half decades have not forced India to play "catch up". Even now India does not feel it necessary to match China's 400-plus nuclear warheads, or to follow China and develop multiple independently targetable re-entry vehicles (MIRVs). India has decided to base its deterrent on a small force of survivable nuclear warheads and delivery systems for a retaliatory strike that can inflict punitive damage on a handful of value targets.

There is no reason why Pakistan should feel compelled to match India's nuclear warheads and missiles, particularly as it has opted for a first strike doctrine and does not have to worry about the survival of its nuclear forces. With a first use doctrine, even for deterring conventional war Pakistan does not need to match India warhead for warhead and missile for missile.

Kenneth Waltz has argued that the distinction between nuclear forces designed for war fighting, that need to be compared with one another, and those designed to deter the use of nuclear weapons, must be clearly understood.

Forces designed for deterrence need not match the adversary's nuclear forces as long as they can do unacceptable damage to the adversary with unacceptable damage sensibly defined. Putting it most appropriately, he has said that "more is not better, if less is enough." Hence, those who are raising the bogey of a nuclear arms race in Southern Asia need to review their alarmist views.

It emerges quite clearly that most of the criticism of the proposed nuclear doctrine stems not from any genuine disagreement with India's no first use doctrine and its professed need to establish a credible minimum nuclear deterrent, but from the desire of many Western countries that India should "cap, reduce and eliminate" its nuclear capability and sign the NPT and the CTBT as a non-nuclear weapons state. Since India's nuclear tests and its declaration of the weaponisation of its nuclear deterrent were based on substantial national security interests, the cap, reduce, eliminate mantra is unlikely to now get anywhere.

INDIA'S NUCLEAR WEAPONS PROGRAM : INDIA'S FIRST BOMB IN 1967-1974

As Ramanna admitted in an interview on 10 October 1997, the "Peaceful Nuclear Explosive" (PNE) program - implying an intention to develop the nuclear explosives for civilian engineering work - was simply a cover for a program aimed from the beginning to develop a weapons capability, in truth there was little if any interest in Plowshare type peaceful applications. On the other hand, there was also no involvement of the military in the development program. There was no attempt to devise a military role for the nuclear explosive, or to seek the military's input for requirements. The military's public statements on nuclear weapons at this time were far from enthusiastic - essentially mirroring Sarabhai's views - so the advocates of nuclear weapons development had little incentive to seek their collaboration. Even with the peaceful cover story, India found it necessary to keep as a low a profile on the project as possible to avoid inevitable attempts by other nations to obstruct it by denying access to nuclear technology and knowledge. During December 1968 - January 1969 P.K. Iyengar visited the Soviet Union with three colleagues and toured the nuclear research facilities at Dubna. He was very impressed by the plutonium fueled pulsed fast reactor he saw there. This type of reactor is an unmoderated fast neutron reactor, that is allowed to go prompt supercritical to produce an intense very short pulse of neutrons. These are all characteristics of the cores of fission bombs, the principal difference between them being that in pulsed reactors the degree of supercriticality is very slight and ordinary thermal expansion of the reactor core is sufficient to shut down the reaction, while in fission bombs the degree is very large and the core cannot expand fast enough to shut down the reaction until vast amounts of energy are released. Pulsed fast reactors provide an excellent laboratory model of fission bomb behavior, having been used for that purpose during the Manhattan Project (the famous Dragon experiments) and afterward (the Godiva, Popsy and Topsy reactors). Recognizing this, Iyengar set about developing just such a reactor for India. The scientific leadership approved the plan in January 1969, the kick-off meeting for this reactor, called Purnima (an approximate acronym for Plutonium Reactor for Neutron Investigation in Multiplying Assemblies), took place in March 1969. Attending this meeting was Iyengar, Ramanna, Homi Sethna, and Sarabhai. Sarabhai's presence clearly indicates that with or without formal approval, the work at BARC toward weapon design now had Sarabhai's support. Chengappa indicates in fact that Sarabhai approved a one million rupee budget for Purnima (about $125,000, a figure could have covered only incidental costs - not the value of the plutonium).

Purnima was designed to use a hexagonal core of 177 stainless steel pencil shaped rods containing 18 kg of plutonium as 21.6 kg of plutonium oxide pellets (enough for three Fat Man type bombs) with a nominal average power of 1 watt. Mahadeva Srinivasan developed a sophisticated physics model for criticality calculations in 1970, and later became the reactor's chief physicist. Construction began that year when sufficient separated plutonium finally became available. Purnima went critical on 18 May 1972. With Purnima as a test bed the Indian physicists were able to refine their understanding of the physics of fast fission and fast neutrons. While not formally part of the later bomb development team Srinivasan's expertise in fast critical systems underlay the nuclear design of the device.

1970 saw expansion of the nuclear weapons program in many ways. Due to the requirements of Purnima the program needed to develop facilities and experience in handling large amounts of plutonium (developed under the supervision of P.R. Roy), and work also began on fabricating plutonium metal alloys for the eventual construction of the bomb core. To advance the development of the essential implosion system V.S. Ramamurthy also began performing numerical implosion simulations on an antiquated Soviet Besm 6 computer

Development of the technology for implosion got underway in April 1970 when Ramanna sent Pranab Rebatiranjan Dastidar, the electronics expert at BARC, to Waman Dattatreya Patwardhan at the Explosive Research and Development laboratory (ERDL) at Pune to begin work on the detonation system for the bomb. Patwardhan was well known to the BARC scientists, since he helped them with the explosives tests years before as part of SNEPP. In July nuclear physicist Dr. Basanti Dulal Nag Chaudhuri took over as science adviser to the Defense Minister, and as Director of the Defense Research and Development Organization (DRDO). The following month, he and Ramanna began working together to recruit the Terminal Ballistics Research Laboratory (TBRL), located in Chandigarh, to develop the explosive lenses for the implosion system.

During 1971 work on weapon design continued. Srinivasan working with K. Subba Rao developed models of the fission process on a nuclear bomb, and equations to predict its efficiency. Chidamabaram completed his work on the plutonium equation of state, and Ramamurthy developed computational models of the implosion, nuclear reaction, and disassembly process to predict the devices behavior. Throughout this period Ramanna and his lieutenant, P.K. Iyengar, held frequest reviews of the projects progress.

In April 1971 Nag Chaudhuri appointed Nagapattinam Sambasiva Venkatesan to Director of TBRL with specific instructions to assist in developing the nuclear device. The 1971 Indo-Pakistani War influenced India's resolve to test a nuclear device, but in a curious and indirect way. This war developed when the bi-regional state of Pakistan, split into East and West Pakistan on either side of India, held its first national election in December 1970. The dominant party of the more populous East Pakistan won a majority of the seats in parliament, but West Pakistan, accustomed to monopolizing political and military power, responded by ignoring the election result. And on 25 March 1971 West Pakistan forces arrested the winner Mujibur Rahman, and launched a campaign brutal military repression on the Bengalis of East Pakistan. This resulted in tens of millions of refugees spilling into India, some of whom took up arms against the Pakistani government.

By autumn the Indian-East Pakistani border had become something close to a combat zone, with India and Pakistan trading intense firing across the border, while armed rebels operated from safe havens in India. In late November PM Gandhi authorized Indian forces to cross the border to "pursue" Pakistani forces.

Pakistan responded by a massive strike against Indian airbases in western India on 3 December, and declaring war on 4 December. India had spent months preparing for this escalation, indeed had deliberately provoked it, and launched an overwhelming 3-pronged attack into East Pakistan. Unable to hold back the Indian invasion, Pakistan attempted to counter with an attack in Kashmir, gaining several miles of territory before being halted by Indian forces. The Indian army on the other hand had surrounded Dacca, the capital of East Pakistan by 15 December, and its garrison surrendered the next day. On 17 December a cease-fire was accepted by both sides, effectively ending the war.

The war had been a crushing defeat for Pakistan, which had lost more than half its population. As the crisis developed throughout 1971 China and Pakistan had grown closer to the U.S. while India had grown closer to the Soviet Union. The keystone of the Nixon administration's foreign policy had been its reapproachment with China (announced 15 July), to place the Soviet Union between the pincers of two major opposing powers. Pakistan had played a critical role in facilitating secret negotiations with China. India had at the same time strengthened its ties to the U.S.S.R. culminating in a formal treaty of friendship on 9 August. Chinese support for Pakistan during the most extreme crisis of Pakistan's existence came to nought however. China failed to provide any significant assistance for Pakistan, such as applying pressure on India's border. The net result was that Pakistan suffered both a serious military defeat, demonstrating its inferiority to India in military terms, and a permanent irreparable loss in its strategic position by the new found independence of East Pakistan. And the much feared Pakistan-China axis had turned out to be a "paper tiger".

Unsurprisingly this did bolster India's sense of security, but it did not stem the momentum toward the testing of a nuclear device as one might have supposed. On 30 December 1971 Sarabhai died, and Homi Sethna - already head of BARC - took his place as chairman of the IAEC. Thus the only prominent voice in Indian government counciling restraint in pursuing the nuclear option was replaced by one of its most ardent advocates.

And the hostile attitude taken toward India by the U.S. during the crisis had along lasting effect on Indian attitudes. Pres. Nixon and Sec. of State Kissinger chose to view India's actions as hostilities aimed at a U.S. ally and thus as an act hostile to the United States, rather than a case of a western-style democracy coming to the defense of a people being brutally persecuted by a military dictatorship for attempting to exercise its democratic rights. The U.S. even went so far as to dispatch an aircraft carrier battle group to the Indian Ocean in an ill-conceived, obscurely reasoned, and ineffectual attempt to pressure India. The feeling that a superpower had attempted to coerce India in affairs affecting India's vital interests became a cause celebre for advocates of the nuclear option (although they never clearly explained how a limited nuclear capability would counter U.S. pressure).

Bhabhani Sen Gupta ably described the shift in India's views toward the nuclear option in the wake of the 1971 war: The Chinese bomb ceased to be the main argument for the Indian bomb, perhaps because of the Chinese inability to help Pakistan in the 1971 war and also because of the initiatives taken by India to normalize relations with China. The arguments for the bomb now were that without it India could not expect to be admitted to the corridors of global power, nor enjoy the status of the dominant regional power; that the bomb might quicken the process of normalizing relations with China; that it would proclaim India's independence of the Soviet Union and compel the United States to change its attitude of hostility or benign neglect. By the beginning of 1972 the basic design for India's first nuclear device was complete, and other parts of the program for developing the necessary expertise to implement the design were coming along. During that year the data from operating Purnima (starting in May) began flowing in allowing confirmation and refinement of the device's nuclear design; and the work in plutonium metallurgy reached the point where the device could be successfully fabricated.

The decision to go ahead and manufacture the device and prepare for a test was made later in the year, while Indira Gandhi was still near the peak of her post-war popularity. Early in the year PM Gandhi had seemed ambivalent about the wisdom of conducting an actual test. But by this time the internal momentum of the nuclear development program, the now well established popularity of the nuclear option among India's literate urban elite, the lack of any significant restraining counsel, and Gandhi's sense of strength all seem to have combined to make the decision one of when, not if, the test would come. The decision to move forward was made by PM Gandhi on 7 September 1972, a day in which she toured BARC on the occasion of the tenth convocation of the Indian Institute of Technology at Bombay. During this tour she was shown a wooden model of the device. Upon seeing the model she gave the scientists present verbal authorization to construct it and prepare for testing, but not to test it without explicit approval from herself.

One change made by Sethna soon after assuming the chairmanship was to split the Indian space program, then part of the Department of Atomic Energy, into a separate agency - observing quite reasonably that to have the DAE developing *both* nuclear explosives and missile technology would wave a red flag for observers concerned about proliferation, no matter what claims were made about the peaceful intent of both programs.

NUCLEAR WEAPONS AND NON-PROLIFERATION TREATY

The Treaty on the Non-Proliferation of Nuclear Weapons, commonly known as the Non-Proliferation Treaty or NPT, is a landmark international treaty whose objective is to prevent the spread of nuclear weapons and weapons technology, to promote cooperation in the peaceful uses of nuclear energy and to further the goal of achieving nuclear disarmament and general and complete disarmament. Opened for signature in 1968, the Treaty entered into force in 1970. On 11 May 1995, the Treaty was extended indefinitely. A total of 190 parties have joined the Treaty, including the five nuclear-weapon States: the United States, Russia, the United Kingdom, France, and China (also the five permanent members of the United Nations Security Council). More countries have ratified the NPT than any other arms limitation and disarmament agreement, a testament to the Treaty's significance. Four non-parties to the treaty are known or believed to possess nuclear weapons: India, Pakistan and North Korea have openly tested and declared that they possess nuclear weapons, while Israel has had a policy of opacity regarding its own nuclear weapons program. North Korea acceded to the treaty in 1985, but never came into compliance, and announced its withdrawal in 2003.

The NPT consists of a preamble and eleven articles. Although the concept of "pillars" is not expressed anywhere in the NPT, the treaty is nevertheless sometimes interpreted as a *three-pillar* system, with an implicit balance among them:

1. *non-proliferation,*
2. *disarmament,* and
3. *the right to peacefully use nuclear technology.*

The NPT is often seen to be based on a central bargain: "the NPT non-nuclear-weapon states agree never to acquire nuclear weapons and the NPT nuclear-weapon states in exchange agree to share the benefits of peaceful nuclear technology and to pursue nuclear disarmament aimed at the ultimate elimination of their nuclear arsenals". The treaty is reviewed every five years in meetings called Review Conferences of the Parties to the Treaty of Non-Proliferation of Nuclear Weapons. Even though the treaty was originally conceived with a limited duration of 25 years, the signing parties decided, by consensus, to extend the treaty indefinitely and without conditions during the Review Conference in New York City on May 11, 1995.

At the time the NPT was proposed, there were predictions of 25-30 nuclear weapon states within 20 years. Instead, over forty years later, only four states are not parties to the NPT, and they are the only additional states believed to possess nuclear weapons. Several additional measures have been adopted to strengthen the NPT and the broader nuclear nonproliferation regime and make it difficult for states to acquire the capability to produce nuclear weapons, including the export controls of the Nuclear Suppliers Group and the enhanced verification measures of the IAEA Additional Protocol. However, critics argue that the NPT cannot stop the proliferation of nuclear weapons or the motivation to acquire them. They express disappointment with the limited progress on nuclear disarmament, where the five authorized nuclear weapons states still have 22,000 warheads in their combined stockpile and have shown a reluctance to disarm further. Several high-ranking officials within the United Nations have said that they can do little to stop states using nuclear reactors to produce nuclear weapons.

Treaty "pillars"

The NPT is commonly described as having three main "pillars": non-proliferation, disarmament, and peaceful use. This "pillars" concept has been questioned by some who believe that the NPT is, as its name suggests, principally about nonproliferation, and who worry that "three pillars" language misleadingly implies that the three elements have equivalent importance.

First Pillar: Non-proliferation

Five states are recognized by the Non-Proliferation Treaty as nuclear weapon states (NWS): China (signed 1992), France (1992), the Soviet Union (1968; obligations and rights now assumed by the Russian Federation), the United Kingdom (1968), and the United States (1968) (The United States, UK, and the Soviet Union were the only states openly possessing such weapons among the original ratifiers of the treaty, which entered into force in 1970). These five nations are also the five permanent members of the United Nations Security Council. These five NWS agree not to transfer "nuclear weapons or other nuclear explosive devices" and "not in any way to assist, encourage, or induce" a non-nuclear weapon state (NNWS) to acquire nuclear weapons (Article I). NNWS parties to the NPT agree not to "receive," "manufacture" or "acquire" nuclear weapons or to "seek or receive any assistance in the manufacture of nuclear weapons" (Article II). NNWS parties also agree to accept safeguards by the International Atomic Energy Agency (IAEA) to verify that they are not diverting nuclear energy from peaceful uses to nuclear weapons or other nuclear explosive devices (Article III).

The five NWS parties have made undertakings not to use their nuclear weapons against a non-NWS party except in response to a nuclear attack, or a conventional attack in alliance with a Nuclear Weapons State. However, these undertakings have not been incorporated formally into the treaty, and the exact details have varied over time. The U.S. also had nuclear warheads targeted at North Korea, a non-NWS, from 1959 until 1991. The previous United Kingdom Secretary of State for Defence, Geoff Hoon, has also explicitly invoked the possibility of the use of the country's nuclear weapons in response to a non-conventional attack by "rogue states". In January 2006, President Jacques Chirac of France indicated that an incident of state-sponsored terrorism on France could trigger a small-scale nuclear retaliation aimed at destroying the "rogue state's" power centers.

Second Pillar: Disarmament

Article VI of the NPT represents the only binding commitment in a multilateral treaty to the goal of disarmament by the nuclear-weapon States. The NPT's preamble contains language affirming the desire of treaty signatories to ease international tension and strengthen international trust so as to create someday the conditions for a halt to the production of nuclear weapons, and treaty on general and complete disarmament that liquidates, in particular, nuclear weapons and their delivery vehicles from national arsenals.

The wording of the NPT's Article VI arguably imposes only a vague obligation on all NPT signatories to move in the general direction of nuclear and total disarmament, saying, "Each of the Parties to the Treaty undertakes to pursue negotiations in good faith on effective measures relating to cessation of the nuclear arms race at an early date and to nuclear disarmament, and on a treaty on general and complete disarmament." Under this interpretation, Article VI does not strictly require all signatories to actually conclude a disarmament treaty. Rather, it only requires them "to negotiate in good faith."

On the other hand, some governments, especially non-nuclear-weapon states belonging to the Non-Aligned Movement, have interpreted Article VI's language as being anything but vague. In their view, Article VI constitutes a formal and specific obligation on the NPT-recognized nuclear-weapon states to disarm themselves of nuclear weapons, and argue that these states have failed to meet their obligation. The International Court of Justice (ICJ), in its advisory opinion on the Legality of the Threat or Use of Nuclear

Weapons, issued 8 July 1996, unanimously interprets the text of Article VI as implying that

"There exists an obligation to pursue in good faith and bring to a conclusion negotiations leading to nuclear disarmament in all its aspects under strict and effective international control." The ICJ opinion notes that this obligation involves all NPT parties (not just the nuclear weapon states) and does not suggest a specific time frame for nuclear disarmament.

Critics of the NPT-recognized nuclear-weapon states sometimes argue that what they view as the failure of the NPT-recognized nuclear weapon states to disarm themselves of nuclear weapons, especially in the post–Cold War era, has angered some non-nuclear-weapon NPT signatories of the NPT. Such failure, these critics add, provides justification for the non-nuclear-weapon signatories to quit the NPT and develop their own nuclear arsenals.

Other observers have suggested that the linkage between proliferation and disarmament may also work the other way, i.e., that the failure to resolve proliferation threats in Iran and North Korea, for instance, will cripple the prospects for disarmament. No current nuclear weapons state, the argument goes, would seriously consider eliminating its last nuclear weapons without high confidence that other countries would not acquire them. Some observers have even suggested that the very progress of disarmament by the superpowers—which has led to the elimination of thousands of weapons and delivery systems —could eventually make the possession of nuclear weapons more attractive by increasing the perceived strategic value of a small arsenal. As one U.S. official and NPT expert warned in 2007, "logic suggests that as the number of nuclear weapons decreases, the 'marginal utility' of a nuclear weapon as an instrument of military power increases. At the extreme, which it is precisely disarmament's hope to create, the strategic utility of even one or two nuclear weapons would be huge."

Third Pillar: Peaceful use of Nuclear Energy

The third pillar allows for and agrees upon the transfer of nuclear technology and materials to NPT signatory countries for the development of civilian nuclear energy programs in those countries, as long as they can demonstrate that their nuclear programs are not being used for the development of nuclear weapons.

Since very few of the states with nuclear energy programs are willing to abandon the use of nuclear energy, the third pillar of the NPT under Article IV provides other states with the possibility to do the same, but under conditions intended to make it difficult to develop nuclear weapons.

The treaty recognizes the inalienable right of sovereign states to use nuclear energy for peaceful purposes, but restricts this right for NPT parties to be exercised "in conformity with Articles I and II" (the basic nonproliferation obligations that constitute the "first pillar" of the Treaty). As the commercially popular light water reactor nuclear power station uses enriched uranium fuel, it follows that states must be able either to enrich uranium or purchase it on an international market. Mohamed ElBaradei, then Director General of the International Atomic Energy Agency, has called the spread of enrichment and reprocessing capabilities the "Achilles' heel" of the nuclear nonproliferation regime. As of 2007 13 states have an enrichment capability. Because the availability of fissile material has long been considered the principal obstacle to, and "pacing element" for, a country's nuclear weapons development effort, it was declared a major emphasis of U.S. policy in 2004 to prevent the further spread of uranium enrichment and plutonium reprocessing (a.k.a. "ENR") technology. Countries possessing ENR capabilities, it is feared, have what is in effect the option of using this capability to produce fissile material for weapons use on demand, thus giving them what has been termed a "virtual" nuclear weapons program. The degree to which NPT members have a "right" to ENR technology notwithstanding its potentially grave proliferation implications, therefore, is at the cutting edge of policy and legal debates surrounding the meaning of Article IV and its relation to Articles I, II, and III of the Treaty.

Countries that have signed the treaty as Non-Nuclear Weapons States and maintained that status have an unbroken record of not building nuclear weapons. However, Iraq was cited by the IAEA with punitive sanctions enacted against it by the UN Security Council for violating its NPT safeguards obligations; North Korea never came into compliance with its NPT safeguards agreement and was cited repeatedly for these violations, and later withdrew from the NPT and tested multiple nuclear devices; Iran was found in non-compliance with its NPT safeguards obligations in an unusual non-consensus decision because it "failed in a number of instances over an extended period of time" to report aspects of its enrichment program; and Libya pursued a clandestine nuclear weapons program before abandoning it in December 2003. In 1991 Romania reported previously undeclared nuclear activities by the former regime and the IAEA reported this non-compliance to the Security Council for information only. In some regions, the fact that all neighbors are verifiably free of nuclear weapons reduces any pressure individual states might feel to build those weapons themselves, even if neighbors are known to have peaceful nuclear energy programs that might otherwise be suspicious. In this, the treaty works as designed.

In 2004, Mohamed ElBaradei said that by some estimates thirty-five to forty states could have the knowledge to develop nuclear weapons.

History

The impetus behind the NPT was concern for the safety of a world with many nuclear weapon states. It was recognized that the cold war deterrent relationship between just the United States and Soviet Union was fragile. Having more nuclear nuclear-weapon states would reduce security for all, multiplying the risks of miscalculation, accidents, unauthorized use of weapons, or from escalation in tensions, nuclear conflict.

The NPT process was launched by Frank Aiken, Irish Minister for External Affairs, in 1958. It was opened for signature in 1968, with Finland the first State to sign. Accession became nearly universal after the end of the Cold War and of South African apartheid. In 1992 China and France signed the treaty, the last of the five nuclear powers named in the treaty to do so. In 1995 the treaty was extended indefinitely. After Brazil acceded to the NPT in 1998 the only remaining non-nuclear-weapons state which had not signed was Cuba, which joined NPT (and the Treaty of Tlatelolco NWFZ) in 2002.

Several NPT signatories have given up nuclear weapons or nuclear weapons programs. South Africa undertook a nuclear weapons program, allegedly with the assistance of Israel in the 1970s, and may have conducted a nuclear test in the Indian Ocean in 1979, but has since renounced its nuclear program and signed the treaty in 1991 after destroying its small nuclear arsenal; after this, the remaining African countries signed the treaty. Several former Soviet Republics, Ukraine, Belarus and Kazakhstan, destroyed or transferred to Russia the nuclear weapons they inherited from the Soviet Union. The former Soviet republics joined NPT by 1994. Successor states from the breakups of Yugoslavia and Czechoslovakia also joined the treaty soon after their independence. Montenegro and East Timor were the last countries to sign the treaty on their independence in 2006 and 2003; the only other country to sign in the 21st century was Cuba in 2002. The three Micronesian countries in Compact of Free Association with the USA joined NPT in 1995, along with Vanuatu. Major South American countries Argentina, Chile, and Brazil joined in 1995 and 1998. Arabian Peninsula countries included Saudi Arabia and Bahrain in 1988, Qatar and Kuwait in 1989, UAE in 1995, and Oman in 1997. The tiny European states of Monaco and Andorra joined in 1995-6. Also signing in the 1990s were Myanmar in 1992 and Guyana in 1993.

United States-NATO nuclear weapons sharing

At the time the treaty was being negotiated, NATO had in place secret nuclear weapons sharing agreements whereby the United States provided nuclear weapons to be deployed by, and stored in, other NATO states. Some argue this is an act of proliferation violating Articles I and II of the treaty. A counter-argument is that the U.S. controlled the weapons in storage within the NATO states, and that no transfer of the weapons or control over them was intended "unless and until a decision were made to go to war, at which the treaty would no longer be controlling", so there is no breach of the NPT. These agreements were disclosed to a few of the states, including the Soviet Union, negotiating the treaty, but most of the states that signed the NPT in 1968 would not have known about these agreements and interpretations at that time.

As of 2005, it is estimated that the United States still provides about 180 tactical B61 nuclear bombs for use by Belgium, Germany, Italy, the Netherlands and Turkey under these NATO agreements. Many states, and the Non-Aligned Movement, now argue this violates Articles I and II of the treaty, and are applying diplomatic pressure to terminate these agreements. They point out that the pilots and other staff of the "non-nuclear" NATO states practice handling and delivering the U.S. nuclear bombs, and non-U.S. warplanes have been adapted to deliver U.S. nuclear bombs which must have involved the transfer of some technical nuclear weapons information. NATO believes its "nuclear forces continue to play an essential role in war prevention, but their role is now more fundamentally political". NATO officials also point out that no nuclear weapons have ever been given over to non-U.S. control by the United States, so therefore there cannot have been a violation of Article I (which prohibits transferring "nuclear weapons or other nuclear explosive devices or control over such weapons or explosive devices") or Article II (which bars "receiv[ing] the transfer from any transferor whatsoever of nuclear weapons or other nuclear explosive devices or of control over such weapons or explosive devices").

U.S. nuclear sharing policies were originally designed to help prevent the proliferation of nuclear weapons—not least by persuading the then West Germany not to develop an independent nuclear capability by assuring it that West Germany would be able, in the event of war with the Warsaw Pact, to wield (U.S.) nuclear weapons in self-defense. (Until that point of all-out war, however, the weapons themselves would remain in U.S. hands.) The point was to limit the spread of countries having their own nuclear weapons programs, helping ensure that NATO allies would not choose to go down the proliferation route. (West Germany was discussed in U.S. intelligence estimates for a number of years as being a country with the potential to develop nuclear weapons capabilities of its own if officials in Bonn were not convinced that their defense against the Soviet Union and its allies could otherwise be met.)

India, Israel, and Pakistan

Three states—India, Israel, and Pakistan—have never signed the treaty. India and Pakistan are confirmed nuclear powers, and Israel has a long-standing policy of deliberate ambiguity. India argues that the NPT creates a club of "nuclear haves" and a larger group of "nuclear have-nots" by restricting the legal possession of nuclear weapons to those states that tested them before 1967, but the treaty never explains on what ethical grounds such a distinction is valid.

India and Pakistan have publicly announced possession of nuclear weapons and have detonated nuclear devices in tests, India having first done so in 1974 and Pakistan following suit in 1998 in response to another Indian test. India is estimated to have enough fissile material for more than 150 warheads. Pakistan reportedly has between 80 and 120 warheads according to the former head of its strategic arms division. India is one of the few countries to have a no first use policy, a pledge not to use nuclear weapons unless first attacked by an adversary using nuclear weapons. India's External Affairs Minister Pranab Mukherjee said during a visit to Tokyo in 2007: "If India did not sign the NPT, it is not because of its lack of commitment for non-proliferation, but because we consider NPT as a flawed treaty and it did not recognise the need for universal, non-discriminatory verification and treatment."

According to leaked intelligence, Israel has been developing nuclear weapons at its Dimona site in the Negev since 1958, and many nonproliferation analysts like David Albright estimate that Israel may have stockpiled between 100 to 200 warheads using the plutonium reprocessed from Dimona. The Israeli government refuses to confirm or deny possession of nuclear weapons, although this is now regarded as an open secret after Israeli low level nuclear technician Mordechai Vanunu—subsequently arrested and sentenced for treason by Israel—published evidence about the program to the British *Sunday Times* in 1986.

In early March 2006, India and the United States finalized an agreement, in the face of criticism in both countries, to provide India with US civilian nuclear technology. Under the deal India has committed to classify 14 of its 22 nuclear power plants as being for civilian use and to place them under IAEA safeguards. Mohamed ElBaradei, then Director General of the IAEA, welcomed the deal by calling India "an important partner in the non-proliferation regime."

In December 2006, United States Congress approved the United States-India Peaceful Atomic Energy Cooperation Act that was cemented during President Bush's visit to India earlier in the year. The legislation allows for the transfer of civilian nuclear material to India. Despite its status outside the Nuclear Non-Proliferation Treaty, India was granted these transactions on the basis of its clean non-proliferation record, and India's need for energy fueled by its rapid industrialization and a billion-plus population. On August 1, 2008, the IAEA approved the India Safeguards Agreement and on September 6, 2008, India was granted the waiver at the Nuclear Suppliers Group (NSG) meeting held in Vienna, Austria. The consensus was arrived after overcoming misgivings expressed by Austria, Ireland and New Zealand and is an unprecedented step in giving exemption to a country, which has not signed the NPT and the Comprehensive Test Ban Treaty (CTBT). While India could commence nuclear trade with other willing countries. The U.S. Congress approved this agreement and the President signed it on 8 October 2008.

The NSG Guidelines currently rule out nuclear exports by all major suppliers to Pakistan and Israel, with very narrow exceptions, since neither has full-scope IAEA safeguards (i.e. safeguards on all its nuclear activities). Attempts by Pakistan to reach a similar agreement have been rebuffed by the United States and other NSG members. The argument put forth is that not only does Pakistan lack the same energy requirements but that the track record of Pakistan as a nuclear proliferator makes it impossible for it to have any sort of nuclear deal in the near future.

On September 18, 2009 the General Conference of the International Atomic Energy Agency called on Israel to open its nuclear facilities to IAEA inspection and adhere to the non-proliferation treaty as part of a resolution on "Israeli nuclear capabilities," which passed by a narrow margin of 49-45 with 16 abstentions. The chief Israeli delegate stated that "Israel will not co-operate in any matter with this resolution."

By 2010, China reportedly signed a civil nuclear deal with Pakistan claiming that the deal was "peaceful" but still it's in direct violation of NPT.

The British government looked askance at the deal purporting that 'the time is not yet right for a civil nuclear deal with Pakistan'. On June 15 2010 *The Times of India* published an article stating, "nuclear deal between China and Pakistan [...] will be violating the Nuclear Non-Proliferation Treaty (NPT) that forbids export of nuclear reactors to countries that have not signed the pact if it goes ahead with the deal. " In the Pakistan-China case, the parties did not seek formal approval from the nuclear suppliers group, and China preferred to "grandfather" the reactor. As of August 2010, *The Times of India* responded, "India is emphatically making the point that China cannot grandfather the reactors to the earlier 1991 deal because Beijing made no mention of it all these years, and that the announcement finally was made after India acquired waiver from NSG to carry out nuclear commerce. As per the NSG guidelines, NSG members can supply nuclear equipment only to countries which have signed Nuclear Non-proliferation Treaty or which have agreed to international inspection of their nuclear facilities.."

Exponents of arms control denounced the China-Pakistan deal as they did in case of U.S.-India deal claiming that both the deals violate the NPT by facilitating nuclear programmes in states which are not parties to the NPT.

As of January 2011, Australia, a top three producer and home to worlds largest known reserves, has continued their refusal to export Uranium to India because it has not signed the NPT despite diplomatic pressure on their part. In November 2011 the Australian Prime Minister announced a desire to allow exports to India, a policy change which was authorized by her party's national conference in December. In 4 December Australia's Prime Minister

Julia Gillard overturned its long-standing ban on exporting uranium to India. She further said "We should take a decision in the national interest, a decision about strengthening our strategic partnership with India in this the Asian century," and said that any agreement to sell uranium to India would include strict safeguards to ensure it would only be used for civilian purposes, and not end up in nuclear weapons.

North Korea

North Korea ratified the treaty on December 12, 1985, but gave notice of withdrawal from the treaty on January 10, 2003 following U.S. allegations that it had started an illegal enriched uranium weapons program, and the U.S. subsequently stopping fuel oil shipments under the Agreed Framework which had resolved plutonium weapons issues in 1994. The withdrawal became effective April 10, 2003 making North Korea the first state ever to withdraw from the treaty. North Korea had once before announced withdrawal, on March 12, 1993, but suspended that notice before it came into effect.

On February 10, 2005, North Korea publicly declared that it possessed nuclear weapons and pulled out of the six-party talks hosted by China to find a diplomatic solution to the issue. "We had already taken the resolute action of pulling out of the Nuclear Non-Proliferation Treaty and have manufactured nuclear arms for self-defence to cope with the Bush administration's evermore undisguised policy to isolate and stifle the DPRK [Democratic People's Republic of Korea]," a North Korean Foreign Ministry statement said regarding the issue. Six-party talks resumed in July 2005.

On September 19, 2005, North Korea announced that it would agree to a preliminary accord. Under the accord, North Korea would scrap all of its existing nuclear weapons and nuclear production facilities, rejoin the NPT, and readmit IAEA inspectors. The difficult issue of the supply of light water reactors to replace North Korea's indigenous nuclear power plant program, as per the 1994 Agreed Framework, was left to be resolved in future discussions. On the next day North Korea reiterated its known view that until it is supplied with a light water reactor it will not dismantle its nuclear arsenal or rejoin the NPT.

On October 2, 2006, the North Korean foreign minister announced that his country was planning to conduct a nuclear test "in the future", although it did not state when. On Monday, October 9, 2006 at 01:35:28 (UTC) the United States Geological Survey detected a magnitude 4.3 seismic event 70 km (43 mi) north of Kimchaek, North Korea indicating a nuclear test. The North Korean government announced shortly afterward that they had completed a successful underground test of a nuclear fission device.

In 2007, reports from Washington suggested that the 2002 CIA reports stating that North Korea was developing an enriched uranium weapons program, which led to North Korea leaving the NPT, had overstated or misread the intelligence. On the other hand, even apart from these press allegations—which some critics worry could have been planted in order to justify the United States giving up trying to verify the dismantlement of Pyongyang's uranium program in the face of North Korean intransigence—there remains some information in the public record indicating the existence of a uranium effort. Quite apart from the fact that North Korean First Vice Minister Kang Sok Ju at one point admitted the existence of a uranium enrichment program, Pakistan's then-President Musharraf revealed that the A.Q. Khan proliferation network had provided North Korea with a number of gas centrifuges designed for uranium enrichment. Additionally, press reports have cited U.S. officials to the effect that evidence obtained in dismantling Libya's WMD programs points toward North Korea as the source for Libya's uranium hexafluoride (UF_6) — which, if true, would mean that North Korea has a uranium conversion facility for producing feedstock for centrifuge enrichment.

Iran

Iran is a party to the NPT but was found in non-compliance with its NPT safeguards agreement and the status of its nuclear program remains in dispute. In November 2003 IAEA Director General Mohamed ElBaradei reported that Iran had repeatedly and over an extended period failed to meet its safeguards obligations, including by failing to declare its uranium enrichment program. After about two years of EU3-led diplomatic efforts and Iran temporarily suspending its enrichment program, the IAEA Board of Governors, acting under Article XII.C of the IAEA Statute, found in a rare non-consensus decision with 12 abstentions that these failures constituted non-compliance with the IAEA safeguards agreement. This was reported to the UN Security Council in 2006, after which the Security Council passed a resolution demanding that Iran suspend its enrichment. Instead, Iran resumed its enrichment program.

The IAEA has been able to verify the non-diversion of declared nuclear material in Iran, and is continuing its work on verifying the absence of undeclared activities. In February 2008, the IAEA also reported that it was working to address "alleged studies" of weaponization, based on documents provided by certain Member States, which those states claimed originated from Iran. Iran rejected the allegations as "baseless" and the documents as "fabrications." In June 2009, the IAEA reported that Iran had not "cooperated with the Agency in connection with the remaining issues... which need to be clarified to exclude the possibility of military dimensions to Iran's nuclear program."

The United States concluded that Iran violated its Article III NPT safeguards obligations, and further argued based on circumstantial evidence that Iran's enrichment program was for weapons purposes and therefore violated Iran's Article II nonproliferation obligations. The November 2007 US National Intelligence Estimate (NIE) later concluded that Iran had halted an active nuclear weapons program in the fall of 2003 and that it had remained halted as of mid-2007. The NIE's "Key Judgments," however, also made clear that what Iran had actually stopped in 2003 was only "nuclear weapon design and weaponization work and covert uranium conversion-related and uranium enrichment-related work"-namely, those aspects of Iran's nuclear weapons effort that had not by that point already been leaked to the press and become the subject of IAEA investigations. Since Iran's uranium enrichment program at Natanz—and its continuing work on a heavy water reactor at Arak that would be ideal for plutonium production—began secretly years before in conjunction with the very weaponization work the NIE discussed and for the purpose of developing nuclear weapons, many observers find Iran's continued development of fissile material production capabilities distinctly worrying. Particularly because fissile material availability has long been understood to be the principal obstacle to nuclear weapons development and the primary "pacing element" for a weapons program, the fact that Iran has reportedly suspended weaponization work may not mean very much. As U.S. Director of National Intelligence Mike McConnell has put it, the aspects of its work that Iran allegedly suspended were thus "probably the least significant part of the program."

Iran states it has a legal right to enrich uranium for peaceful purposes under the NPT, and further says that it "has constantly complied with its obligations under the NPT and the Statute of the International Atomic Energy Agency". Iran also states that its enrichment program is part of its civilian nuclear energy program, which is allowed under Article IV of the NPT. The Non-Aligned Movement has welcomed the continuing cooperation of Iran with the IAEA and reaffirmed Iran's right to the peaceful uses of nuclear technology. UN Secretary General Ban Ki-moon has welcomed the continued dialogue between Iran and the IAEA, and has called for a peaceful resolution to the issue.

In April 2010, Washington stepped up its efforts to impose a new round of sanctions on Iran over its nuclear program. But key Asian powers such as India and China oppose the adoption of a new round of sanctions against Tehran.

South Africa

South Africa is the only country that developed nuclear weapons by itself and later dismantled them – unlike the former Soviet states Ukraine, Belarus and Kazakhstan, which inherited nuclear weapons from the former USSR and also acceded to the NPT as non-nuclear weapon states.

During the days of apartheid, the white South African government developed a deep fear of both a black uprising and the threat of communism.

This led to the development of a secret nuclear weapons program as an ultimate deterrent. South Africa has a large supply of uranium, which is mined in the country's gold mines. The government built a nuclear research facility at Pelindaba near Pretoria where uranium was enriched to fuel grade for the Koeberg Nuclear Power Station as well as weapon grade for bomb production.

In 1991, after international pressure and when a change of government was imminent, South African Ambassador to the United States Harry Schwarz signed the Nuclear Non-Proliferation Treaty. In 1993, the then president Frederik Willem de Klerk openly admitted that the country had developed a limited nuclear weapon capability. These weapons were subsequently dismantled before South Africa acceded to the NPT and opened itself up to IAEA inspection. In 1994 the IAEA completed its work and declared that the country had fully dismantled its nuclear weapons program.

Libya

Libya had signed and ratified the Nuclear Non-Proliferation Treaty and was subject to IAEA nuclear safeguards inspections, but undertook a secret nuclear weapons development program in violation of its NPT obligations, using material and technology provided by the A.Q. Khan proliferation network —including actual nuclear weapons designs allegedly originating in China. Libya began secret negotiations with the United States and the United Kingdom in March 2003 over potentially eliminating its WMD programs. In October 2003, Libya was embarrassed by the interdiction of a shipment of Pakistani-designed centrifuge parts sent from Malaysia, also as part of A. Q. Khan's proliferation ring. In December 2003, Libya announced that it had agreed to eliminate all its WMD programs, and permitted U.S. and British teams (as well as IAEA inspectors) into the country to assist this process and verify its completion. The nuclear weapons designs, gas centrifuges for uranium enrichment, and other equipment—including prototypes for improved SCUD ballistic missiles—were removed from Libya by the United States. (Libyan chemical weapons stocks and chemical bombs were also destroyed on site with international verification, with Libya joining the Chemical Weapons Convention.) Libya's noncompliance with its IAEA safeguards was reported to the U.N. Security Council, but with no action taken, as Libya's return to compliance with safeguards and Article II of the NPT was welcomed.

Leaving the treaty

Article X allows a state to leave the treaty if "extraordinary events, related to the subject matter of this Treaty, have jeopardized the supreme interests of its country", giving three months' (ninety days') notice. The state is required to give reasons for leaving the NPT in this notice. NATO states argue that when there is a state of "general war" the treaty no longer applies, effectively allowing the states involved to leave the treaty with no notice. This is a necessary argument to support the NATO nuclear weapons sharing policy, but a troubling one for the logic of the treaty. NATO's argument is based on the phrase "the consequent need to make every effort to avert the danger of such a war" in the treaty preamble, inserted at the behest of U.S. diplomats, arguing that the treaty would at that point have failed to fulfill its function of prohibiting a general war and thus no longer be binding. Many states do not accept this argument.

North Korea has also caused an uproar by its use of this provision of the treaty. Article X.1 only requires a state to give three months' notice in total, and does not provide for other states to question a state's interpretation of "supreme interests of its country". In 1993, North Korea gave notice to withdraw from the NPT. However, after 89 days, North Korea reached agreement with the United States to freeze its nuclear program under the Agreed Framework and "suspended" its withdrawal notice. In October 2002, the United States accused North Korea of violating the Agreed Framework by pursuing a secret uranium enrichment program, and suspended shipments of heavy fuel oil under that agreement. In response, North Korea expelled IAEA inspectors, disabled IAEA equipment, and, on January 10, 2003, announced that it was ending the suspension of its previous NPT withdrawal notification. North Korea said that only one more day's notice was sufficient for withdrawal from the NPT, as it had given 89 days before. The IAEA Board of Governors rejected this interpretation. Most countries held that a new three-months withdrawal notice was required, and some questioned whether North Korea's notification met the "extraordinary events" and "supreme interests" requirements of the Treaty. The Joint Statement of September 19, 2005 at the end of the Fourth Round of the Six-Party Talks called for North Korea to "return" to the NPT, implicitly acknowledging that it had withdrawn.

Recent and coming events

The 2000 Review Conference had as main outcome the definition in practical terms of the nuclear weapons states' disarmament obligations, summarized in the so called Thirteen Steps. On 18 July 2005, US President George W. Bush had met Indian Prime Minister Manmohan Singh and declared that he would work to change US law and international rules to permit trade in US civilian nuclear technology with India. Some, such as British columnist George Monbiot, argue that the U.S.-India nuclear deal, in combination with US attempts to deny Iran (an NPT signatory) civilian nuclear fuel-making technology, may destroy the NPT regime, while others contend that such a move will likely bring India, an NPT non-signatory, under closer international scrutiny.

In the first half of 2010, it was strongly believed that China had signed a civilian nuclear deal with Pakistan claiming that the deal was "peaceful". Arms control advocates critcised the reported China-Pakistan deal as they did in case of U.S.-India deal claiming that both the deals violate the NPT by facilitating nuclear programmes in states which are not parties to the NPT. Some reports asserted that the deal was a strategic move by China to balance US influence in South-Asia.

According to a report published by Department of Defense in 2001, China had provided Pakistan with nuclear materials and has gave them critical technical assistance in the construction of Pakistan's nuclear weapons development facilities, in violation of the Nuclear Non-Proliferation Treaty, of which China even then was a signatory.

At the Seventh Review Conference in May 2005, there were stark differences between the United States, which wanted the conference to focus on non-proliferation, especially on its allegations against Iran, and most other countries, who emphasized the lack of serious nuclear disarmament by the nuclear powers. The non-aligned countries reiterated their position emphasizing the need for nuclear disarmament.

The 2010 Review Conference was held in May 2010 in New York City, and adopted a final document that included a summary by the Review Conference President, Ambassador Libran Capactulan of the Philippines, and an Action Plan that was adopted by consensus. The 2010 conference was generally considered a success because it reached consensus where the previous Review Conference in 2005 ended in disarray, a fact that many attributed to the U.S. President Barack Obama's commitment to nuclear nonproliferation and disarmament. Some have warned that this success raised unrealistically high expectations that could lead to failure at the next Review Conference in 2015.

The "Global Summit on Nuclear Security" took place April 12–13, 2010. The summit was proposed by President Obama in Prague and is intended to strengthen the Nuclear Non-Proliferation Treaty in conjunction with the Proliferation Security Initiative and the Global Initiative to Combat Nuclear Terrorism. Forty seven states and three international organizations took part in the Summit, which issued a communiqué and a work plan.

Criticism and Responses

Over the years the NPT has come to be seen by many Third World states as "a conspiracy of the nuclear 'haves' to keep the nuclear 'have-nots' in their place". This argument has its roots in Article VI of the treaty which "obligates the nuclear weapons states to liquidate their nuclear stockpiles and pursue complete disarmament. Some argue that the NWS have not fully complied with their disarmament obligations under Article VI of the NPT. There has been disappointment with the limited progress on nuclear disarmament, where the five authorized nuclear weapons states still have 22,000 warheads between them and have shown a reluctance to disarm further.

As noted above, The International Court of Justice, in its advisory opinion on the Legality of the Threat or Use of Nuclear Weapons, stated that "there exists an obligation to pursue in good faith and bring to a conclusion negotiations leading to nuclear disarmament in all its aspects under strict and effective international control. Such an obligation requires that states actively pursue measures to reduce the numbers of nuclear weapons and the importance of their role in military force structures. Some critics of the nuclear-weapons states contend that they have failed to comply with Article VI by failing to make disarmament the driving force in national planning and policy with respect to nuclear weapons, even while they ask other states to plan for their security without nuclear weapons.

The United States responds to criticism of its disarmament record by pointing out that since the end of the Cold War it has eliminated over 13,000 nuclear weapons and eliminated over 80% of its deployed strategic warheads and 90% of non-strategic warheads deployed to NATO, in the processing eliminating whole categories of warheads and delivery systems and reducing its reliance on nuclear weapons. U.S. officials have also pointed out the ongoing U.S. work to dismantle nuclear warheads. When current accelerated dismantlement efforts ordered by President George W. Bush have been completed, the U.S. arsenal will be less than a quarter of its size at the end of the Cold War, and smaller than it has been at any point since the Eisenhower administration, well before the drafting of the NPT. The United States has also purchased many thousands of weapons' worth of uranium formerly in Soviet nuclear weapons for conversion into reactor fuel. (As a consequence of this latter effort, it has been estimated that the equivalent of one lightbulb in every ten in the United States is powered by nuclear fuel removed from warheads previously targeted at the United States and its allies during the Cold War.) The U.S. Special Representative for Nuclear Nonproliferation agreed that nonproliferation and disarmament are linked, noting that they can be mutually reinforcing but also that growing proliferation risks create an environment that makes disarmament more difficult. The United Kingdom, France and Russia likewise defend their nuclear disarmament records, and the five NPT NWS issued a joint statement in 2008 reaffirming their Article VI disarmament commitments.

According to Thomas Reed and Danny Stillman, the "NPT has one giant loophole": Article IV gives each non-nuclear weapon state the 'inalienable right' to pursue nuclear energy for the generation of power. A "number of high-ranking officials, even within the United Nations, have argued that they can do little to stop states using nuclear reactors to produce nuclear weapons". A 2009 United Nations report said that: The revival of interest in nuclear power could result in the worldwide dissemination of uranium enrichment and spent fuel reprocessing technologies, which present obvious risks of proliferation as these technologies can produce fissile materials that are directly usable in nuclear weapons.

Moreover, the NPT says nothing about aspects of the nuclear fuel cycle "such as uranium mines and mills, from which terrorists could easily acquire fissile material". Dozens of nations remain potential "weak links" in the global defense against nuclear terrorism and tacitly ignore UN mandates on controls over fissile material at uranium mines. Niger, a major uranium exporter, and the Democratic Republic of the Congo, the source of uranium for the first atomic bomb, are "among the states falling short in complying with UN Security Council Resolution 1540".

According to critics, those states which possess nuclear weapons, but are not authorized to do so under the NPT, have not paid a significant price for their pursuit of weapons capabilities. Also, the NPT has been explicitly weakened by a number of bilateral deals made by NPT signatories, notably the United States.

NUCLEAR WEAPONS OF PAKISTAN

Pakistan's nuclear energy program dates back to the 1950s, but it was the loss of East Pakistan (now Bangladesh) in a war with India that probably triggered a January 1972 political decision (just one month later) to begin a secret nuclear weapons program.

Deterring India's nuclear weapons and augmenting Pakistan's inferior conventional forces are widely believed to be the primary missions for Islamabad's nuclear arsenal. Observers point to India's 1974 "peaceful" nuclear explosion as the pivotal moment that gave additional urgency to the program. Pakistan produced fissile material for its nuclear weapons using gas-centrifuge-based uranium enrichment technology, which it mastered by the mid-1980s. Highly-enriched uranium (HEU) is one of two types of fissile material used in nuclear weapons; the other is plutonium. The country's main enrichment facility is a centrifuge plant located at Kahuta; Pakistan may have other enrichment sites. Islamabad gained enrichment-related technology from many sources. This extensive assistance is reported to have included uranium enrichment technology from Europe, blueprints for a small nuclear weapon from China, and missile technology from China.

The United States had information during the 1970s that Pakistan was constructing a uranium enrichment facility. A. Q. Khan has stated that Pakistan began enriching uranium in 1978 and produced HEU in 1983.10 Although Pakistan subsequently told the United States that it would produce only low-enriched uranium (which is not used as fissile material in nuclear weapons.

U.S. and Pakistani officials who were in government in 1990 indicated during a 1994 meeting that Islamabad decided sometime after October 1989 to resume producing HEU. However, another Pakistani official suggested during the same meeting that the decision may have happened sooner.

The United States had information during the 1970s and early 1980s that Pakistan was pursuing nuclear weapons designs, but exactly when Pakistan produced a workable nuclear explosive device is unclear.

A 1985 National Intelligence Council report stated that Pakistan "probably has a workable design for a nuclear explosive device" and was "probably... a year or two away from a capacity to produce enough" highly enriched uranium for such a device. A 1987 National Security Council (NSC) memorandum described Pakistan's "continued pursuit... of its nuclear weapons option." A 1993 NSC report to Congress stated that Islamabad's nuclear weapons efforts "culminated with the capability to rapidly assemble a nuclear device if necessary by the end of the 1950s. A. Q. Khan stated in an interview published in May 1998 that Islamabad "attained" the capability to detonate such a device "at the end of 1984."

Similarly, Khan reportedly stated in a January 2010 speech that Pakistan "had become a nuclear power" in 1984 or 1985. Moreover, "senior Pakistani politicians" told a Canadian parliamentary committee in June 1998 that Pakistan had "reached the nuclear 'threshold' by 1984-85," according to a 1998 report. In any case, President Bush's failure to certify in 1990 that Pakistan did not "possess a nuclear explosive device" led to a cut-off in military and financial aid under the Pressler Amendment.

After India conducted nuclear weapon tests on May 11 and May 13, 1998, Pakistan's government responded on May 28 and May 30 with six tests in western Pakistan. Test yields were about 10 kilotons and 5 kilotons, according to seismic analysis. The United States imposed additional sanctions after the tests, but these were lifted after the September 11, 2001, terrorist attacks on the United States.

According to public estimates, Pakistan has about 90-110 nuclear weapons, though it could have more. Pakistan's HEU-based nuclear warheads use an implosion design with a solid core of approximately 15-20 kilograms of HEU. Islamabad reportedly continues to produce HEU for weapons at a rate of at least 100 kilograms per year.

Pakistan has also pursued plutonium-based warheads and continues to produce plutonium for weapons. Islamabad has received Chinese and European assistance for at least some of its plutonium program.

The 40-50 megawatt heavy-water Khushab plutonium production reactor has been operating since 1998.27 It appears that Islamabad is constructing at least two additional heavy-water reactors, which will expand considerably Pakistan's plutonium production capacity, at the same site. Whether one of those reactors is already operating is unclear.

Additionally, Pakistan has a reprocessing facility. at the Pakistan Institute of Science and Technology (PINSTECH) and is apparently constructing other such facilities. *Nuclear Fuel* reported in 2000 that, according to "senior U.S. government officials," Islamabad had begun operating a "pilotscale" reprocessing facility at the New Laboratories facility at PINSTECH. Pakistan also appears to be constructing a second reprocessing facility at the site and may be completing a reprocessing facility located at Chasma.

Pakistani plutonium-based nuclear warheads likely contain approximately 4-6 kilograms of plutonium, according to one expert estimate. Islamabad's construction of additional nuclear reactors and expansion of its reprocessing capabilities could indicate plans to increase and improve Pakistan's nuclear weapons arsenal in the near future. Indeed, then DIA Director Michael Maples told the Senate Armed Services Committee on March 10, 2009, that "Pakistan continues to develop its nuclear infrastructure, expand nuclear weapon stockpiles and seek more advanced warheads and delivery systems." Similarly, Admiral Mullen confirmed during the May 14, 2009, hearing that the United States has "evidence" that Pakistan is expanding its nuclear arsenal. DIA Director Burgess's assessment during a March 10, 2011, hearing before the Senate Armed Services Committee was the same as his predecessor's.

PAKISTAN'S CIVIL NUCLEAR PROGRAM

Pakistan also has a civil nuclear power program, with two reactors currently operating—the Karachi Nuclear Power Plant, which went critical in 1971, and the Chasma Nuclear Power Plant, which went critical in 2000. Prime Minister Gilani announced May 12, 2011, that a second nuclear reactor at Chasma, constructed with Chinese assistance, had become operational. Beijing has also apparently agreed to construct two additional power reactors at Chasma, according to both Chinese and Pakistani officials. Pakistan Atomic Energy Commission Chairman Ansar Parvez stated May 12, 2011, that concrete has been poured for one of these reactors and that ground breaking for the other reactor would take place the next month. The first reactor is to come on line in 2016, with the next to follow 10 months later. Acting Assistant Secretary Van Diepen stated July 22, 2010, that such a sale would appear to be inconsistent with current Nuclear Suppliers Group (NSG) guidelines. Additionally, Pakistan and China are reportedly close to finalizing an agreement for Beijing to construct a third, larger, reactor in Pakistan. As noted, the NSG changed its guidelines in 2008 to allow nuclear trade with India. Secretary of State Clinton suggested July 20, 2010, that the United States does not currently support a similar change for Pakistan. Assistant Secretary of State Robert Blake reiterated Van Diepen and Clinton's positions March 18, 2011.

Pakistan is also operating two research reactors—Pakistan Research Reactor 1, which went critical in 1965,170 and Pakistan Research Reactor 2, which went critical in 1989. Pakistan Research Reactor 1, which was originally supplied by a U.S. firm, was converted from using highly-enriched uranium (HEU) to low-enriched uranium fuel in 1992.172 A "small amount" of the HEU fuel remains in Pakistan.

Delivery Vehicles

Pakistan has two types of delivery vehicles for nuclear weapons: aircraft controlled by the Pakistan Air Force and surface-to-surface missiles controlled by the Pakistan Army. Pakistan could deliver its nuclear weapons using F-16 fighter aircraft purchased from the United States, provided that modifications are made. It is widely believed that Islamabad has made the relevant modifications to the F-16s previously sold to them by Washington.

Although concerns have been raised about the impact of these sales on the strategic balance in South Asia. the U.S. government maintains that the sale of additional F-16s to Pakistan will not alter the regional balance of power. The contract for provision of an additional 18 aircraft was signed in 2006, as was the contract for the weapons for those aircraft and a contract to perform the mid-life upgrade on Pakistan's F-16A/B model aircraft. Pakistan's F-16 fleet will, therefore, be expanded, but it is unclear what portion of the fleet will be capable of a nuclear mission. Mirage V aircraft may also be used as delivery vehicles.

DIA Director Burgess told the Senate Armed Services Committee March 10, 2011, that Pakistan is developing new missile systems which, when deployed and added to Islamabad's current ballistic missiles, will enable Pakistan "to strike a variety of targets at ranges of 200-2000 kilometers with both conventional and nuclear payloads." Islamabad has three types of ballistic missiles thought to be nuclear-capable: the solid-fuel *Hatf-III* (*Ghaznavi*), with a range of approximately 300-400 kilometers; the solid-fuel *Hatf-IV* (*Shaheen*), with a range of over 450 kilometers; and the liquid-fuel *Hatf-V* (*Ghauri*), with an approximate range of almost 1,300 kilometers; The solid-fuel *Hatf-VI* (*Shaheen-2*) missile, when deployed, will be "capable of reaching targets out to 2,000 kilometers," former DIA Director Maples stated March 10, 2009,72 adding that Islamabad has made "significant progress" on the missile.

A 2009 National Air and Space Intelligence Centre (NASIC) report appears to support this conclusion, stating that the missile "probably will soon be deployed." Pakistan's Inter Services Public Relations announced April 19, 2011, the first successful flight test of a "newly developed Short Range Surface to Surface Multi Tube Ballistic Missile Hatf IX (NASR)."

The missile has a range of 60 kilometers and "carries nuclear warheads of appropriate yield with high accuracy," according to the press release. Islamabad continues to carry out ballistic missile tests, but notifies India in advance in accordance with an October 2005 bilateral missile pre-notification pact. Maples also indicated that Pakistan is developing nuclear-capable cruise missiles: the Babur (ground-launched) and the Ra'ad (air-launched), both of which will have estimated ranges of 320 kilometers, according to the NASIC report. In an April 29, 2011, announcement of a successful flight test of the Ra'ad, the Pakistani government gave the missile's range as 350 kilometers; In an October 28, 2011, announcement of a flight test of the Babur, the Pakistani government gave the missile's range as 700 kilometers.

Nuclear Doctrine

Pakistan's strategic doctrine is undeclared, and will probably remain so, but prominent officials and analysts have offered insights concerning its basic tenets. Describing the guiding principle as minimum credible nuclear deterrence. high-level officials' statements point to four policy objectives for Islamabad's nuclear weapons: deter all forms of external aggression; deter through a combination of conventional and strategic forces; deter counterforce strategies by securing strategic assets and threatening nuclear retaliation; and stabilize strategic deterrence in South Asia.

Pakistani officials have also indicated that this nuclear posture is designed to preserve territorial integrity against Indian attack, prevent military escalation, and counter its main rival's conventional superiority.

Pakistan has pledged no-first-use against non-nuclear-weapon states, but has not ruled out firstuse against a nuclear-armed aggressor, such as India. Some analysts say this ambiguity serves to maintain deterrence against India's conventional superiority; the Foreign Ministry spokesperson stated May 21, 2009, that "there are acquisitions of sophisticated weaponry by our neighbour which will disturb the conventional balance between our two countries and hence, lower the nuclear threshold." Other analysts argue that keeping the first-use option against New Delhi allows Islamabad to conduct sub-conventional operations, such as support for low intensity conflict or proxy war in Kashmir, while effectively deterring India at the strategic level. Pakistan has reportedly addressed issues of survivability through pursuing a second strike capability, possibly building hard and deeply buried storage and launch facilities, deploying roadmobile missiles, deploying air defenses around strategic sites, and utilizing concealment measures.

Command and Control

Pakistan's command and control over its nuclear weapons is compartmentalized and includes strict operational security. The government's command and control system is based on "C4I2SR" (command, control, communication, computers, intelligence, information, surveillance and reconnaissance). Islamabad's Strategic Command Organization has a three-tiered structure, consisting of the National Command Authority (NCA), the Strategic Plans Division (SPD), and the Strategic Forces Commands.

The NCA, established in 2000, supervises the functions and administration of all of Pakistan's organizations involved in nuclear weapons research, development, and employment, as well as the military services that operate the strategic forces. The prime minister, as head of government, is chairperson of the NCA. The NCA also includes the chair of the joint chiefs of staff; the ministers of defence, interior, and finance; the director general of the SPD; and the commanders of the Army, Air Force, and Navy. The final authority to launch a nuclear strike requires consensus within the NCA; the chairperson must cast the final vote. The NCA is comprised of two committees, the Employment Control Committee (ECC) and the Development Control Committee (DCC), each of which includes a mix of civilian and military officials. The ECC's functions include establishing a command and control system over the use of nuclear weapons. The DCC "exercises technical, financial and administrative control over all strategic organisations, including national laboratories and research and development organisations associated with the development and modernisation of nuclear weapons.

The SPD is headed by a director general from the Army and acts as the secretariat for the NCA. The SPD's functions include formulating Islamabad's nuclear policy, strategy, and doctrine; developing the nuclear chain of command; and formulating operational plans at the service level for the movement, deployment, and use of nuclear weapons. The Army, Air Force, and Navy each have their own strategic force command, but operational planning and control remains with the NCA. The SPD coordinates operational plans with the strategic forces commands. According to current and former Pakistani officials, Islamabad employs a system which requires that at least two, and perhaps three, people authenticate launch codes for nuclear weapons. On December 13, 2007, then-President Musharraf formalized these authorities and structure in the "National Command Authority Ordinance, 2007."89 The NCA was established by administrative order, but now has a legal basis. Analysts point out that the timing of this ordinance was meant to help the command and control system weather political transitions and potentially preserve the military's strong control over the system. The ordinance also addresses the problems of the proliferation of nuclear expertise and personnel reliability. It outlines punishable offenses related to breach of confidentiality or leakage of "secured information," gives the SPD authority to investigate suspicious conduct, states that punishment for these offenses can be up to 25 years imprisonment, and applies to both serving and retired personnel, including military personnel, notwithstanding any other laws. As a result, Pakistani authorities say that the ordinance should strengthen their control over strategic organizations and their personnel.

Security Concerns

According to a 2001 Department of Defence report, Islamabad's nuclear weapons "are probably stored in component form," which suggests that the nuclear warheads are stored separately from delivery vehicles. According to some reports, the fissile cores of the weapons are separated from the non-nuclear explosives. But whether this is actually the case is unclear; one report states that the warheads and delivery vehicles are probably stored separately in facilities close to one another, but says nothing about the fissile cores. And, according to an account of a 2008 experts' group visit to Pakistan, Lieutenant General Khalid Kidwai, the head of the SPD, suggested that the nuclear warheads (containing the fissile cores) may be mated with their delivery vehicles. According to Kidwai, the report says, the SPD's official position is that the weapons "will be ready when required, at the shortest notice; [but] the Pakistani doctrine is not endorsing a USUSSR model with weapons on hair trigger alert." The 2001 Defence Department report says that Pakistan can probably assemble its weapons fairly quickly.

It warrants mention that, although separate storage may provide a layer of protection against accidental launch or prevent theft of an assembled weapon, it may be easier for unauthorized people to remove a weapon's fissile material core if it is not assembled. Dispersal of the assets may also create more potential access points for acquisition and may increase the risk of diversion.

As the United States prepared to launch an attack on the Afghan Taliban after September 11, 2001, President Musharraf reportedly ordered that Pakistan's nuclear arsenal be redeployed to "at least six secret new locations." This action came at a time of uncertainly about the future of the region, including the direction of U.S.-Pakistan relations. Islamabad's leadership was uncertain whether the United States would decide to conduct military strikes against Pakistan's nuclear assets if the government did not assist the United States against the Taliban. Indeed, President Musharraf cited protection of Pakistan's nuclear and missile assets as one of the reasons for Islamabad's dramatic policy shift.

These events, in combination with the 1999 Kargil crisis, the 2002 conflict with India at the Line of Control, and revelations about the A. Q. Khan proliferation network, inspired a variety of reforms to secure the nuclear complex. Risk of nuclear war in South Asia ran high in the 1999 Kargil crisis, when the Pakistani military is believed to have begun preparing nuclear-tipped missiles. It should be noted that, even at the high alert levels of 2001 and 2002, there were no reports of Pakistan mating the warheads with delivery systems.

In the fall of 2007 and early 2008, some observers expressed concern about the security of the country's arsenal if political instability were to persist. Former Prime Minister Benazir Bhutto said in a November 5, 2007, interview that, although then-President Musharraf claimed to be in firm control of the nuclear arsenal, she feared this control could weaken due to instability in the country. Similarly, Michael Krepon of the Henry L. Stimson Centre has argued that "a prolonged period of turbulence and infighting among the country's President, Prime Minister, and Army Chief" could jeopardize the army's unity of command, which "is essential for nuclear security." During that time, U.S. military officials also expressed concern about the security of Pakistan's nuclear weapons. Then-IAEA Director General Mohamed ElBaradei also has expressed fears that a radical regime could take power in Pakistan, and thereby acquire nuclear weapons. Experts also worry that while nuclear weapons are currently under firm control, with warheads disassembled, technology could be sold off by insiders during a worsened crisis." However, U.S. intelligence officials have expressed greater confidence regarding the security of Islamabad's nuclear weapons. Deputy Secretary of State John D.

Negroponte in testimony to Congress on November 7, 2007, said he believed that there is "plenty of succession planning that's going on in the Pakistani military" and that Pakistan's nuclear weapons are under "effective technical control." Similarly, Donald Kerr, Principal Deputy Director of National Intelligence, told a Washington audience May 29, 2008, that the Pakistani military's control of the nuclear weapons is "a good thing because that's an institution in Pakistan that has, in fact, withstood many of the political changes over the years." More recently, former DIA Director Maples stated March 10, 2009, that Islamabad "has taken important steps to safeguard its nuclear weapons," although he pointed out that "vulnerabilities exist." As noted, current DIA Director Burgess articulated a similar assessment in March 2011.

U.S. officials have also conveyed confidence in the security of Islamabad's nuclear weapons. General Petraeus stated on May 10, 2009, that "[w]ith respect to the—the nuclear weapons and—and sites that are controlled by Pakistan ... we have confidence in their security procedures and elements and believe that the security of those sites is adequate." Admiral Mullen echoed this assessment during a May 14, 2009, hearing before the Senate Armed Services Committee. More recently, Secretary of Defence Robert Gates stated in a January 21, 2010, interview that the United States is "very comfortable with the security of Pakistan's nuclear weapons." Then-State Department spokesperson P.J. Crowley told reporters April 9, 2010, that Pakistan "has demonstrated that it can secure its own nuclear weapons program." Similarly, Under Secretary of Defence Michele Flournoy stated during an April 29, 2010, hearing that "we believe that Pakistan has a very solid command-and-control system for their nuclear weapons," adding that "they have made a great deal of investment in the security of their nuclear arsenal." As noted, this confidence has continued into 2011. James Clapper, Director of National Intelligence, told the House Intelligence Committee February 10 that "our assessment is that the nuclear weapons in Pakistan are secure." General Petraeus told the Senate Armed Services Committee March 15 that "[t]here is quite considerable security for the Pakistani nuclear weapons." Asked about the security of Pakistan's weapons following a May 2011 insurgent attack on a military installation in Karachi, Assistant

Secretary of State Robert Blake stated June 21 that "there is much more heightened security around" Pakistan's nuclear weapons facilities than at the Karachi installation. U.S. knowledge of Pakistan's arsenal, however, remains limited, according to U.S. officials. For example, Mullen stated that "we're limited in what we actually know" about Islamabad's nuclear arsenal. Leon Panetta, Director of the Central Intelligence Agency, similarly acknowledged in a May 18, 2010, speech that the United States does not possess the intelligence to locate all of Pakistan's nuclear weapons-related sites.

Other governments have also voiced opinions regarding the security of Pakistan's nuclear arsenal. For example, Indian National Security Adviser M. K. Narayanan said that the arsenal is safe and has adequate checks and balances. Similarly, then-Secretary of State for Foreign and Commonwealth Affairs David Miliband told the *Charlie Rose Show* December 15, 2008, that Islamabad's nuclear weapons "are under pretty close lock and key." Furthermore, according to Director of the French General Directorate of External Security Erard Corbin de Mangoux, Pakistan's military and civilian leaders have a "sense of responsibility" to maintain control over the country's nuclear weapons; these leaders "know that the international status to which they aspire depends directly on their ability to exercise complete control over such an instrument of power," he argued in an interview published in spring 2010. Other non-U.S. officials, however, have sounded somewhat less optimistic. For example, Russian Deputy Prime Minister Sergei Ivanov said in a March 24, 2009, television interview that Moscow is "very much concerned" about the security of Pakistan's arsenal. Indian officials expressed concerns about the security of Pakistan's nuclear arsenal following the May 2011 insurgent attack on the Karachi military installation.

Pakistani officials have consistently expressed confidence in the security of the country's nuclear arsenal. Then-President Musharraf stated in November 2007 that Pakistan's nuclear weapons are under "total custodial controls." More recently, President Asif Ali Zardari told *CNN* December 2, 2008, that the country's nuclear command and control system "is working well."

Additionally, a Pakistani Foreign Ministry spokesperson stated May 21, 2009, that "there is simply no question of our strategic assets falling into the wrong hands. We have full confidence in our procedures, mechanisms and command and control systems."

Pakistani Prime Minister Yousaf Raza Gilani stated May 8, 2010, that Islamabad has "laid to rest" concerns about its nuclear arsenal's security. The May 2011 U.S. strike that killed Al Qaeda leader Osama bin Laden generated a public discussion in Pakistan as to whether a country such as India or the United States could successfully attack and destroy Pakistan's nuclear weapons.

Responding to these concerns, Prime Minster Gilani stated May 25, 2011, that the country's "strategic assets are well protected and our capability to defend our sovereignty, territorial integrity and liberties of our people, is very much in place." In addition to the above scenarios, the security of Pakistan's nuclear weapons could also be jeopardized by another conflict between India and Pakistan, Michael Krepon argued, explaining that an "escalating war with nuclear forces in the field would increase the probability of accidents, miscalculations, and the use of nuclear weapons."

This is because [w]hen tensions rise precipitously with India, the readiness level of Pakistan's nuclear deterrent also rises. Because the geographical coordinates of Pakistan's main nuclear weapon storage sites, missile, and air bases can be readily identified from satellites—and therefore targeted by opposing forces—the dictates of deterrence mandate some movement of launchers and weapons from fixed locations during crises. Nuclear weapons on the move are inherently less secure than nuclear weapons at heavily-guarded storage sites. Weapons and launchers in motion are also more susceptible to "insider" threats and accidents.

Such a war, Krepon added, would also place stress on the army's unity of command. Krepon has also pointed out that Islamabad faces a dilemma, because less-dispersed nuclear weapons may be more vulnerable to a disarming military strike from India."

4

Arms Industry and its Modernisation

The arms industry is a global industry and business which manufactures and sells weapons and military technology and equipment. Arms producing companies, also referred to as Defence companies or military industry, produce arms mainly for the armed forces of states. Products include guns, ammunition, missiles, military aircraft, military vehicles, ships, electronic systems, and more. The arms industry also conducts significant research and development.

It is estimated that yearly, over 1 trillion dollars are spent on military expenditures worldwide (2% of World GDP). Part of this goes to the procurement of military hardware and services from the military industry. The combined arms sales of the top 100 largest arms producing companies amounted to an estimated \$315 billion in 2006. In 2004 over \$30 billion were spent in the international arms trade (a figure that excludes domestic sales of arms). The arms trade has also been one of the sectors impacted by the credit crunch, with total deal value in the market halving from US\$32.9bn to US\$14.3bn in 2008.

Many industrialized countries have a domestic arms industry to supply their own military forces. Some countries also have a substantial legal or illegal domestic trade in weapons for use by its citizens. The illegal trade in small arms is prevalent in many countries and regions affected by political instability.

Contracts to supply a given country's military are awarded by the government, making arms contracts of substantial political importance.

The link between politics and the arms trade can result in the development of what US President Dwight D. Eisenhower described as a military-industrial complex, where the armed forces, commerce, and politics become closely linked.

Various corporations, some publicly held, others private, bid for these contracts, which are often worth many billions of dollars. Sometimes, such as the contract for the new Joint Strike Fighter, a competitive tendering process takes place, where the decision is made on the merits of the design submitted by the companies involved.

Other times, no bidding or competition takes place. In the Cold War Era, arms exports were used by both the Soviet Union and the United States to influence their standings in other countries, particularly Third World Countries. Since the fall of the Soviet Union, global arms exports initially fell slightly, but have since grown again to cold war levels. The United States is the overall top supplier of weapons. The United States is also the top supplier of weapons to the developing world, accounting for around 36% of worldwide weapons sales, followed by Russia, Britain, Germany and China.

The Control Arms Campaign, founded by Amnesty International, Oxfam, and the International Action Network on Small Arms, estimated in 2003 that there are over 639 million items of small arms in circulation, and that over 1135 companies based in more than 98 different countries manufacture small arms as well as their various components and ammunition. According to Oxfam, an estimated 500,000 individuals die in small arms-conflicts every year, approximately one death per minute.

SECTORS

Land-based Weapons

This category includes everything from light arms to heavy artillery, and the majority of producers are small. Many are located in Third World countries. International trade in handguns, machine guns, tanks, armored personal carriers and other relatively inexpensive weapons is substantial. There is relatively little regulation at the international level, and as a result, many legitimately produced weapons fall into the hands of rebel forces, terrorists, or regimes under sanctions.

Aerospace Systems

Encompassing military aircraft (both land-based and naval aviation), conventional missiles, and military satellites, this is the most technologically advanced sector of the market. It is also the least competitive from an economic standpoint, with a handful of companies dominating the entire market.

The top clients and major producers are virtually all located in the West, with the United States easily in first place. Prominent aerospace firms include Dassault Aviation, EADS,Finmeccanica, Thales Group, Lockheed Martin, Boeing, and Britain's BAE Systems.

There are also several multinational consortia mostly involved in the manufacturing of fighter jets, such as the Eurofighter. The largest military contract in history, signed in October 2001, involved the development of the Joint Strike Fighter.

Naval Systems

All of the world's major powers maintain substantial maritime forces to provide a forward presence and enhance overall mobility, with the largest nations possessing aircraft carriers, nuclear submarines and advanced anti-air defense systems. The vast majority of military ships are conventionally powered, but some are nuclear-powered. There is also a large global market in second-hand naval vessels, generally purchased by developing countries from Western governments.

World's Largest Defence Budgets

This is a list of the fifteen countries with the highest defence budgets for the year 2006. The information is from the Stockholm International Peace Research Institute. Total world spending amounted to $1.158 trillion USD in 2006, with nearly half of the total amount spent by the United States. The actual budget for the PRC's armed forces is unknown, the figure given is an official estimate of government fund allocation, with much of the net budget funds coming from extra-budgetary sources.

Military expenditure in market exchange rate dollar terms, 2006

Rank	Country	Spending ($b.)	%GDP
–	World Total	1,158	2.41
1	United States	985.7	12.99
2	United Kingdom	59.2	2.49
3	France	53.1	2.38
4	People's Republic of China	49.5	1.88
5	Japan	43.7	1.00
6	Germany	37.0	1.28
7	Russia	34.7	3.54
8	Italy	33.9	1.61
9	Saudi Arabia	29.0	8.32
10	India	24.2	2
11	South Korea	21.9	2.47
12	Canada	14.6	1.10
13	Australia	13.8	1.83
14	Brazil	13.4	1.26
15	Spain	12.3	1.00

1. Data for China and Russia are estimates, their expenditures are not well known.

2. Data for Saudi Arabia include expenditure for public order and safety and might be slight overestimates.

3. In the percentage spending per GDP, the GDP list (2006) of the International Monetary Fund was taken.

4. One quarter of the world total is illicit and/or black market trade.

World's Largest Arms Exporters

The unit in this table are so-called trend indicater values expressed in millions of US dollars. These values do not represent real financial flows but are a crude instrument to estimate volumes of arms transfers, regardless of the contracted prices, which can be as low as zero in the case of military aid.

Supplier	2000	2001	2002	2003	2004	2005	2006	2007
USA	7505	5801	4984	5581	6616	7026	7821	7454
Russia	4190	5631	5458	5355	6400	5576	6463	4588
Germany	1622	825	910	1707	1017	1879	2891	3395
France	1033	1235	1342	1313	2267	1688	1586	2690
Netherlands	259	192	243	342	218	611	1575	1355
UK	1356	1116	772	624	1143	871	978	1151
Ukraine	280	649	440	530	600	700	1000	1200
South Korea	100	240	140	140	410	260	260	844
Italy	192	224	407	321	216	787	860	562
Sweden	46	7	120	158	73	116	803	529
Israel	308	850	125	468	287	536	472	414
China	228	498	544	553	271	223	564	355
Canada	83	129	182	279	305	193	227	343
Spain	321	298	365	309	533	244	258	238
Switzerland	104	120	109	139	201	166	144	211
Bulgaria	N/A	N/A	N/A	250[1]	N/A	190	149	192

The information is from the Stockholm International Peace Research Institute or from the national defence commissions where available and is updated at least once a year. Next to SIPRI there are several other sources that provide data on international transfers of arms.

These include national reports by national governments about arms exports, the UN register on conventional arms and an annual publication by the US US Congressional Research Service that includes data on arms exports to developing countries as compiled by US intelligence agencies.

A list of such sources can be found at the SIPRI website. Due to the different methodologies and definitions used different sources often provide significantly different data.

For example, according to Statistisk sentralbyrå (Norway state statistics), Norway exports a greater value (in USD) of arms than many of the nations listed above.

Some of the differences are possibly due to deliberate over or under reporting by some of the sources. Governments may claim high arms exports as part of their role in marketing efforts of their national arms industry or they may claim low arms exports in order to be perceived as a responsible international actor.

List of Major Weapon Manufacturers

Major arms industry corporations by nation

Country	Weapon manufacturers and Arms Traders
Argentina	Fábrica MilitarFábrica Militar de Aviones
Austria	GlockSteyr Mannlicher
Australia	TenixAustralian Defence IndustriesAustralian Submarine CorporationCommonwealth Aircraft Corporation
Bangladesh	Defence Advancement Trading Company (DATCO)
Belgium	Fabrique Nationale de Herstal
Bosnia and Herzegovina	Zrak dd
Brazil	Ares Aeroespacial e DefesaAvibras
	CBC - Companhia Brasileira de Cartuchos
	Embraer
	Helibras
	IMBEL - Indústria Brasileira de Material Bélico, belonging to the Brazilian Army
	Taurus
Bulgaria	TEREMArsenal Corporation
Canada	Colt Canada
	Bombardier
	SNC-Lavalin Group
China	Norinco
	AVIC IAVIC II
	Chengdu Aircraft Industry Group
	China Nanchang Aircraft Manufacturing Corporation
	Changhe Aircraft Industries Corporation
	China State Shipbuilding Corporation (CSSC)
	China National Nuclear Corporation
	China Aerospace Science & Technology Corporation (CASC)
Denmark	Skandinavisk Aero Industri
	Hydrema
	Terma
Egypt	AOI

France	EADS
	Dassault Aviation
	DCNS
	Thales Group
	GIAT Industries
Germany	Carl Walther GmbH Sportwaffen
	Diehl BGT Defence
	EADS
	Heckler & Koch
	Krauss-Maffei
	Rheinmetall
	Mauser
	Lürssen
	Thyssenkrupp
	MBDA
Greece	EASHAI
India	DRDO
	Hindustan Aeronautics Limited
Indonesia	PT Pindad
	Perindustrian Angkatan Darat
Israel	Israel Aerospace Industries
	Israel Weapon Industries
	Rafael Advanced Defense Systems
	Elbit
Italy	Beretta
	Finmeccanica
	Fincantieri
	AvioAgusta
	Westland
	Benelli (firearms)
Mexico	ALFA
	DGIM
	Hydra Technologies of Mexico
	Mabe
	Mendoza
	Mondragon
	San Luis Rassini
	SEDENA

	SEMAR
	Valdez Industria
	Xiuhcoatl
Myanmar	Reliable Technology Limited
Norway	Kongsberg Defense & Aerospace
	Nordic Ammunition Group
Poland	Bumar
	PZL
Pakistan	Pakistan Aeronautical Complex
	Heavy Industries Taxila
	Pakistan Ordnance Factories
Portugal	INDEP
Russia	Sukhoi
	Mikoyan
	Mil Moscow Helicopter Plant
	Tupolev
	Ilyushin
	Yakovlev
	Tikhomirov Scientific Research Institute of Instrument Design
	Moscow Institute of Thermal Technology
	IZH
	Kartsev-Venediktov Design Bureau
	Almaz Scientific Industrial Corporation
	Vympel NPO
	Beriev
	FSUE "Splav"
Serbia	Zastava Arms
	Yugoimport
South Africa	Denel
South Korea	Hyundai Rotem
	Samsung Techwin
Spain	EADS-CASA
	Navantia
	Santa Barbara (General Dynamics)

Sweden	BAE Systems Bofors
	Kockums
	Saab
Switzerland	Astra Arms
	SIGARMS
	RUAG
	Pilatus Aircraft
	Armasuisse
	MOWAG (General Dynamics)
Thailand	Chaiseri Metal & Rubber
	Thailand Aviation Industries TAI
Turkey	MKEK
	TAI
	Aselsan
Ukraine	Antonov
	KMDB
	Malyshev Factory
	RPC Fort
	Yuzhmash
	Yuzhnoye Design Bureau
United Kingdom	BAE Systems
	Cobham plc
	MBDA
	Rolls-Royce
United States	AAI Corporation
	BAE Systems Inc.
	Boeing
	Bushmaster Firearms International
	Carlyle Group
	Colt's Manufacturing Company
	General Atomics
	General Electric (primarily through GEAE)
	General Dynamics
	Honeywell
	Lockheed-Martin
	Northrop Grumman Corporation
	Raytheon Corporation
	United Technologies (primarily through Pratt and Whitney, Sikorsky Aircraft Corporation)

CONTROL AND INTERNATIONAL TREATY

We are committed to upholding, implementing and further strengthening the multilateral disarmament and non-proliferation framework in the fight against threats which are tending to escape the control of national sovereignty, the challenges deriving from destabilising accumulation and spread of small arms and light weapons, from illicit or irresponsible arms trade, and from the proliferation of weapons of mass destruction, which are creating new and growing hot-spots of international tension. In this regard, the EU welcomes the growing support in all parts of the world for an International Arms Trade Treaty and is firmly committed to this process.

Institutes Participating in Weapon Research and Warfare Simulation

- Netherlands Organisation for Applied Scientific Research
- Bolt, Beranek and Newman
- QinetiQ
- World Security Institute

Ethical Dimension

For many people, arms exports may pose an ethical challenge, as they may see supplying the weapons for a conflict as morally akin to becoming involved with negligible personal, national or corporate risk. Essentially, they view the arms industry as a means of profiting from war and death when failure to supply arms could lead to an early disengagement.

On the other hand, exporting arms to groups (or nations) with "laudable" goals—e.g. a rebel group overthrowing a fascist regime—can be an invaluable equalizer in the conflict. And there is no shortage of parties to a conflict that can wreak incalculable destruction without the assistance of modern armaments—for instance, the Hutus of the Rwandan Genocide conducted most of their carnage using simple machetes and other low-tech implements.

Of course—and this is endemic of nearly every debate over arms trade—the terminology used and the people it refers to can be frustratingly fluid. As years pass, governments decide on new "interests" and circumstances change accordingly. "Freedom fighters" become "insurgents". "Terrorists" become "invaluable allies", and "religious zealots" morph into "agents of stability". Entire nations, to use the parlance of the early 21st century, can go from the "Coalition of the Willing" to the "Axis of Evil" in very little time, and every change affects policy and the distribution of arms in the world.

THE ETHICS AND ECONOMICS OF THE ARMS TRADE

Every sensible market economist should accept that a market must operate within a framework of law and moral convention.Investment Bankers are not permitted to finance firms that sell poison and there are strong constraints on the emission of lead into rivers or on pollutants into the chain of foodstuffs.My contention is that exports of arms to dubious regimes should come within the sphere of what is out of bounds – and more decisively so than at present. Would we have to pay a heavy economic price for such restraint? There is indeed sometimes a conflict between national self-interest and ethical actions, just as there can be a conflict between personal self-interest and moral behaviour. But in both cases this is often exaggerated. In the national case it is exaggerated by an inflated view of the role of arms and export promotion in the British economy.

The promotion and *de facto* subsidisation of arms sales is – like most other industrial subsidies – wealth destroying; there would be very little, if any, sacrifice involved in doing away with the whole effort. Behind the arms promotion lobby is the primitive belief that if one source of overseas sales dries up, the workers and other resources involved would waste away. This is rubbish in view of the millions of people who change jobs every year. If other countries want to compete with us in foolish subsidies, let them.

The Ethical Case

It might be best to examine the ethical case before the economic arguments. It is not my intention to argue against all arms sales. It would be absurd for each member of an alliance to try to make a full range of weapons, simply out of *amour propre,* when specialisation would pay far better. In 1998-99 the Ministry of Defence spent 13% of its equipment budget on 64 co-operative equipment programmes involving 19 partner nations. The most important of these, by far, were France, Germany, the USA, Italy and the Netherlands.

Subsidised credit for exports of arms or major capital goods have far worse effects than just the economic ones. Western nations are undoubtedly rich enough to waste some resources. As Adam Smith said: 'There is an awful lot of ruin in a nation.'

The worst effects are political and moral. They are both illustrated by the instance of the Pergau Dam in Malaysia in the mid 1990s when the Conservative government overturned a publicly minuted reservation by the Permanent Secretary of the Department of Overseas Development and insisted on supporting credits for this dam. One of the unstated arguments for going ahead was that this would act as a sweetener to persuade the Malaysian government to buy other goods, including arms, from Britain. On the other hand arms sales are justified because they are supposed to persuade governments that buy them to use British equipment in their capital projects. Thus one bad consequence is called in aid to support another; and Third World despots are encouraged to devote still more resources to military spending on prestige projects of dubious value.

More recently, the Labour Prime Minister was said to have overruled the Foreign Secretary when he authorised a statement by Stephen Byers on 21 December 1999 that he was 'minded', subject to certain conditions, to grant export credit for the Ilisu dam project in Turkey, which will flood several valleys with sites of unique cultural and religious value to the Kurds. You can imagine what this will do to promote ethnic harmony inside Turkey. In the spring of 2001 we were still waiting for a decision.

We cannot leave out of account the enormous part that bribery plays in this trade. A forthcoming study by Joe Roeber concludes that: 'Because of the structure, complexity and capacity of the market, and above all, because of the secrecy that surrounds every aspect of its activities, the international arms trade is the most corrupt of all legal trades.' He finally asks: 'Can we justify bribing people to buy arms they may not need with money their taxpayers cannot afford, simply to inflate the number of jobs in a declining industry?'

All these follies are supported by the myth that exports are valuable for their own sake, however small the return the British nation gets from them. Business lobbyists are able to persuade a succession of prime ministers, ranging from ultra-dry Conservatives to New Labour that, if the government does not support them, their overseas rivals will win the contracts instead.

Orders of Magnitude

The official estimate for British arms sales is that they amounted in 1999 to about £4bn or appreciably less 0.5% of GDP. A great part consisted of aircraft and aerospace parts. A good academic estimate of the direct cost of government support is about £400m per annum. This does not cover the arms promotion aspects of many royal, political and military visits and activities, which are ostensibly for other purposes. Indirect support for what is known as the Defence Industrial Base is a good deal larger. The number of workers employed is put at 90,000 or just over 0.33% of UK employment. There are two practical inhibitions that limit official export promotion. The first and obvious one is the Exchequer cost. Secondly there is the fear that official promotional activities will be self-defeating, and still more expensive, if all governments follow them in a competitive race. Accordingly, international organisations such as the European Union, the World Trade Organisation, the OECD and the Berne Credit Union have set rules to limit – but not stop – government support. Unfortunately these agreements do not prevent the never-ending procession of royalty, ministers and ambassadors who promote arms sales abroad, to say nothing of the military and trade attachés. Then there is the Defence Export Services Organisation, which provides marketing and military assistance. Above all, arms sales are often backed by the Export Credits Guarantee Department (ECGD), which provides 'insurance and finance packages for exporters of capital goods and services and political risk insurance' – in other words, taxpayer support for sales that would not pass muster on purely commercial terms. While public enterprises are set a target real rate of return of six per cent, the ECGD has to do no more than break even on average. The ECGD covers medium to long-term capital goods exports from three years up to 16 years duration. In a typical year it underwrites about £7bn of cover. The business is concentrated almost entirely on civil engineering projects and military and civil aerospace. The largest recipient is China. The military share of ECGD business has averaged over 25% in the most recent five years.

The much-maligned Treasury tends to fight many ECGD deals, but is often defeated. Huw Evans, a former Treasury deputy secretary, has said that the ECGD is too vulnerable to intensive lobbying of ministers by large corporations and that it should become an independent agency. As Andrew Tyrie MP, a former adviser to Conservative chancellors has written, 'It is illogical to indulge in a competition to give away our own exports through an auction of subsidies.'

THE DEVELOPMENT OF A SMALL ARMS DATABASE

There is no comprehensive database of small arms acquisitions and inventories available that is comparable to the one on large conventional weapons maintained by the Stockholm International Peace Research Institute (SIPRI). An attempt to develop such a database would be challenging but not impossible. Some countries in Asia are still hesitant about the confidence-building values of transparency and consider such an act disadvantageous because it supposedly would expose their military weaknesses. However, this view may be changing as precedents, such as declaring weapon acquisitions to the UN Register, instills trust and confidence in military transparency. If the legal trade in small arms becomes more transparent, the task of developing a comprehensive database would become less challenging. In turn, the development of such a database would allow better assessments of policies implemented to counter the illicit proliferation of small arms.

Further Exploration of the ARF Option

ARF considerations might consist of giving more attention to developing a regional convention against the illicit trafficking of small arms, as well as researching the possibility of establishing a regional small arms register. Although a small arms register is often seen as an arms control mechanism, it is also an effective way to approach concerns related to illicit trafficking. Some Southeast Asian countries may react coolly to such a proposal because they may perceive it as a "foreign/western" construct. However, the development of an arms register appears to suit the countries' preference for confidence-building measures (CBMs) as well as consensus building and nonconfrontational approaches to security relations. The ARF itself would not be responsible for creating and running the register. Instead, it would act as forum in which the topic can be deliberated. Although the ARF meets only once a year, members have observed the value of this forum and therefore, have created several inter-sessional meetings to deal with specific security topics. The forming of an ARF inter-sessional group to address illicit small arms trafficking will indeed enhance regional cooperation. The trans-border nature of illicit movement of small arms has rendered the issue a regional problem. Thus, cooperation through frequent dialogues and workshops would bring the region closer to understanding the small arms phenomenon comprehensively.

The ARF is important in that it is the only forum in which Southeast Asian countries as well as major regional players are able to gather and discuss security issues. In short, getting the countries to sit and talk about the feasibility of a small arms register (its pros and cons) or other actions to address the small arms problem is the most important step of the process.

Since its creation, ASEAN countries have dominated the ARF agenda. Therefore, in order to allow the small arms concern to be included in the agenda of the forum, at least one of the ASEAN members will have to recognize the importance of addressing the issue. It is in Canada's interest that small arms proliferation be discussed within the forum, given the issue's implications for North America. Canada is in a strategic position to suggest some of the paths that could be followed to address the problem adequately. However, Canada must not do so in a patronizing way. As Canadian diplomats already know, Southeast Asian officials are sensitive about incorporating "foreign" ideas into regional policies. Nonetheless, small arms proliferation is too important of an issue for Canada to be left out of the ARF discussions. The creation of a regional small arms register seems feasible as long as Canada introduces the idea to the forum with previous support from the ASEAN members. Only then will the discussion be taken more seriously (once they realize the seriousness of the problem). The manner in which such an idea is packaged matters a great deal.

Concluding Remarks

Past studies on small arms proliferation and its impacts on societies have indicated Central-South America, Central-Southern Africa and South Asia as the most problematic areas. However, this study indicates that the problem is also affecting Southeast Asia. The illicit trafficking of small arms in the region has a security character that is distinct from that in some of the other regions (except for Central-South America, where there are similar features). The implications of illicit trade in such weapons are linked closer to criminal activities than they are related to issues of post-conflict peacebuilding. The exception to this may be Cambodia. But even there the impact of small arms proliferation has not led to the chaos seen in parts of South Asia and Southern Africa. Nonetheless, security conditions in Southeast Asia are of considerable concern to Canada because of its possible implications.

Countries in the region have taken some steps to control the illicit movement of small arms at the national level through methods such as imposing strict laws, increasing border surveillance and training officials. Bilateral approaches such as joint maritime patrols have also taken place among Indonesia, Malaysia and Singapore. However, as the study indicates, overcoming the problem effectively would require more cooperation and coordination among the countries in the region. Acting as a neutral third party (yet having great interest in the situation within the region), Canada may be in a position to help catalyse such cooperation. There may be a lack of interest among some of the Southeast Asian countries because of their inability to project a long-term view of non-military/human security in the region. Canada could play a role in raising awareness of the concerns related to illicit trafficking of small arms and small arms proliferation in general. In any case, it is not in Canada's best interest to remain idle and wait for the regional countries to come to their senses.

This study shows that a number of approaches can be pursued to achieve regional cooperation in tackling the small arms problem. As reports demonstrate a trend of increasing illicit small arms transfers, countries cannot afford to wait longer in reacting if the problem is to be managed effectively. The conditions will not improve by themselves. This is important to bear in mind, especially considering that small arms are harder to retrieve once they have entered a society.

MILITARY EXPENDITURE TRENDS

On March 4, 2011, Beijing announced a 12.7 percent increase in its military budget to approximately $91.5 billion. This increase continues more than two decades of sustained annual increases in China's announced military budget. Analysis of 2000-2010 data indicates China's officially disclosed military budget grew at an average of 12.1 percent in inflation-adjusted terms over the period. Although the military budget increases are slightly larger than the percentage increases of its overall economic growth of 10.2 percent over the same period, the actual change in the implied burden of the official defense budget on the economy appears negligible.

Estimating China's Actual Military Expenditures

The Department of Defense estimates China's total military-related spending for 2010 was over $160 billion, using 2010 prices and exchange rates. Estimating actual PLA military expenditures is a difficult process due to the lack of accounting transparency and China's still incomplete transition from a command economy. Moreover, China's published military budget does not include major categories of expenditure, such as foreign procurement. China's legislature has not made public any details of the role, if any, that it plays in exercising oversight of the PLA budget. However, public calls within China for greater budget transparency, generally in response to sustained and systemic official corruption, suggest that improvement in government transparency as a whole could develop over time.

The United States and other countries continue to urge China to increase transparency in military spending. In August 2010, China submitted a report on its military expenditures to the UN Secretary General, the third such report in as many years. China's report was submitted in the UN Simplified Reporting Form, which provides minimal information on major budget categories, in contrast to the more detailed Standardized Reporting Form used by countries practicing greater defense transparency.

CHINA'S ADVANCING DEFENSE INDUSTRIES

Since the late 1990s, China's state-owned defense and defense-related companies have undergone a broad-based transformation. Beijing continues to improve its business practices, streamline bureaucracy, broaden incentives for its factory workers, shorten developmental timelines, improve quality control, and increase overall defense industrial production capacity. Beijing is also emphasizing integration of defense and non-defense sectors to leverage the latest dual-use technologies and the output from China's expanding science and technology base. Augmented in part by direct acquisition of foreign weapons and technology, these reforms have enabled China to incorporate mid-1990s technology into the development and production of most of its advanced weapon systems. Some systems, particularly ballistic missiles, incorporate cutting-edge technologies in a manner that rivals even the world's most modern systems.

Civil-Military Integration. Developing innovative dual-use technology and an industrial base that serves both military and civilian needs is a high priority for China's leadership. President Hu expressed in his political report to the CCP's 17th Party Congress in October 2007:

> *We must establish sound systems of weapons and equipment research and manufacturing… and combine military efforts with civilian support, build the armed forces through diligence and thrift, and blaze a path of development with Chinese characteristics featuring military and civilian integration.*

China's defense industry has benefited from integration with a rapidly expanding civilian economy and science and technology sector, particularly elements that have access to foreign technology. Progress within individual defense sectors appears linked to the relative integration of each, through China's civilian economy, into the global production and research and development (R&D) chain. For example, the shipbuilding and defense electronics sectors, benefiting from China's leading role in producing commercial shipping and information technologies, have witnessed the greatest progress over the last decade. Information technology companies in particular, including Huawei, Datang, and Zhongxing, maintain close ties to the PLA.

In contrast, enterprises producing high-performance computers, advanced applications software, and specialized top-end semiconductors/microprocessors—key to the evolution of increasingly advanced and capable defense microelectronics and applications, but with limited counterparts in the PRC civil-industrial sector—have experienced slower progress. The aviation and ordnance sectors have similarly suffered from a limited number of spin-off benefits, despite partnerships between foreign multinational corporations and domestic industry.

Sector-by-Sector Analysis. Progress across China's defense industry sectors has been uneven. Production trends and resource allocation appear to favour missile and space systems, followed by maritime assets (both surface and sub-surface), aircraft, and ground force materiel. In all areas, China is increasing the quality of its output and surge production capabilities, if not capacities. However, many of China's most advanced systems are still based heavily on foreign designs copied through reverse engineering, highlighting a persistent weakness in China's capability for overall system design and integration.

Missile and Space Industry: China produces a broad range of sophisticated ballistic, cruise, air-to-air, and surface-to-air missiles. Many of China's primary final assembly and rocket motor production facilities have received upgrades over the past few years, likely increasing production capacity.

In addition to supplying China's military, complete systems and missile technologies could also be marketed for export. Surge production for these systems could result in a significantly higher output of SRBMs and perhaps double the number of MRBMs per year. China's space launch vehicle industry is expanding to support satellite launch services and the manned space program.

Shipbuilding Industry: China operates a vibrant and globally competitive shipbuilding industry. By some measures, China is the largest shipbuilder in the world. Shipyard expansion and modernization have increased China's shipbuilding capacity and capability, generating benefits for all types of military projects, including: submarines; surface combatants; naval aviation, including aircraft carriers; and lift assets. China continues relying on foreign suppliers for some propulsion units and to a much lesser degree, fire control systems, cruise missiles, surface-to-air missiles, torpedo systems, sensors, and other advanced electronics. Modular shipbuilding techniques will allow China to spread production across multiple locations, increasing both efficiency and output. China has already demonstrated an ability to surge submarine and amphibious production.

Armament Industry: China's ground force modernization includes production of new tanks, armored personnel carriers, and artillery pieces. There have been advances in almost every area of PLA ground forces with new production capacity to accommodate surge requests. China's reliance on foreign partners to fill gaps in critical technical capabilities could still limit actual surge output.

THE RISE OF CHINA'S MARITIME SECURITY INTERESTS

Historically a continental power, China increasingly looks to the maritime domain as a source of economic prosperity and national security. China's evolving maritime consciousness, as reflected in senior-level rhetoric and resource allocation, has potentially far reaching consequences in the Asia Pacific region and beyond. Many PRC officials and citizens view maritime power as a prerequisite to becoming a great power. This chapter addresses China's attention to the maritime domain, with a particular focus on the security dimension. It identifies the catalysts influencing PRC thinking on maritime interests and the steps China has taken to address these challenges, including naval development, legislation, improving civilian maritime enforcement, and diplomatic initiatives. Finally, it addresses China's specific maritime interests and addresses how China's posture could evolve in the future.

In its 2010 China Ocean's Development Report, China's State Oceanic Administration (SOA) proclaimed, building maritime power is China's historic task for the 21st century, and the decade from 2010-2020 is the key historic stage for realizing this task. Although China appears to lack an official maritime strategy, PRC officials, military strategists, and academics are focused on the growing relevance of maritime power to China's interests.

SMALL ARMS TRADE AND MANUFACTURE IN PAKISTAN

In the case of South Asia and more specifically Pakistan, some very interesting aspects come forth. The source of weapons supply and acquisition has been myriad: ranging from illicit influx, transfer or trade to the local production facilities. Several countries in the region produce SA/LW in the government-owned or public sector enterprise, which is licitly regulated, with India and Pakistan possessing the most developed weapon manufacturing capabilities. But as such the predominant from of acquisition of LW by the state security forces continues to be the import or foreign technology transfer.

Although LW have somewhat always been available in the arms bazaars within the North West Frontier Province of Pakistan, such as Darra Adamkhel and Landi Kotal, the major impetus and free flow of modern light weapons has increased manifold after the Soviet occupation of Afghanistan. The December 1979 Soviet invasion resulted in Pakistan's proactive support to various Mujahideen outfits engaged in fighting the occupationist forces. This effort was practically driven by its own security interest but mainly on behalf of the US, which provided material and financial assistance to these Afghan guerrillas though Pakistan. The failure or ignorance of the incumbent government of the time to pay adequate attention to this dangerously spiraling trend of weapons accumulation and free flow in the hands of non-state actors aggravated this problem. In spite of the cessation of Soviet occupation, Afghanistan to date remains bitterly embroiled in a civil war, which has cast very severe shadows on the Pakistani civil society.

Before moving further the point to be stressed that when studying weapons proliferation, an important aspect is to keep in perspective the demand and supply factor. The motives for which suppliers and recipients engage in weapons transaction may be mixed. Suppliers may have political or commercial incentives or a combination of both. For this reason, excessive and destabilizing accumulation and transfer of small arms are closely related to the increased incidence of conflicts and high level of crime and violence. It is observed that sub-state or non-state forces make extensive use of such arsenal due to its merits of easy accessibility, storage and handling. Insurgent forces, irregular troops and freedom fighters, criminal groups and sub-state actors harbouring ethnic, religious and sectarian agenda use SA/LW for their particular motives with impunity. Generally speaking the most perturbing aspect of these conflicts is that more than 80% of the causalities are civilian, non-combatants-mostly women and children.

Market Trends and Origins of Arms Proliferation in Pakistan: The main focus with respect to weapons proliferation in Pakistan remains on the unorganized private enterprise at the Landi Kotal, where arms trade continues without any state supervision. In comparison to this, the POF as mentioned earlier creates mainly the military-specific ammunition, the production cost of is relatively expensive. Secondly, the POF manufactured ammunition has a very limited and restricted clientele. Another contributing factor is that POF sells only through designated distributors.

Secondly, the organized sector manufacturers are also bound to sell their products only to licensed buyers. This again limits their sale capacity. The overall number of licensed gun owners is not more than 80,000-90,000 people of the entire country's population. This makes the legal market a very small one, which is adequately served by the private producers

But recent trends indicate that the estimated number of weapons in circulation is much higher than tabulated. The rising ethno-sectarian strife, civil war in Afghanistan, and an enhanced sense of insecurity arising out of factors such as poor economic conditions, bad governance and deteriorating law and order situation, have given rise to a level of frustration and discontent. It is witnessed that this rising sense of apathy and social injustice has strengthened the appeal of SA/LW. Darra and its cheaper rates attract not only non-state actors, who purchase these weapons in bulk, but also a second category of buyers, such as officials, aw enforcing agents, influential politicians, feudal and tribal lords who regard possession of light weapons as a status symbol. Moreover the various governments too have contributed to exacerbating this situation by giving licenses for prohibited bore weapons to politicians and influential interest arming one (ethnic/ sectarian) group against another from time to time.

A principal source of weapons proliferation and supply to areas of regional and domestic conflict, the unorganized sector has a minimal manufacturing capacity of producing per unit a hundred weapons per day. With a very sudden and dramatic termination of the Afghan conflict, the political governments after Zia's military rule proved to be ineffective in solving this menace. Although attempts were made in the past and present to curb the proliferation and indiscriminate usage of small arms, they are very much an indicator of a dysfunctional state apparatus.

In Pakistan, the failure of governance-especially with regard to narcotics production and smuggling-coupled with the country's proximity to Afghanistan and involvement in the attempts to end the Soviet occupation of the country, has aggravated an already dire law-and-order situation. In many cases, access to light weapons has facilitated or intensified conflicts, often by emboldening the protagonists. Consequently, the ability of security forces has declined corresponding with the increased firepower enjoyed by the forces pitted against them. As regards the leakage of these illicit arms, the Soviet invasion of Afghanistan unshared in a new era in the light weapons trade in South Asia, with millions of tons of military material including SA/LW, being imported into the region. Other countries also contributed in one way or indirect assistance in both material and finances. For example, China wary of Soviet designs contributed weaponary, while Saudi Arabia came forth with financial assistance. As a front line ally, Pakistan became the main conduit for this massive military assistance programme, with its top intelligence outfit, inter-services intelligence (ISI), managing the receipt and distribution and the American CIA coordinating the supply of weapons. With a bitter Vietnam experience still fresh in memory, the United States, at least initially, did not want to be seen as providing direct military assistance for the Mujahideen, and for these reason massive amounts of arms were purchased from the Chinese government. Interesting trends could be witnessed in this undercover arms pipeline; the CIA would procure through Egypt large amounts of antipersonnel mines originally produced in Italy. During this period, weapons even of Israeli and as Indian makes could also be found in circulation. The CIA would then arrange for the arms to be either flown to Islamabad or shipped, via Oman, to Karachi.

The US-orchestrated arms shipments had a fundamental impact on the war in Afghanistan. Moreover, the autonomy given to the Pakistan intelligence services in controlling the distribution of weapons was to have a profound effect on subsequent security conditions in the region. Washington's "hand-off" policy of allowing the ISI to control the arms pipeline was largely the product of Oakley's belief that the United States had failed in Vietnam because of excessive governmental interference and mismanagement.

One factor contributing to the availability of small arms and light weapons in many areas (of conflict) is their earlier supply by Cold War opponents. Much of the supply and acquisitions of arms in the regions of conflict dealt with by the UN has been conducted by Governments or by legal entities authorized by the Governments. Some states have exercised insufficient control and restraint over transfers and holdings of small arms and light weapons. Moreover, arms supplies associated with foreign interference in areas of conflict are still a feature of current realities. In general, the lines of supply often are complex and difficult to monitor, facilitated by the relative ease with which small arms and light weapons can be concealed.

Not surprisingly, the arms pipeline to the Mujahideen leaked significantly. By the time the weapons reached Mujahideen field commanders, they had been loaded and off-loaded at least fifteen times while transported over the distance of several thousand kilometers by trucks, ships, trains, and pack animals. How many weapons leaked out of the pipeline is unknown, but the estimates run into millions of unaccounted for weapons. One glaring proof of this is the April1988 Ojhri camp blast in the Rawalpindi metropolis, which claimed not less than 100 civilan lives. Although no official version of the inquiry conducted came out, it is generally speculated that the blast was engineered to cover-up for the undelivered and hoarded weapons, and there is also a major link between this incident and the Iran Contra scandal.

Another contributing factor, however diminutive is that Afghans returning to their country after months or years in the refugee camps in the North West Frontier Province have left their weapons behind in Pakistan. This again forms a cause for weapons proliferation. Under the Geneva Accord, it was agreed that any surplus weapons that were left off the pipeline would be handed over to the Afghans, and interestingly there was a frantic arms transfer to Afghanistan, before the agreement came into effect. Most of these were smuggled back into Pakistan and sold in arms bazaars of the tribal area.

Besides, Afghanistan has a significant number of small arms manufacturing units. The trade of these arms is a ready source of income for the war-ravaged Afghan population. With a long porous border that stretches the entire Pakistan-Afghanistan belt, coupled with corrupt and inefficient border control forces, the mechanism fails miserably in effectively checking and curbing the inflow of not only weapons but other forms of smuggling as well. This has made the availability of arms in the commercial market considerably high and in some cases prices have fallen, attracting buyers from all over the country and region to purchase unlicensed weapons. The various weapons on sale in this regard, can be grouped in to four categories;

1. Weapons that lecked from the US-supported arms pipelines.
2. The stocks of Soviet weapons captured by the Mujahideen during the conflict.
3. The third category of weapons is those manufactured by small-scale producers within the region.
4. Finally, the arms bazaars of the NWFP are full of miscellaneous weapons that must have arrived in the region though extremely circuitous and unpredictable routes-from Vietnam or the Middle East. For instance, G-3s have appeared from Iran, given that border controls between Iran and Pakistan were relaxed after the fall of the shah.

Though there is clear evidence that light weapons are proliferating at an alarming rate from the North to the South, there are also south-to-north movements from Sri Lanka, Singapore, and other starting points in Southeast Asia. There are also discernible east-to west and west-to east movements.

In Pakistan, it is not only the Afghan crisis alone that was instrumental in introducing the Gun Culture. Another very important but relatively ignored aspect was the Baluchistan insurgency of the 1970s, that witnessed a massive inflow of weaponry from the traditional leakage points

There is a dire need for the government to take control of the drug trade and prevent the proliferation and flow of weapons, domestically, regionally and particularly with the help of the international community. What will be difficult, if not impossible to implement is an effective gun control agenda-such as the present regime's Seven-Stage De-Weaponization Programmes. This 7- stage formula includes a ban on arms license, and a proliferation on carrying weapons in the first stage, which became effective from March 1, 2000. The other proposals or possibilities under the same action plan were to recover illicit/unlicensed arms, canceling of the prohibited arms licenses and also to regulate and bring under state control arms manufacturing units in the tribal areas. The problem is so acute that there is a need to implement such policies and reforms in their true spirit. Bringing Darra under the state umbrella is an issue that the governments past and present have seriously deliberated upon. As a necessary first step the tribal areas were awarded with the right to Adult Franchise as well, but the possibility of Darra manufacturers agreeing to any state supervision or taxation seems impossible an evidence of which is reaction faced by the government over its attempt to document and evaluate the economy. The government needs to stick to a given time frame and implement the necessary reforms, otherwise the situation could be one as identified by Pamela Constable, in one of her recent Washington post articles, "Pakistani Retreats in Battle for Reform"- that there is found a tendency on part of the Pakistani government to announce bold reforms, only to backtrack later when opposition surfaces.

At the practical level, this new de-weaponisation policy will face many problems, especially in the NWFP and tribal areas where it is part of local culture and tradition to carry a weapon and in fact it also forms a part of their attire. This plan will definitely discourage open display of weapons in major urban centers, but again this will not be able to redress the problem fully.

Efforts made by the past governments were inadequate for either they were not properly articulated or they failed to deal with the real root cause of the problem that is the illicit trafficking of weapons. Whatever measures enforced affected only the manufacturers, thus giving the illegal trading cartels a free hand to conduct their business with impunity.

Although light weapons have always circulated within Pakistan, the impact of the American-sponsored arms pipeline to the Afghan Mujahideen stands head and shoulders above any other adverse development in recent years. The flood of weaponry into the region has clearly played a major part in the erosion of low and order over the past decade. The growing proliferation of and access to small arms are increasing both the communal polarization and the incidence of violence. The very availability of weapons is providing a short-term solution for a long-term problem. At the very point when political discourse and sound governance are required to overcome these problems, the need is to harness our efforts together to combat this menace.

5

Proliferation of Small Arms and Light Weapons in South Asia

According to the UN Deputy Secretary General, Louise Fréchette, 'No region, no country is immune from the devastating consequences of the proliferation of small arms and light weapons..., [which] severely hampers social and economic development.' South Asia is no exception to how SALW poses a non-traditional security threat. Regardless of age, gender, status or location, all are targets. Moreover, even children can be trained on how to use them. Private ownership of SALW is widespread and they can be obtained very cheaply.

The SALW firearms in South Asia mostly originate from western nations. The spread of SALW grew in the wake of Afghan War during the 70s and 80s as refugee communities and volunteers were co-opted along side the regular cadres to fight the Soviet Army, and they had to be armed. Similarly, the end of declared war in Cambodia made available large numbers of small weapons that eventually found their way into Sri Lanka and northeastern India.

There are now an estimated 75 million firearms in South Asia, 63 million of which are in civilian hands. India and Pakistan overwhelmingly account for most of the weapons (40 million and 20 million respectively) where there is local production as well, while civilians in Nepal and Sri Lanka own an estimated 3 million weapons. Non-State actors are getting hold of government weapons and re-exporting them to armed groups fighting insurgencies in other countries. The possession of small arms by politicians is also a growing problem across the subcontinent as owning private militia has become both a status symbol, as well as political clout against adversaries. Despite state regulations, several political leaders have not surrendered their arms to their government and still hold unlicensed arms. Politicians use these weapons to intimidate opponents and voters, patronise the underworld and criminal syndicates in order to protect themselves and thus pose a serious threat to the democratic process itself.

In Bangladesh, most of the weapons in circulation are those that were not collected after its 1971 independence war. Bangladesh is also being used as a corridor for smuggling firearms. Currently, Bangladesh has more than 200,000 small arms and most of these are with various organised criminal gangs and their political godfathers. There are about 80 crime syndicates around the country of which more than 28 are active in Dhaka alone. Politicians, too, use armed private militia to protect themselves, as well as to intimidate opponents. Law-makers are also turning a blind eye both to border patrol agents who are poorly equipped and to police officers who rent out their arms to criminals and terrorists. Clandestine manufacturers operate small operations that can be set up, dismantled and relocated overnight. In 2002, Bangladesh introduced tighter controls on firearms, but the problem remains.

Indian's record of small arms is the highest in the region which accounts for around 40 million contraband firearms. In India, all possible problems associated with the proliferation of small arms are to be found: illegal manufacture, theft from State arsenals, licensing loopholes, lax enforcement, cross-border smuggling, political violence, unregulated private security and a movie culture that often glorifies firepower and revenge by those defiant of authority. In India, small arms have eroded human rights, weakened democratic institutions, and polarised ethnic, religious, economic and political differences between citizens. Tensions between Hindu and Muslim groups in India under state patronage are one of the country's major sources of violence. In early 2002, up to 2000 Muslims were massacred in India in state of Gujarat. India also banned 32 organisations under the Prevention of Terrorism Act

(POTA) for their activities. Although the Government of India (GoI) has taken several steps it still faces the problems of proliferation of SALW. Currently New Delhi is in the process of drafting a proposal to the United Nations seeking a global ban on small-arms sales to non-state actors. According to reports from a senior Home Ministry official, 'If a global ban is achieved, it would help to improve the security situation in the country.'

Nepal has been suffering from destabilising effects of SALW in the hands of its Maoists. About a decade ago, an aerial fire or the use of tear gas in Nepal would have caused a national hue and cry and national/international coverage of the news. Now, even two digit death statistics have become routine news. Deaths and injuries from small arms have become like an 'epidemic' in Nepal. While the main sources of proliferation of small arms are the Maoist insurgency, criminality and the political elite are no less responsible.

The Maoists rebels have stolen their weapons from police outposts and other government arsenals, while other criminal gangs are engaged in smuggling drugs for guns and money-laundering along the Indian border. Women are often used as carriers of small arms in illicit trafficking. It is estimated that one-third of the Maoist fighters are women. At the community level it is often known who owns arms and where they are kept. After the restoration of democracy in 1993, politicians resorted to all available means to win elections, including armed intimidation. Although a tentative ceasefire agreement was signed between the Government and the Maoists, but the proliferation of SALW remains unabated.

The ratio of SALW proliferation in Pakistan is the second highest in the region. In Pakistan there is a close linkage between organised groups, narcotics, money-laundering, terrorism activities and illicit trade in SALW. The proliferation of SALW and terrorism emerged as one of the main problems after the 1979 Soviet invasion of Afghanistan, when the US covertly armed thousands of 'Mujahedeen' with millions of SALWs, a great number of which eventually found their way into Pakistan along with the refugees who sought asylum. Pakistan's indigenous arms manufacturing cottage industry in the northwest tribal areas named as 'Darra Adamkhel' has fuelled-up the conflict-prone legacy of society with millions of small arms.

Darra's 'father-and-son' arms industry has existed for generations as a family legacy and traditionally, as a cottage arms production industry, has been outside the jurisdiction of central authorities. According to recent estimates, Darra employs more than 400,000 people. Prior to the Soviet invasion of Afghanistan in 1979, these shops produced mainly repeating rifles. The steady influx of weapons from various sources during the war enhanced the local manufacturer's knowledge, skills and production capacities.

The Darra region annually produces approximately 20,000 units of all kinds of weapons, including AK-47. It is estimated that in the past 20 years as a result of on going antagonisms between tribes, sectarianism, ethnicity, terrorism, organised crimes and poor law and order situation have sharpened into ethnic and community divides. Gun-related violence has resulted in more than 500,000 killings around the country. In 2001, the Government of Pakistan (GoP) launched a country-wide anti-arms drive in a bid to curb the 'Kalashnikov culture.' The Government devised a multi-pronged and phased 'de-weaponisation' strategy which includes: banning the display of weapons in public, the buying back of arms, recovering illicit arms and regulating production in the tribal areas. Initially a public awareness campaign was launched with an amnesty period for the surrender of illicit SALWs. After the expiry of the amnesty period, campaign for weapons collection and recovery were launched. Until 2003, around 250,000 illicit SALW firearms of different categories and types were recovered or confiscated, in addition to large amount of ammunition. While this ambitious effort has been praised nationally and internationally, Pakistan civil society is calling for a broader policy framework to address the underlying challenges of under-development which lead to proliferation, namely: the need for economic incentives as an alternative for 'culture of weaponisation'. Despite the official ban on sale and purchase of non-licensed weapons, unauthorised arms and ammunition remain in circulation and the illegal arms trade and gunrunning continues.

The status of proliferation of SALW in Sri Lanka can be attributed to many factors such as the internal armed conflicts, arms and political campaigns, arms held by deserters and criminals, as well as arms owned by private security firms and deteriorating public safety due to criminal activities. One of the main primary sources of SALW proliferation is the internal conflict between Government and the LTTE which has caused more than 65,000 deaths. Although a ceasefire was signed in February 2002, between Government and the LTTE, the circulation of weapons will continue to be a security threat to ordinary Sri Lankans. Meanwhile, it has now become common practice for politicians to raise private armies to literally fight elections for them; and, the generous funding these mercenary armies receive are drawing even government soldiers to join their ranks. Furthermore, politicians offer protection to members of criminal gangs who become allies thus impeding the efforts of police to combat the growing problem of organised crime in the country. According to some rough open source estimates there are more than 2 million firearms in circulation in Sri Lanka. 90% of the illegal arms in circulation are said to come from the Government. Finally, all smuggling from outside Sri Lanka comes by sea routes, and coastal patrols are lacking. The Sri Lankan Government has taken several steps to address the problem through the implementation of relevant legislation, namely amnesty for surrender of illegal arms, registration of existing arms, and attempts to collect weapons and so forth. In January 2002, an amnesty for surrender of illegal arms was offered by the Ministry of Interior but did not produce the expected results. In 2004, disarmament, demobilisation and reintegration (DDR) of ex-combatants, including in many cases child soldiers, started in Sri Lanka which still has to yield its results.

MAJOR ROUTES OF SMALL ARMS PROLIFERATION

Russian weapons are systematically moving to Vietnam, Cambodia and Laos by sea from Vladivostok and Nakhodka to Haiphong and Saigon (Ho Chi Min City) and further through Vietnamese territory. It is also reported that they are often resold by Vietnamese and Cambodian authorities. Certain amounts of firearms might also be transported from Russia to Vietnam by air.

We can suppose that some quantities of Russian weapons might be transported from the Russian Far East to Vietnam via Chinese territory, but as of today, no reports on that possible route have been seen.

Considerable numbers of Chinese-made light weapons are regularly passing across the Chinese-Russian border to Russia through two major points:

- Zabaikal'sk (Chita province)/Manchouli (Inner Mongolia) border crossing placed astride Hailar-Chita highway. Since March 1, 1998 (after revamping), this crossing has 14 lanes and is capable of handling 10,000 to 20,000 people and 1,500 cars daily. As of today, about 60 percent of trade between Russia and China passes through this point.
- Blagoveschensk (Amur territory) border crossing astride the Qiqihar-Blagoveschensk highway. This crossing has only eight lanes handling daily not more than 10,000 people and 950 cars. Most Chinese-made firearms are brought to Russia from China by commercial trailers, often accompanied by false papers indicating other types of goods (for example, mechanical toys). Certain amounts of firearms are smuggled by Chinese and Russian private citizens (the so-called "Chelnoks" or "Shuttle-traders"). Actual forms of Russian-Chinese border trade and smuggling in combination with corrupt and under-equipped custom officers and border guards do not permit even approximate calculations of the amount of Chinese-made arms smuggled into Russian federation within the last three years.

We should also mention the secondary direction of small arms (both Russian-and Chinese-made) proliferation in East Siberia and the Far East. This direction runs from south to the north down the rivers Lena, Aldan, Nizhnaya Tunguska, Angara and Yenisey to the cities lying along these rivers and to small rural communities and settlements scattered in their basins.

Some high-quality Russian-made light weapons might be sold to North Korea (at least until 1991 this was one of the regular routes of Russian weapons). Several reported cases of drug smuggling across the Russian-North Korean border (from Korean side) suggest that this might also be one of the routes of small arms trade. (Experience has shown that drug smuggling routes are in most cases the routes of small arms smuggling as well). It is possible that an arms-smuggling route might run through the tiny section of Russian-Korean border Najin-Ungghi (N. Korean side) — Khasan-Posyette (Russian side), limited by the Sea of Japan on the south and the "Kyonghung sack" of Chinese territory on the north.74 One of the possible sea routes of small arms proliferation might lead from Russian Far East (Vladivostok-Nakhodka) to Central and South America. Another reported sea route goes from Vladivostok to Japanese ports — possibly Osaka, Kobe and Yokohama.

Russian-made assault rifles and submachine guns, as well as ammunition have been reported in Nicaragua, El-Salvador and Colombia. As of today, we have discovered no materials tracing the delivery of the above mentioned arms across the Pacific Ocean. However this assumption does not seem unreasonable. We could also assume that if that delivery really took place, some amounts might be reloaded and stored in some ports at the Pacific coast of the USA and Canada.

NUCLEAR ARMS RACE

The nuclear arms race was a competition for supremacy in nuclear warfare between the United States, the Soviet Union, and their respective allies during the Cold War. During the Cold War, in addition to the American and Soviet nuclear stockpiles, other countries also developed nuclear weapons, though none engaged in warhead production on nearly the same scale as the two superpowers.

World War II

The first nuclear weapon was created by the American Manhattan Project during the Second World War and was developed to be used against the Axis powers. Scientists of the Soviet Union, then an ally of the United States, were aware of the potential of nuclear weapons and had also been conducting research in the field. The Soviet Union was not officially informed of the

American experiments until Stalin was briefed at the Potsdam Conference on July 24, 1945. The Americans did not trust the Soviets enough to keep the information safe from German spies but also distrusted the Soviets and their intentions generally, despite their wartime military alliance. Even during the war several government and military figures in the USA saw the USSR as a potential enemy in the future.

Despite their official ignorance, the Soviets were well aware of the program due to a ring of spies operating within the American nuclear program. The atomic spies (including Klaus Fuchs and Theodore Hall) kept Stalin well informed of American progress. When U.S. President Harry S. Truman informed Stalin of the weapons, he was surprised at how calmly Stalin reacted to the news and thought that Stalin had not understood what he had been told. In fact Stalin had long been aware of the program. The program was top classified meaning even Truman did not know about it or the weapons until he became president.

In August 1945, atomic bombs were dropped on Truman's orders on designated Japanese cities. The first bomb was dropped on Hiroshima, and later another bomb was dropped on Nagasaki by the B-29 bombers *Enola Gay* and *Bock's Car* respectively.

Early Cold War

In the years immediately after the Second World War, the United States had monopoly on specific knowledge of and raw materials for nuclear weaponry. Initially, it was thought that uranium was rare in the world, but this turned out to be wrong. American leaders hoped that their exclusivity would be enough to draw concessions from the Soviet Union, this proved ineffective. Behind the scenes, the Soviet regime was working on building their own atomic weapons. During the war Soviet efforts had been limited due to a lack of uranium, but new supplies in Eastern Europe were found and provided a steady supply while the Soviets developed a domestic source. While American experts had predicted that the USSR would not have nuclear weapons until the mid-1950s, the first Soviet bomb was detonated on August 29 of 1949, shocking the entire world. The bomb, named "Joe One" by the West, was more or less a copy of the bomb the United States had dropped on Japan, "Fat Man".

Governments spent massive amounts to increase the quality and quantity of their nuclear arsenal. Both nations quickly began working on the hydrogen bombs and the United States detonated their first of these on November 1, 1952. Again, the Soviets surprised the Americans by exploding a deployable thermonuclear device next August, though it was not a real multi-stage hydrogen bomb, which followed in 1955.

The most important development in terms of delivery in the 1950s was the introduction of intercontinental ballistic missiles, ICBMs. Missiles had long been regarded the ideal platform for nuclear weapons, and were potentially a more effective delivery system than strategic bombers, which was the primary delivery method at the beginning of the Cold War. On October 4, 1957, the Soviet Union showed the world that they had missiles able to reach any part of the world when they launched the Sputnik. The United States launched their own satellite on the 31 October 1959. The Space Race showcased technology critical to the delivery of nuclear weapons, the ICBM boosters, while maintaining the appearance of being for science and exploration.

This period also saw some of the first attempts to defend against nuclear weapons. Both superpowers built large radar arrays to detect incoming bombers and missiles. Fighters to use against bombers and anti-ballistic missiles to use against ICBMs were also developed. Large underground bunkers were constructed to save the leaders, and citizens were told to build fallout shelters and taught how to react to a nuclear attack. These measurements were called civil defense.

Mutual Assured Destruction (MAD)

None of these defensive measures were secure, and in the 1950s both the United States and Soviet Union had nuclear power to obliterate the other side. Both sides developed a capability to launch a devastating attack even after sustaining a full assault from the other side (especially by means of submarines), called a second strike. This policy was part of what became known as

Mutual Assured Destruction: both sides knew that any attack upon the other would be devastating to themselves, thus in theory refraining them from attacking the other.

Both Soviet and American experts hoped to use nuclear weapons for extracting concessions from the other, or from other powers such as China, but the risk connected with using these weapons was so grave that they refrained from what John Foster Dulles referred to as brinkmanship. While some, like General Douglas MacArthur, argued nuclear weapons should be used during the Korean War, both Truman and Eisenhower opposed.

Both sides were unaware of the capacity of the enemy's arsenal of nuclear weapons. The Americans suffered from a lack of confidence, and in the 1950s they believed in a non-existing bomber gap. Aerial photography later revealed that the Soviets had been playing a sort of Potemkin village game with their bombers in their military parades, flying them in large circles, making it appear they had far more than they truly did. The 1960 American presidential election saw accusations of a wholly spurious missile gap between the Soviets and the Americans. On the contrary, the Soviet government exaggerated the power of Soviet weapons to the leadership and Nikita Khrushchev.

An additional controversy formed in the United States during the early 1960s concerned whether or not it was certain if their weapons would work if the need should occur. All of the individual components of nuclear missiles had been tested separately (warheads, navigation systems, rockets), but it had been infeasible to test them all combined. Critics charged that it was not really known how a warhead would react to the gravity forces and temperature differences encountered in the upper atmosphere and outer space, and Kennedy was unwilling to run a test of an ICBM with a live warhead. The closest thing to an actual test was 1962's Operation Frigate Bird, in which the submarine USS *Ethan Allen* launched a Polaris A1 missile over 1,000 miles to the nuclear test site at Christmas Island. It was challenged by, among others, Curtis LeMay, who put missile accuracy into doubt to encourage the development of new bombers. Other critics pointed out that it was a single test which could be an anomaly; that it was a lower-altitude SLBM and therefore was subject to different conditions than an ICBM; and that significant modifications had been made to its warhead before testing.

THE FINANCIAL VALUE OF THE ARMS TRADE

It is not possible to ascribe a precise financial value to the international arms trade. However, by aggregating financial data on the value of their arms exports as released by the main suppliers, it is possible to make an indicative estimate. According to official government data, the estimated financial value of the international arms trade in 2007, the last year for which data is available, was $51.1 billion, which represents 0.3 per cent of world trade. This figure is likely to be lower than the true figure since a number of significant exporters, including China, do not release data on the financial value of their arms exports. Although the SIPRI data on international arms transfers and official government data on the financial value of the arms trade are based on different methodologies, both have tended to increase since 2001. According to official government data, the USA was the largest arms exporter in 2007, with exports worth $12.8 billion; Russia was in second place, with $7.4 billion; France was in third place, with $6.2 billion; Israel was in fourth place, with $4.4 billion; and the UK was in fifth place, with $4.1 billion.

Comparing SIPRI's data on international arms transfers with national data on the financial value of arms exports reveals some of the differences in the methodologies used to create these data sets. For example, a significant proportion of Israel's arms exports consists of electronics and other components, which are not included in the SIPRI Arms Transfers Database. This partly explains why Israel is among the five largest arms exporters according to reported financial values but not according to SIPRI data on international arms transfers. Meanwhile, a significant proportion of German arms exports consists of military aid and the sale of second-hand equipment. Since the SIPRI data is based on the notional equivalent values of the weapon systems (the TIV), and not their cost at the point of sale, these transfers may be valued more highly in the SIPRI data on international arms transfers than in Germany's national data on the financial value of its arms exports. This may partly explain why Germany appears among the five largest arms exporters according to the SIPRI TIV, but not among the five largest according to reported financial values.

PROLIFERATION OF SMALL ARMS AND LIGHT WEAPONS

The end of the Cold War removed constraints inherent to superpower rivalry, and contributed to an outbreak of inter-state and intra-state wars and conflicts, often of a religious or ethnic character and often involving unusual violence and cruelty. In addition, some of the proxy wars fuelled during the Cold War decades within states remained unresolved. These wars and conflicts were fought not only by regular armies, but also by militias and armed civilians, in support of the regular forces. They had to be armed and in the process this led to an excessive and uncontrolled proliferation of small arms and light weapons (SALW). The decade of the 90s particularly saw expanding civil wars, in former Yugoslavia, mass starvation in Somalia and so forth, arising out of civil wars enlarging into ethnic cleansing. To control the increasing incidents of regional and inter-state conflicts, Boutros Boutros Ghali, the new Secretary-General of the United Nations at the time, came up with an 'Agenda for Peace' in June 1992, stressing a central role that ought to be played by the UN, and reviewed the various methods for a more effective role of the Security Council in preventing, controlling or resolving disputes through preventive diplomacy, peace-keeping, peace-making and peace-related efforts, as well as for arms control and disarmament. By 1993, the 'Agenda for Peace' was already under criticism for UN's ineffectiveness, given that fratricide grew into ethnic cleansing in Yugoslavia, the peace mission to Somalia failed miserably, there was a political standoff in Haiti, and civil chaos surfaced in Zaire and Tajikistan.

At that point, SALW were considered responsible for deaths and violence in most conflicts and for the collapse of state institutions, especially the police and judiciary, with resulting paralysis of governance, a breakdown of law and order, and general anarchic conditions of banditry and chaos. The SALW used in these conflicts and civil wars were mainly acquired during the

Cold War. However, after the Cold War, the SALW used in these conflicts were proliferated through arms black markets, private production, and smuggling. As a result, the full extent of the destabilising consequences of an excessive accumulation, proliferation, transfer and use of small arms and light weapons began to be felt as a major global threat. It led to the re-evaluations of security in international forums such as the UN.

In 1995, in a position paper, entitled 'Supplement to Agenda for Peace' the UN Secretary-General noted that while there were some agreed upon global norms and standards against weapons of mass destruction, there were no such norms or standards that could be used against the excessive and destabilising accumulation of small arms and light weapons. It was then realised that uncontrolled proliferation of small arms and light weapons posed, and continues to pose, a major non-traditional threat to international as well as regional peace and security. The 1995, General Assembly resolution 50/70B first raised the issue of proliferation of SALW. In this resolution, the UNGA, by reaffirming the role of the UN in the field of disarmament stated its realisation regarding SALW in the following words.

'That arms obtained through the illicit arms trade are most likely to be used for violent purposes and that even small arms when so obtained, directly or indirectly, by terrorist groups, drug traffickers or underground organisations can pose a danger to regional and international security, and certainly to the security and political stability of the countries affected.' As a result, the UN Secretary-General established a panel Group of Governmental Experts on Small Arms to report on types of SALW, nature and causes of their proliferation, and the ways and means to prevent and reduce the excessive and destabilising accumulation and transfer of small arms and light weapons, as they cause or exacerbate conflict. At that time many prevailing conflicts inflicted heavy causalities on the people involved, and the victims were mostly women and children. It was estimated that, by 1996, over 35 million people in 23 countries throughout the world were at risk of facing civil strife, either owing to ongoing humanitarian crises, or as a result of a slow recovery from past ones.

The Group of Governmental Experts on Small Arms held a number of different regional and international workshops and finally presented its consolidated report in 1997 on types of SALW, nature and causes of their proliferation, and recommendations to control and prevent their proliferation. In this report, Bangladesh, Sri Lanka, Nepal, Pakistan and India shared the growing concern over the trans-boundary movement of illicit and covert arms trade from Afghanistan, and emphasised on the need for a worldwide campaign to raise global consciousness of the consequences of the inflow to, and outflow of, weapons from Afghanistan. The 1997 report by Governmental Experts on Small Arms acted as a catalyst and placed the issue of SALW on the international agenda. On December 9, 1997, the UNGA endorsed all issues raised by the report in its resolution 52/38J. In 1998, the UNGA established another Group of Governmental Experts on Small Arms to assist the UN Secretary-General to prepare a report on the progress made in the implementation of the recommendations of the 1997 report and further actions recommended to be taken. On August 19, 1999 the UN Secretary-General presented the report of Group of Governmental Experts on Small Arms to the UNGA, in preventing and reducing the excessive and destabilising accumulation of small arms and light weapons. As a result of these efforts the UNGA decided to convene an international conference on the illicit arms trade in all its aspects no later than 2001.

In October 2000, the UN Secretary-General Kofi Annan, in his Millennium Report, 'We the People', presented to the UNGA, attached a special concern to the problems associated with proliferation of SALW. Significantly, Annan described small arms as 'weapons of mass destruction' because the death toll from small arms dwarfed that of all other weapons systems, and in most years greatly exceeded the toll of the atomic bombs that had devastated Hiroshima and Nagasaki. Annan further said that

'The proliferation of small arms, and munitions and explosives has also aggravated the violence associated with terrorism and organised crime. Even in societies not beset by civil war, the easy availability of small arms has in many cases contributed to violence and political instability. These, in turn, have damaged development prospects and imperilled human security in every way. Small arms proliferation is not merely a security issue; it is also an issue of human rights and of development. The proliferation of small arms sustains and exacerbates armed conflicts. It endangers peacekeepers and humanitarian workers. It undermines respect for International Humanitarian Law (IHL). It threatens legitimate but weak governments and it benefits terrorists as well as the perpetrators of organised crime.'

In his Millennium Report, Annan urged the Member States to participate fully in the UN Conference on Small Arms in order to take serious actions to curtail the illicit trade in small arms. From July 9-20, 2001, the UN Conference on the Illicit Trade in Small Arms and Light Weapons in All Its Aspects took place at New York. In order to combat and eradicate the illicit trade in SALW, the States adopted a wide range of political undertakings at the national, regional and global levels. The significant step was the adoption of the Programme of Action (PoA) with consensus by the Member States. The PoA mainly covers the areas of legislation, destruction of weapons that were confiscated, seized, or collected, as well as international cooperation and assistance to strengthen the ability of States in identifying and tracing illicit arms and light weapons. Finally, the Member States agreed to hold a review conference in 2006, as well as biennial meetings along the way. These meetings would allow NGOs and governments to keep the momentum moving forward on the small arms issue under the PoA framework.

On December 23, 2003, the UNGA passed resolution 58/241 and established an open-ended working group to negotiate an international instrument to enable States to identify and trace, in a timely and reliable manner, illicit small arms and light weapons. The working group is making its every effort to ensure that a positive outcome would be achieved.

In February 2005, the United Nations Secretary-General presented its report of 'Small Arms' to the UNSC and recommended that the UNSC and the UNGA should establish a committee to look into how the two organs could work together in the areas of illicit SALW brokering. The UNSC declaring its primary responsibility for maintaining international peace and security, also appealed to the arms-exporting countries 'to exercise the highest responsibility in small arms and light weapons transactions' in accordance with international law.

Currently, more than 640 million items of SALW are in circulation around the world. Around 59% of it are owned or controlled by civilians while the rest are owned by governments, armed forces, police, insurgents and other non-state forces. The annual trade in small arms is about $40 billion. Two-thirds of global arms deliveries go to the developing countries. Small arms are produced by more than 1,000 companies in at least 98 countries, with about 7 million new arms produced annually. Since 1990, more than four million people have been killed, the majority of them were civilians (90%) of whom an overwhelming 80% were women and children. According to a recent report from the UN, 'two million children have been killed in the last ten years in conflicts where small arms have been used; five million have been disabled, and twelve million left homeless.' A 'small arm' thus exists for every twelve persons in the world.

The same is the case with South Asia where proliferation of SALW is very high. In South Asia the proliferation of SALW is linked to insurgencies, ethnic and sectarian violence, organised crimes, political movements and private militias, terrorist activities, inter-state wars, guerrilla warfare and many other violence-related activities. Proliferation of SALW is not only threatening human security, but also impacting on the societal peace, livelihood and economic development of the countries and the communities of the region. It is not an easy task to control the menace of SALW so as to end human misery and sufferings in South Asia.

Since the introduction of the PoA, Pakistan, India, Sri Lanka, and Bangladesh have implemented PoA and submitted their respective national reports on voluntary basis. These reports deal with legal, administrative and procedural measures to combat proliferation of SALW. Despite these measures, the menace of small arms is still prevailing in their respective societies. There is a need to identify weaknesses and problems in these measures to devise a coherent regional approach to address the problems of

SALW. There is a growing need that South Asian states should proactively participate in the first UN review conference in 2006 to curb proliferation of SALW, since South Asia itself has such a proliferation of SALW. A coherent regional approach would contribute towards strengthening an international mechanism to curb the proliferation of SALW in all its aspects, because a regional approach is an effective mechanism to curb proliferation of SALW which is a trans-border phenomenon.

Against this background, this paper provides a brief comparative survey of SALW in the South Asian region, and follows that up with an evaluation of the current measures adopted by the South Asian states to address the problems associated with effective legislation, administrative regulations and procedures to curb proliferation of SALW, as signatories to the PoA. It is difficult to have a precise number of small arms users in South Asia. Statistics available from country to country are scarce and not updated enough and yet they present a dismal and a grim picture. Sources of arms proliferation, illegal private ownerships, and illegal smuggling are also additional problems that need to be seriously studied for their impact areas. Lastly the study would discuss the possibilities of regional cooperation in order to develop a more coherent regional solution in line with the international efforts to curb the proliferation of SALW.

MAJOR RECIPIENTS OF SMALL ARMS IN THE AREA

In Siberia and the Russian Far East, there are at least four groups of regular recipients of small arms coming from both foreign and domestic sources:

- criminals belonging both to highly organized "Mafia" groups ("syndicates" and "brotherhoods") and to smaller, spontaneously organized gangs;
- private citizens interested in purchasing firearms predominantly for self-defence;
- private security formations; and,
- different opposition and separatist groups.

Russian criminal groups in Siberia and the Far East, with their major headquarters in the cities of Vladivostok, Nakhodka,

Khabarovsk, Blagoveschensk, Irkutsk and Yakutsk, (as well as criminal groups scattered all over Russian Federation) prefer Russian-and Western-made (American, German, and Israeli) weapons for permanent use and storage.

Those groups regularly purchase a considerable amounts of Russian-made firearms and ammunition which comes either directly from the military plants (from Tula province, the Urals and other arms-producing areas of the country), or is stolen from army barracks and stores. Some small amounts of Western-made (predominantly American and German) firearms have also been detected in possession of criminals in Siberia and the Far East. These weapons, as well as the ammunition they acquire might be sporadically coming from North America (predominantly via Vladivostok and Nakhodka) and/or from Western Europe (probably through the Trans-Siberian railway).

However, for contract killings and for arming the lowest-class recruits, organized mobsters of Russia tend to use Chinese products mainly because of their low price. According to information provided by the Moscow Nizam Research Group, the black-market price for the latest model of Russianmade AKM assault rifles may vary from $US 1000 to $US 1200 depending on the area and season, while Chinese-made AKM assault rifles are sold in the range of $US 400 to $US 600. The similar ratio ($US 6 for one box of 20 Russian-made AKM cartridges to $US 4 for the similar but made in China one) exists for ammunition.

For contract killings, acts of terror and property destruction, the "Russian Mafia" also uses various sorts of mines and explosives, most of which are produced by specialists working in state laboratories and using state equipment. However, some parts and elements are partially stolen from the stores of the Russian Army, or imported from abroad.

Millions of private citizens of the Russian Federation not involved in organized criminal activities, are also regular purchasers of Russian-and Chinese-made firearms. Often illegally, they acquire firearms at their own risk believing that it might protect their lives, their families and property. Urban residents tend to purchase pistols and revolvers, while rural residents prefer to buy rifles, automatic and even assault rifles. Since the end of the nineteenth century, wearing firearms was a tradition and part of a way of life for rural residents of the Russian-Chinese frontier and remote northern areas of East Siberia and the Far East (both descendants of settlers from European Russia/Eastern Europe and Native Siberians). The main reasons for this tradition were:

- hunting as one of the important means of survival;
- the need to protect human lives from wild animals;
- dangerous atmosphere of the frontier with often and unexpected attacks from China;
- petty and high criminal activity, and regular escapes of inmates from prisons and concentration camps; and,
- low density of population in combination with poor activity of law enforcement structures.

After the end of Civil War (1917-1922), the Communists tried to ban the private ownership of small arms in the area, but that policy was not effective, and semi-illegal possession of small arms by private citizens finally became tolerated by the authorities. Thus almost every family residing in the area keeps and regularly updates its own small arsenal of small arms. Although it is absolutely obligatory that every small arm in the country should be registered, most Siberians tend to neglect this legal prescription. In most cases, residents of frontier and northern areas tend to acquire Russian or Chinese arms (depending on the purchasers' wealth), but some copies of American rifles have also been noted. A similar situation is observed with respect to small arms acquisition and registration by various private security and detective companies in the area, as well as in numerous prospectors' and explorers' teams operating in the remote northern territories.

The Russian and international media have been regularly reporting the presence of small arms in the arsenals of various paramilitary opposition groups. Among those groups worthy of mention are several right-wing and nationalist organizations having branches in Siberia and the Russian Far East, namely: Kossacks, Pamyat', Russian National Union, Skinheads, Young Patriots of Russia, and the leftist terrorist "Revvoyensovet RSFSR" ("Revolutionary Council of Russian Soviet Socialist Republic.")

Several representatives of other radical organizations, among them the Liberal Democratic Party, leftist Union of Russian Communists and different associations of Afghan War veterans, have also mentioned in their public speeches that their branches might also have small arms arsenals. Separatist movements in some autonomous areas of Russian Siberia and Far East, namely the Republics of Sakha-Yakoutia and Tannu-Tuva might be also recipients of small arms both from Russian Army stores and from China. Vietnam and Cambodia are still the main recipients of Russian weapons in East Asia. They acquire Russian weapons for their domestic army and police use, as well as for further sale to Myanmar, Malaysia and the Philippines. The North Korean Army might still be one of the recipients of some highquality Russian weapons, including small arms.

Certain amounts of Russian-made firearms are exported from the Russian Maritim Territory to Japan in exchange for Japanese cars. This "business" has been organized by the Kovalsky Mafia Syndicate (with its headquarters in Vladivostok) and supposedly the Yakuza. We can assume that various separatist movements of China — among them Uigur and Tibetan separatists, as well as guerilla movements in Myanmar, Thailand, Indonesia and Philippines — might have been, or will be, explored and approached by Russian arms traders looking for new markets.

Some Tibetan tribes and communities in remote areas of the Tibetan "Autonomous Region" and the province of Qinghai (for example the tribe of Golog which officially has still not surrendered to Chinese communist troops) have been reported to possess arsenals of Chinese-made firearms, including assault rifles, and to purchase ammunition on a regular basis.

At present, there are about 157,000 Russian troops deployed in the area (the forces of Trans-Baykal and Maritim military districts). Keeping in mind the equipment saved for tactical and strategic reserves, together with some out-of-date weapons, there should be deployed at least 1.5-2 million units of small arms at various military stores. Widespread embezzlement of small arms belonging to the army may have resulted in the transfer of at least 5 to 10% of the above amounts to underground stores of criminal groups, as well as into the hands of private citizens. About 350,000 units of small arms (pistols, submachine guns and assault rifles) should be deployed at MVD (Federal Police), OMON (Special Police Forces) and FSB (Federal Security Service) stores in the area.

In spite of widespread corruption and collaboration with criminal structures typical of Russian law enforcement structures within the last years, the stores of the above forces have never been reported as objects of embezzlement. Private citizens (both involved and relatively non-involved in criminal activity) residing in the research area, are expected to hold at least 2,000,000 small arms (rifles, automatic rifles, carbines, assault rifles pistols and revolvers). The possible number of small arms in underground ("Mafia"-controlled) arsenals in the area is estimated at 3,000 to 10,000 items including Kalashnikov assault rifles and machine guns, TT and TM pistols, Uzi rifles and submachine guns, as well as antitank weapons and grenade launchers (RPG-22-1 "Mukha").

SMALL ARMS PROLIFERATION: THE ARMS CONTROL CHALLENGE

Over the course of the past decade small arms have become the primary choice of weapons for political and criminal groups in fueling armed conflicts, wars, massacres, ethnic cleansing and human rights violations. That, in no small measure is due to the fact that small arms are too readily available and too inexpensive, while at the same time requiring only minimal training, logistics and support to maintain and operate. 300 manufacturers in 74 countries produce small arms, of which well over 500,000,000 are believed to be in circulation, inside or outside of state regulatory controls. Between 1985 and 1995, there has been a twenty-five per cent increase in the number of producers. Moreover, low-end sell-offs or give-aways of "surplus" small arms increase supply as well. As a result, there is an overabundance of inexpensive small arms glutting the world market.Yet, to date the international trade in small arms remains largely unregulated.

Principal sources of small arms include: small arms acquired for legal purposes and misused (e.g. human rights violations and external aggression), small arms acquired for legal purposes and sold/stolen; small arms for crime and unintentional injuries (gray market), and illegally manufactured or trafficked small arms (black market).

Whatever the perspective, i.e. peace-building versus crime prevention or arms control, draining these supply sources is imperative. Measures must be devised to limit the access to small arms (licensing, storage, embargoes), to reduce the supply of small arms (control of manufacture, identification, tracing etc.) and to reduce the demand for small arms (amnesties, buy-backs). The weapons of violence must be brought back into the control of the state, with the state itself being made accountable for its deeds. This essentially means empowering the state at one level, and using all tools available to induce more responsible behaviour on its part, at another. The two approaches must be mutually compatible.

The permanent members of the UN Security Council alone are responsible for 85% of the global arms trade. 40% of the worldwide flow of small arms is attributed to illicit trafficking and the majority of illicit weapons are proven to originate in the licit trade. Getting these governments to tighten national controls and to accept strengthened international standards for legal arms transfers should lend itself to reducing supply, significantly. Small arms transfer policies should be designed to support transfers that do not destabilize or threaten regional peace and security. With production monitored and limited and exports restricted and tighter controlled a reduced supply should restrict access and decrease overall circulation.

Given that small arms are produced, acquired and exported for legitimate purposes it is not, as opposed to the global campaign to ban landmines, appropriate to seek a ban. Rather, EPG's overall objective is to assist in efforts to curtail the supply of illicit small arms.

Such an objective will require a constructive parallelism among a range of politically and legally binding instruments, involving operative and normative measures which pertain both to the licit as well as the illicit trade, and which address both conflict prevention and conflict resolution. As one building block toward this overall objective, the group's goal is to promote a cooperative regulatory approach built around a small arms control regime (SACR), broad in scope and global in reach and to consist of, on the preventive side, (1) a Small Arms Register, (2) strengthened national export controls, and (3) an international code of conduct. On the reduction side, to consist of weapons collection programs as integral to peace agreements and post-conflict demobilization and reconstruction programs as well as to conflict prevention strategies.

Universal, comprehensive and non-discriminatory SACR would integrate current efforts based on a variety of approaches: crime prevention, arms control, firearms regulation, human rights, development, gun safety etc. It should, therefore, not be viewed as detracting from or interfering with ongoing, local, national or regional efforts. Rather, SACR can be said to provide a set of common standards around which these efforts can be harnessed.

Cooperative arms regulation and disarmament must address security and developmental concerns as functional corollaries and must be integrated into national programs as well as into international cooperation efforts.

While the task is a daunting one, many international development agencies have already taken steps to incorporate security sector reform and other conflict prevention strategies into their assistance programs.

Integral to cooperative disarmament, preventive measures must pursue two objectives: first, to limit and control availability and access to small arms (supply side) and secondly, to reduce the demand for such weapons (demand side). On the supply side such an approach necessitates measures aimed at effectively regulating legal transfers between states based on a principle of responsible restraint, controlling the availability, use and storage of small arms within states, preventing and combating illicit transfers, collecting and removing surplus arms from both civil society and regions of conflict, increasing transparency and accountability, support for research and information sharing.

Correspondingly, on the demand side, the international community must commit to helping reverse cultures of violence through support for the reform of the security sector (both police and military) in affected states as fundamental to good governance, through the promotion of norms of civilian non-possession and of government restraint, by enhancing demobilization and reintegration programs for ex-combatants, by halting the abhorrent use of child fighters and by effectively combating the culture of impunity that fuels the illicit arms trade.

Also, reduction measures must be devised to secure, destroy or otherwise responsibly dispose of small arms that are already in circulation, inside or outside of legal possession.

The international donor community should establish collection and buy-back programs as well as other mechanisms to identify and promote best practices and to ensure adequate financial support. This is of particular importance with respect to "surplus" military weapons during a peace process.

Integral to peace accords, combatants must be demobilized, disarmed and weapons surrendered safely destroyed.

There are important lessons to be learned from small arms collection and destruction (Mozambique, Mali, Liberia) reintegration of ex-combatants into productive civilian life (Cambodia, Philippines), post-conflict reconstruction (Cambodia, Bougainville) and the reform of police, judicial and penal systems (Cambodia, Papua New Guinea).

Law enforcement efforts in States where the illicit use of small arms is particularly severe should be supported as well.

The international donor community should cooperate with affected states in the establishment of incentive-based weapons collection programs as well as other mechanisms to identify and promote best practices and to ensure adequate financial support.

The UN can develop centres for excellence pertaining to certain aspects of the problem area, such as arms collection programs, security sector reform and security arrangements for post-conflict development.

Technical and financial resources are needed and the UN can play a role in mobilizing these resources.

THE IMPACT OF ILLICIT SMALL ARMS ON HUMAN SECURITY

Terrorism and Insurgency

The number of insurgency movements in Southeast Asia receiving frequent supplies of small arms is limited. These movements exist in Indonesia, Myanmar and the Philippines. As well, there is continued fighting among different political factions in Cambodia.

The insurgents in Indonesia (Acehnese, East Timorese and West Irian) are among the least likely to receive small arms from abroad. Their numbers are small and they do not have the mechanisms to raise adequate funds for weapons purchase. The Indonesian government and military have been effective in isolating these movements and preventing any contact with the outside. The East Timorese resistance, for example, mainly uses weapons taken from Indonesian soldiers. Therefore, although the demand for small arms may exist in these insurgent areas, the threat of actual acquisition is minimal. This argument is strong especially considering that profits have become the main goal of today's small arms trade. The most likely recipients of small arms in Indonesia are criminal elements. And even this situation is questionable because there is not a network of organized crime, such as the Triad in China or the drug cartels in Myanmar, that have the resources to sustain any form of arms transfer. In the Philippines, separatist groups on Mindanao have engaged in sporadic armed confrontation with central government forces for years. The insurgents have admitted to obtaining weapons from foreign sources. Photographs of rebel soldiers show them to be well equipped with small arms and ammunition, and it is unlikely that these are solely from stealing and confiscating weapons from government forces. Further fighting not only threatens human security in the Philippines, but also could have a significant impact on the country's economic growth.

Since last year's coup in Cambodia, incidents of political violence have been high. "Hundreds of [Hun Sen's] oppositions remain in Thailand in exile or are fighting in the jungles." Although

Hun Sen's faction has been accused internationally for committing such violence against Norodom Ranarindh's supporters, the latter often are perpetrators as well. Prior to the coup, during the United Nations sponsored peacebuilding process, it was feared that disarmament efforts would result in small arms moving out of the country and into neighbouring states. However, while the movement of small arms from Cambodia to places such as northern Myanmar is possible, the demand for weapons in Cambodia is rising. Small arms are probably re-circulating within the country and foreign sources may be involved in further re-supply. While Hun Sen's faction could be receiving small arms shipment from Vietnam, Ranarindh loyalists could be receiving theirs from China. To make things even more complicated, the Khmer Rouge is still actively seeking ways to become involved in this political power play.

Criminal Activities

Criminal elements have profited most from easier access to illicit weapons, and there are signs of increasing gun related violence. In China, there is a steady growth in gun-related crimes since 1994 and the government warns of the threat this poses to public security. The problem is intensified by the growing brutality of such crimes. As numbers and levels of criminal violence escalate, citizens seek security through acquiring small arms for personal use. In turn, this trend exacerbates overall conditions as it allows the small arms trade to flourish by raising the demand for such weapons. This becomes the case especially when the government is perceived to be slow and ineffective in implementing measures to manage the problem. Such a situation is not unique to China and can be observed throughout East Asia. The links between small arms proliferation and criminal activities in Southeast Asia is especially problematic when one also factors in the estimated high volume of drug trade in the region. In Myanmar, the sales of small arms to drug lords such as Khun Sa have allowed them to strengthen their power. With easy access to such weapons, the drug cartels have formed well-equipped private armies, which increasingly pose serious threats to state sovereignty. The state monopoly on violence — one of the main characteristics of the modern state system — is increasingly undermined. Through the flourishing illicit trade in small arms, these private armies occasionally appear at least as well equipped and trained than the national security forces. This situation provides drug cartels with the tools to strengthen their grip over communities of peasants who are enslaved by the trade. Small arms proliferation is also associated with the drug trade in the form of common channels of supply.

The transfer of small arms may be different from that of drugs because the former carry more bulk and are easier to trace in their origins. However, the manner in which they are transported is comparable. For example, drugs and small arms transfers across the Thai-Cambodian border are sometimes carried out by concealing these products inside the gas tanks of shipping trucks. In addition to the similarities in methods, these goods are moving through similar patterns of supply channels. This argument is supported by reports claiming that weapons and drugs are often exchanged along such supply lines. The trades in small arms and drugs complement each other; the flourishing of one trade certainly induces growth in the other.

While the small arms/drug trades model also applies to illicit maritime activities, piracy is the more serious problem at sea. The most recent International Maritime Bureau (IMB) report shows that Southeast Asia remains the region with the highest rate of piracy in the world. These criminal activities are frequent in the South China Sea (especially within the Hong Kong-Luzon-Hainan triangle), the Strait of Malacca and the Gulf of Thailand. While trends have been on the rise for the last five years or so, last year's report indicates another problem; the level of violence committed during pirate attacks have dramatically increased.

Acts of piracy in the region are usually carried out using homemade explosives and small arms such as rifles and machine guns. The increasing level of violence during pirate attacks could possibly be linked to the growing availability of small arms. Considering that the number of pirate attacks reported did not increase dramatically, the surge in levels of violence which accompany these acts can only be explained by the widening use of small arms. Consequently, in addition to facing the fear of being robbed, the personal security of ship crews is also increasingly threatened.

Implications for State Sovereignty in the Region

The situations discussed in the previous section indicate that the most predominant threats to security caused by the growth in illicit small arms trafficking are of non-military nature. Insurgency movements, factional fighting and criminal activities flourish with easy access to small arms. While regional states may not see these threats as serious in the short term, their implications in the long run may cause disruption in state legitimacy and stability.

One of the most important features of the modern state is its monopoly on internal violence. However, as non-state, non-military elements gain power, they pose a challenge to the norm. Having just gained their independence from European powers in the latter part of the century (except for Thailand, which was never ruled by a foreign power) countries in Southeast Asia are still undergoing statebuilding processes. Most of them are still concentrating on developing mechanisms against encroachment from other countries (especially considering the existence of historical animosities and unending territorial disputes among the regional countries). As a result, small-scale insurgencies and criminal activities are often overlooked as possible threats to the state.

The growth of drug smuggling and piracy poses threats to the region's economic activities. As the current economic downturn deepens, there is a strong possibility that these activities may grow even faster. For example, the tough anti-drug policies in Thailand, which has been responsible for the declining production of opium on the Thai section of the Golden Triangle, could lose its effectiveness as officials try to relieve their economic hardship through corruption. Also, the hundreds of Indonesians who are fleeing to the Malaysian peninsula could become easy targets for pirates operating in the Malacca Strait. These descriptions are mainly speculative, but they are important considerations for governments in the region. The current economic meltdown represents a tough challenge to statehood in Southeast Asia. The erosion of state legitimacy by internal, non-military, non-state elements renders the task of overcoming the meltdown more difficult. Therefore, it is in these countries interest to attribute more attention to the trafficking of illicit small arms, which enhances the power of these non-state actors.

Implications for Canada

The problem of illicit small arms movement in Southeast Asia could also have repercussions that extend beyond the region's border. Having close relations with most of the countries in the region, there are a number of implications that Canada may suffer if the illicit proliferation of small arms is allowed to grow in Southeast Asia and the rest of Asia in general. These implications can be divided into those that are of a direct nature and those that could affect Canada indirectly.

There has not been any substantial evidence yet that Asian small arms are circulating illicitly on Canadian soil. However, the possibility of this happening is real. The demand for military small arms may not be high, but criminal elements in Canada — as in any country — certainly have some interest in such weapons. Recognizing the *potential* for problem, instead of reacting to it *"after the fact,"* is important considering efforts to extract small arms from society has been proven to be difficult. As Canada becomes more involved in the Asian economies, the volume of transshipment entering the Port of Vancouver is rapidly growing. This expansion could potentially stretch the abilities of Canadian customs officials to monitor the entrance of goods. The experience in Hong Kong indicates that as the volume of transshipment increases, so does the susceptibility of ports to illicit activities. The most recent drug bust at the Vancouver port indicates that criminals are already taking advantage of increased transshipment volume to smuggle illicit goods. Since the channels for drug smuggling are often used for illicit weapons transfer as well, attention should be paid to the possibility of small arms entering Canada through Vancouver and efforts should be taken to avoid this.

In addition to direct shipments of small arms from Asia, Canada should also be on alert for Asian weapons that may have been introduced to North America through U.S. ports. The confiscation of Chinese machine guns at the San Francisco port two years ago indicates the possible existence of a supply channel. Once the weapons have reached North America, they could enter Canada by land in spite of controls along the borders. The Firearms Smuggling Work Group claims that small arms are smuggled into north of the border through means as simple as courier services. Also, gun running from the United States seems to be in association with other types of smuggling such as tobacco, alcohol and drugs. The indirect implications of small arms proliferation to Canada mainly stem from our economic relations with countries of the Asia-Pacific. In 1993, the region was the market for more than $16.6 billion of Canadian exports while imports from the region numbered about $25.1 billion. While Canadian investment in the Asia-Pacific region figured at about $12.2 billion in 1996.51 Furthermore, Southeast Asian countries such as Indonesia, the Philippines, Singapore and Thailand are among the top 25 most promising markets for Canadian export. The indirect implications of Southeast Asia's growing illicit arms trade can be observed in at least three ways.

First, small arms proliferation has the potential to undermine government legitimacy. As mentioned, the proliferation of small arms has strong destabilizing elements. However, increasing crime and insurgency, fueled by the availability of small arms, is not likely to cause immediate chaos. Instead, the process of undermining government legitimacy will be gradual and in turn, this regression will certainly affect susceptible countries' economic performance. Such a condition would be disadvantageous because Canadian trade and investment interests in the region are high. Second, the rising trend of piracy could present serious obstructions to regular economic activities. The waterways of the region are highly trafficked by ships connecting the region with the rest of the world. The East Asian sea-lanes of communication (SLOC) are the lifelines to the region's economies as well as a major channel for Canadian export and imports. The rising violence related to pirate attacks would hamper the movement of shipping vessels and increase the cost of conducting trade (e.g., higher insurance cost, extra costs for re-routing). Although the negative effects may not be apparent now, their long-term repercussions are reasons enough to become involved in preventative measures such as limiting the flow of illicit small arms in the region. Third, Canada's involvement in humanitarian and development projects in the region is at risk of being undermined by violence caused by the growth in illicit small arms trafficking. For example, the Canadian International Development Agency (CIDA) is funding the six-year, $7.8 million Canada-Cambodia Development Program (CCDP), to aid the process of reconstruction and rehabilitation in this war torn country. This is one of the largest and most active development assistance projects in Cambodia. However, the success of this project could be eroded if political instability and armed violence continue. CIDA and many Canadian Non-Governmental Organizations (NGOs) are also involved in similar development assistance programs in Vietnam and Thailand. In these cases as well, violence caused by easy access to small arms is certainly a factor which limits the accomplishment of these organizations in promoting prosperity, security and Canadian values in the region.

POLICY OPTIONS

UN Based Efforts

The United Nations remains one of the best institutions for promoting efforts to manage the problem of small arms proliferation. Former UN Secretary General Boutros Boutros Ghali's Agenda for Peace was important as a beginning, and last year's Report of the Small Arms Panel provided some guidelines to further treatment of the issue. The greatest advantage to UN based efforts is its inclusiveness, especially when considering that illicit small arms proliferation is a global security problem as much as it is a regional or national one.

One of the most talked about suggestions is the possible expansion of the UN Register of Conventional Weapons to promote transparency about the legal trade in small arms. However, since its creation, the UN Register has had mixed results. Not all states have submitted reports of their weapons acquisitions, but the leading arms exporting countries have responded. The export/import information provided by states often contain discrepancies, but it has revealed some previously unknown data as well as represents a modest step towards enhancing transparency. The expansion of the Register (beyond the seven original weapon categories and to include small arms) seems an efficient and logical progression, however the goal will be difficult to achieve. The creation of the Register in the first place was a difficult enough process and some states are unhappy about its current scope and coverage (hence, the lack of universal participation). For a number of states, the current situation represents the limit of their willingness to cooperate in transparency measures. Although the expansion of the Register may be the most desired goal for countries such as Canada, its actual realization is difficult. Nevertheless, this should not deter attempts to proceed with such an approach.

The UN, through its Centre for International Crime and Prevention, has also increased its activity in the study of domestic firearm regulations. Concerns related to the illicit trafficking of small arms figure prominently in this study.

At the moment, there may be a move towards developing a convention dealing with illicit trafficking within the Commission on Crime Prevention and Criminal Justice. With further development — including more participation among member states — these efforts represent an important step towards a more comprehensive treatment of the illicit small arms trade. The UN's work in this field allows for a multi-dimensional approach (when combined with UN studies on post-conflict disarmament, arms control, norm building and education) to tackling problems related to the small arms phenomenon.

As mentioned in the previous paragraph, the UN is heavily involved in developing effective ways to manage post-conflict disarmament. The provision of disarmament goals in peacekeeping missions is important because they are essential to the creation of lasting peace and stability. This is usually done through the process of norm building as well as educating the people living in post-conflict areas. The UN Disarmament Committee has conducted a series of studies on the role of UN peacekeeping missions in disarming, demobilizing and reintegrating post-conflict societies. These efforts do not necessarily address directly how the movement of small arms affects trends in criminal activities (considering such activities are more predominant in Southeast Asia). However, they provide insights on how small arms originating from countries such as Cambodia, Myanmar and Vietnam can be stemmed.

Regional Based Efforts

In order to complement the achievements of the UN, the Panel on Small Arms also suggested in its report the development of regional initiatives. The ASEAN Regional Forum (ARF) has emerged as a forum for discussions on security, although it is not a formal regional security structure. With the lack of a structured regional security mechanism, the ARF has become an important body for the promotion of policies aimed at managing the illicit trade in small arms.

For example, one of the confidence building measures (CBMs) listed for discussion within the ARF and its sub-bodies is "preventing and combating illicit trafficking in conventional small arms." By introducing ideas in the ARF and working within this framework of thinking, regional efforts would most likely be debated and pursued in a more productive fashion.

One of the initiatives could be the creation of regional small arms registers. To ensure efficient exchanges of ideas, policies and information, registers from different regions would be interconnected through a forum within the UN body. In Southeast Asia, Malaysia has indicated a desire to initiate the development of such a register for the purposes of tackling the illicit trade in small arms as well as enhancing regional confidence-building. Since Malaysia is one of the core members of the ARF, there is a possibility that it may decide to introduce such an initiative through this forum. Another idea that seems feasible is the creation of a regional convention against the illicit trafficking of small arms, as we have seen occur in the Organization of American States (OAS). There appears to be common features between small arms proliferation in the Americas and Southeast Asia. These include:

- criminal uses of illicit small arms;
- close relations between the small arms and drug trades (e.g., the cases of Myanmar and Colombia);
- possible proliferation of small arms as a result of post-conflict conditions (e.g., the cases of El Salvador, Nicaragua and Cambodia);
- organized insurgent and separatist movements (e.g., the Shining Path in Peru and Bolivia, the Zapatistas in Mexico and the MNLF/MILF in the Philippines; and,
- existence of relatively stable governments.

These similarities suggest that important lessons can be learned from the OAS experience. In the OAS Convention, there are a number of elements which deserve to be highlighted because of their potential applicability to conditions in Southeast Asia and possibly the rest of East Asia. These include:

- marking of small arms during production to enable increased facility in tracing the origins and movement of weapons;
- strengthening export controls by identifying destination of small arms transfers;
- enhancing cooperation, coordination and exchange of information and monitoring technologies among regional states; and,
- establishing of national bodies that would serve as contact points among the regional states.

The development of a regional convention on the illicit trafficking of small arms would certainly complement similar efforts at the UN level.

Regional countries that face difficulties controlling the inflow of illicit small arms may be interested in pursuing the above suggestions. Thailand, for example, has indicated in the past that it is willing to accept suggestions on how to manage trans-border criminal activities. Importantly, such a convention addresses the problems related to illicit proliferation but does not interfere with legal government-to-government trade in small arms. The ARF might act as a forum for initial discussions on the topic, after which regular multi-lateral discussions would be set up to ensure that focused deliberations evolve.

A GLOBAL PERSPECTIVE ON LIGHT WEAPONS

The twentieth century has been marked by a global scattering of violence and the material vehicles of violence – light weapons. Increased intergroup violence is a major characteristic of the contemporary world, with particularly harsh outbreaks in Bosnia, Burundi, Croatia, Kashmir, Nagorno-Karabakh, Georgia, Rwanda, Sri Lanka, Somalia, Sudan, Yemen and the Kurdish areas of Iraq and Turkey. This violence is often explained by essentialist arguments about a primordial ethnic identity. The dangers of the reliance on a primordialist theory of ethnicity are illustrated in the case of Rwanda. The theory assumes that people are born into particular cultural identities which command their deepest loyalties. The violence in Rwanda between the Hutus and Tutsis – and the violence in former Yugoslavia between Serbs and Croats – is explained in terms of fixed, inherited identities. However, many scholars have emphasised that ethnic antagonism did not cause the 1994 Rwandan genocide, although the form it took involved the systematic manipulation of ethnic identities for political ends.

The 1994 Rwandan genocide also illustrates the impact of the systematic accumulation of modern weaponry. It shows how the growing global diffusion of small arms is contributing to the incidence and intensity of violence in the post-Cold War era. 'Western journalists have made much of the fact that a good deal of the killing was performed with knives and machetes, giving this episode a distinctive air of primitive savagery. It should be noted, however, that the killings began in a relatively systematic fashion . . . and that the earliest massacres were conducted by the army and organised militias equipped with grenades and assault rifles imported from France, Egypt and South Africa by the Rwandan (Hutu) government' (Klare, 1995:36). There is evidence that some of the mass murders – for example, of 20 000 people in a stadium – were carried out using machine-guns. This is an item South Africa exported to Rwanda in 1992, but the managing director of

Armscor, in a letter to Amnesty International, also used arguments about machetes and ethnicity to minimise South African responsibility.

The Rwandan case is part of a larger pattern; since 1989 there have been global changes in the nature of violence and armed conflict. There has been a shift away from war between states involving major weapon systems, to intra-state war involving light weapons. Instead of wars being fought between states with well-organised armies equipped with major weapons systems confronting each other across defined geographic boundaries, today's violent conflict is usually an internal struggle with irregular forces using light weapons. This set of changes 'constitutes a remarkable break with the past'. The international disarmament agenda has focused on weapons of mass destruction and neglected light weapons. The threat of nuclear war has not disappeared – a threat captured in E.P. Thompson's warning of 'exterminism' – but it is one that has diminished, while light weapons proliferate.

The global diffusion of light weapons is part of recent changes in the global arms trade pattern. Michael Klare has conceptualised these changes as a shift from the 'proliferation/arms race' model that focused on the transfer of arms and technology involved in major weapons systems from one state to another, to what he terms the 'diffusion/global violence' model. The proliferation model was concerned largely with state-to-state transfers of major weapon systems from six or seven major industrial powers; under the diffusion model, there are more actors involved in the transfer of light weapons. The changes in the nature of armed conflict in the post-Cold War world have led not only to shifts in the global flow of weapons but to dramatic changes in the social organisation of violence. In intra-state conflicts involving light weapons 'it is members of the opposing group who are seen as the enemy, not the armed forces of a hostile state'. The boundaries of opposing group identities are socially constructed and defined.

The current predominance of light weapons has reversed the trajectory whereby warfare was becoming increasingly impersonal: a process of killing and maiming by pushing a button or moving a lever. The technology of major weapons systems made its victims invisible 'as people ... seen through the sights of firearms could not be'.

Small arms are responsible for most of the deaths in current conflicts, the most common being the automatic assault rifle. The majority of actors in these conflicts are sub-state groupings. All the violent conflict under way in the world involves violence between internal groups, often ethnically defined, rather than states. According to one estimate, 'only 4 of the 82 armed conflicts recorded in 1989-92 were of a classic inter-state character, while all of the remainder entailed some degree of internal warfare, usually along ethnic and religious lines'. Instead of the 'cats paw' wars of the Cold War era fought by the superpowers using proxy forces, there are civil wars taking place within failed states, in what have been termed 'teacup wars' (Gelb, 1994:36). States are losing their monopoly of legitimate violence. 'The key narrative of the new world order is the disintegration of states' and the 'key language of that dissolution is ethnic nationalism'. This implies the reversal of another historic trend: the disarmament of civilians in the process of Western state formation. 'Well-armed groups of citizens are forming all over the world' (Tilly, 1991: 7) and this process threatens to subvert democracy.

SDUs were initially armed with knobkieries, spears and homemade weapons, but later obtained access to a variety of firearms including AK-47s and R4 rifles (Rosenthal, 1994). Rosenthal found that SDUs were not armed by MK, but by gun-runners operating in commercial rather than political interests. The vast majority of licensed gun owners in South Africa are white. Whites were granted firearm licences more easily than blacks. It was customary during the apartheid era to demand that blacks, coloureds and Indians have training before they were granted firearm licences, although whites were not required to undergo such training. The number of licensed firearm owners has increased dramatically since 1976. At the end of 1996, the total number of licensed firearms in South Africa was 4,1 million.

Licences are easily available and enforcement is minimal. At present, you can get a licence if you are mentally stable (established in a ten-minute conversation, according to one police informant), have never been convicted of a serious (violent) crime in the last 10 years and are at least 16 years old. A number of informants maintained that there is a massive amount of police corruption in processing firearm licences, which extends deep into the Central Firearm Register. Increasing numbers of licensed firearms are ending up in criminal possession. In contemporary South Africa, widespread poverty and unemployment have contributed to violence as increasing numbers of citizens have come to rely on criminal violence as a means of livelihood.

Analysing gun violence as a social phenomenon involves more than exploring individual biographies, motives and meanings; it involves examining the diverse social organisations, cultural frameworks, social practices, group attachments and institutions built up around guns. Collectively, these constitute a robust 'gun culture'. Overall, this culture provides a social sanction to the possession of guns and much gun violence follows culturally defined repertoires of behaviour. The values, social practices and institutions which constitute this gun culture include what Raymond Williams calls 'consumerist militarism'. It involves the normalisation, legitimation and even glorification of war, weaponry, military force and violence through television, films, books, songs, dances, games, sports and toys. None of these are insignificant in the light of Mann's definition of militarism as 'a set of attitudes and social practices which regards war and the preparation for war as a normal and desirable social activity'.

All of these cultural forms constitute a kind of 'banal militarism' which operates near the surface of social life. Banal militarism is embedded in everyday activities; it works through prosaic routines and rituals to make war, weaponry and violence appear natural and inevitable. It is exemplified in war games such as paintball, which has become increasingly popular among white South Africans since 1985. At its core, paintball simulates the sequence of killing. One Johannesburg informant involved in this 'gun culture' spent much of his leisure time playing paintball, practising at shooting ranges and cleaning and 'stroking' (his word) the 12 guns he owned. This behaviour is chillingly reminiscent of that of the killer responsible for Britain's worst mass murder, the Dunblane school shooting of 16 children and their teacher in 1996.

This gun culture not only operates to glamorise war and weaponry, but to 'normalise' these social arrangements. Part of this 'normalisation' is the notion that private gun ownership is legitimate; a right, not a privilege. A key institution which promotes this notion is the South African Gun Owners' Association (SAGA). This is not as powerful as the National Rifle Association in the United States, but in 1995 SAGA organised petitions to the Constitutional Assembly stating that the Constitution should be amended to recognise the right to own firearms and to place a limitation on government's power to disarm the civilian population. SAGA maintains that 'the anti-gun lobby's emphasis shouldn't be on guns – it should be on people. Guns are to crime as cameras are to pornography but they don't ban cameras.'

The notion that private gun ownership is legitimate is linked to the notion that guns are an effective and necessary form of protection. The gun combines two contradictory images: it is a means of order and of violence; paradoxically it is believed to provide protection from violence through the potential threat of violence. A common theme articulated by many informants who had purchased guns for self-protection was a sense of being powerless, of being victims of social forces beyond their control. But the psychodynamic power of the gun as protection is largely illusionary. Legally owned weapons contribute to the problem of violent crime.

6

Arms Race Developing in the Asia-Pacific Region

Many analysts believe that growing friction between the United States and China will define the coming decades. Certainly, China is in the midst of an ambitious bid to modernize its military by the middle of this century. A key part of this effort is to downsize its army—the world's largest—while beefing up its air force and navy. This will enable China to project military force farther beyond its borders. China's total spending is second only to that of the United States, but it is low as measured by per capita spending. However, China has expanded its military spending at a double-digit pace in the past decade, and it became the world's second-largest military power, surpassing France, in 2009. In March 2011, the Chinese government announced that it would be raising its official military budget by 12.7%, to US$91.5 billion. This marks a surge forward in military spending and reverses the government's 2010 position, when it reined in military spending to a mere 7.5% increase. The 2010 military budget was the first to fall below 10% since 1989. Military experts in the United States and elsewhere have said Beijing's real military spending is at least double the announced figure. A 2009 Pentagon report estimated China's total military spending to be between US$105 billion and US$150 billion. While growing rapidly, China's military spending is still dwarfed by that of the United States.

China clearly now intends to develop a military capability to match its new-found economic status, and is spending more on its navy and air force, and cutting back on its land forces. The idea is to put the country in a better position to project force outside its own borders. China's insatiable appetite for raw materials and energy has also widened the military's mission to protect China's strategic economic interests overseas. The country's naval and air forces certainly appear determined to impose their dominance in the South China Sea—through which vital oil supplies pass, and where several islands are in dispute—and in the East China Sea, where China and Japan are in dispute over mineral rights, and a number of contested islands. The government says that most of the increased military expenditure is focused on improving the historically poor living conditions of soldiers in the People's Liberation Army.

In addition, the authorities intend to increase spending on "informatization," in an attempt to close the gap on the United States's use of "smart" technology. Defence companies in the West could benefit from China's attempts to upgrade its military technology, although it is extremely doubtful whether Washington would allow American companies to supply technology to China.

Some analysts contend that if China's economic growth remains robust, and the country is thus able to continue to expand its defence spending significantly each year, it will pose a threat to the United States' military dominance of the globe by the mid-21st century, or earlier. In early 2009, Beijing confirmed plans to build aircraft carriers, with the apparent intent of projecting "blue water" naval power eastwards into the Pacific, bringing it into potential conflict with the United States. For its part, Beijing fears that the United States is trying to "encircle" China, by using India, and allies such as Japan and Australia, as proxies to contain China's increasing military strength. China's concerns have some validity—military ties between Washington and New Delhi, for example, are growing in a number of areas. India is also growing into a major purchaser of US military equipment, an about-turn for a country that relied on Soviet weapons during the Cold War. In a groundbreaking deal, India agreed to buy six Lockheed C130J transport planes for around US$1 billion in January 2008—New Delhi had previously procured transport aircraft from the USSR or Russia. India is expected to spend US$100 billion in the next decade on its military. India's defence minister, Arackaparambil Kurien Antony, has made it clear that he expects military spending, currently 2.5% of GDP, to increase substantially as the nation's robust economy continues to grow.

OTHER MAJOR TRENDS

The Environment

It might appear surprising, but the US military is arguably doing more to save the planet than any other organization on earth. The US Defence Department is investing huge sums in the search to develop renewable sources of energy, as well as improving energy efficiency. The key drivers behind this trend include: national security—the United States does not want to be dependent upon energy imported from politically unstable regions; cost reasons—even a 5% cut in the fuel bill would save the Department of Defence US$635 million (based on the 2007 figure); and, finally, because it makes sound military sense—many lives are lost transporting fuel to the frontline in vulnerable convoys.

The US military is already one of the largest consumers of renewable energy in the world, and it has set a goal that 25% of its energy should come from renewable sources by 2025. The US Air Force's goal is that 50% of all the fuels used in domestic training flights will come from synthetic, or non-petroleum, sources by 2016. The US military is also investing heavily in solar and wind power.

Technological Advances

The military is one of the key drivers of technological advances. There are certainly some remarkable developments taking place. The F-35 Joint Strike Fighter, being developed by Lockheed Martin, Northrop Grumman, and BAE Systems, for example, features some extraordinary features. These include technology that allows the pilot to look through the structure of the aircraft. The aircraft also features voice commands that significantly reduce the pilot's workload.

The military is also investing heavily in information technology on land. Military units constantly transmit huge amounts of data back and forth to report their position, generate situational awareness, and share information on enemy tactics. Soldiers with access to laptops, for example, can provide vital information to military commanders. Real-time management of information enables rapid decision-making, meaning that military operations can proceed quickly, possibly providing a decisive advantage during a battle.

Cyberspace: The New Battlefield

Unsurprisingly, given the new emphasis on information technology, governments around the world are investing heavily in measures to protect their computer networks from attacks, and to launch their own cyber attacks. In 2010, the *Guardian* reported (January 13, 2010) that the Chinese military has been developing capabilities to spy on, infiltrate, and compromise adversaries' computer networks for years. "Informatized war" is an integral component of its "three warfares" (*san zhong zhanfa*) strategic concept, and the achievement of information superiority is viewed as a requirement for battlefield supremacy. Many large defence companies have already branched out into cyber-security and information-technology services.

THE INTERNATIONAL ARMS TRADE: DIFFICULT TO DEFINE, MEASURE, AND CONTROL

The international arms trade apparently has weathered the financial crisis quite well. Available data indicate that the impact to date on the volume of orders and deliveries has been limited. As has been shown in the past, financial resources—from domestic budgets or foreign military assistance—are not the only factor that influences arms acquisitions. Perceived internal or external threats to national security, the need to replace or upgrade military inventories, demonstrations of international status, development of domestic arms industries via licensed production and offsets, the desire to strengthen ties with suppliers, and the influence of the military play important roles in the arms acquisition process. Before permitting exports of arms and military equipment, suppliers will assess the potential economic gains and the potential impact of the transfer on their strategic interests and foreign policy. Will the transfer harm or help friendly states or the supplier's international commitments, reputation, or standing?

For several reasons, there is no straightforward answer to the question, "How big is the international arms trade?" First, there is no globally agreed definition of "arms." States and international organizations that seek to measure or control the arms trade use lists of items that vary in their complexity and coverage, most notably with regard to their inclusion of "dual-use goods," items with both military and civilian applications. Second, there is no common agreement on what types of activities constitute the arms trade. Examples of areas where differences exist include arms leased to other states; gifts and donations; the transfer of technology to produce arms and military equipment; and upgrades, parts, and services related to the transfer of arms and military equipment. Third, the lack of openness and transparency by many arms suppliers and recipients regarding the value and volume of their arms exports and imports makes it difficult to collect accurate data. As a result, a variety of different definitions of the international arms trade and estimates of its scale exists. This has implications for efforts to establish controls on arms transfers via a future international arms trade treaty (ATT). This article will outline some of the challenges in defining, measuring, and controlling the international arms trade.

Definitions and Estimates

The national lists of arms and military equipment to be subject to export controls (control lists) maintained by most states and all major arms exporters provide a useful starting point for defining "arms" and the international arms trade. The Munitions List and Lists of Dual-Use Goods and Technologies of the Wassenaar Arrangement on Export Controls for Conventional Arms and Dual-Use Goods and Technologies provide the basis for the control lists of the 40 states that are members of the group. The Munitions List covers a wide range of arms and military equipment, from small arms to ships, as well as ammunition, information and communication technologies, training equipment, and equipment for producing arms. Several significant arms-exporting nonmembers, including China, have fully or partially aligned their national control lists with the Munitions List. As a result, all of the top 10 arms suppliers during 2005-2009 have control lists derived from the Wassenaar Arrangement.

National control lists serve as the basis for national reports on arms exports. As of January 2010, 32 states had published at least one national report on arms exports since 1990, and a further nine states provided information on the value of their export licenses and exports to the 2009 European Union (EU) Annual Report on Arms Exports. These reports vary in detail but, at a minimum, tend to provide data on the financial value of arms export licenses or arms exports. Several major exporters (e.g., Russia) do not produce such reports, but do release official data on the financial value of their arms exports. Using national reports and official statements, the Stockholm International Peace Research Institute (SIPRI) has attempted to provide estimates of the financial value of the international arms trade.

The now-defunct U.S. Arms Control and Disarmament Agency (ACDA) created the following comprehensive definition of the arms trade, which has been widely used by researchers: weapons of war, parts thereof, ammunition, support equipment, and other commodities designed for military use.... Dual-use equipment...when its primary mission is identified as military. The building of defence production facilities and licensing fees paid as royalties for the production of military equipment.... Military services such as training, supply operations, equipment repair, technical assistance and construction are included where data are available.

A similar definition of the arms trade is used to compile the U.S. Congressional Research Service's (CRS) annual report, "Conventional Arms Transfers to Developing Nations." In spite of the name, the report contains estimates for the value of the global arms trade, not just trade with developing countries. The CRS estimated the financial value of deliveries of arms to be $34.5 billion for 2007. Despite using a narrower definition of arms transfers than the CRS, SIPRI's accounting of official financial data contained in national reports and official statements for 2007 generated a figure of $51.1 billion for arms exports, representing 0.3 percent of world trade. This figure is likely to be lower than the true figure because a number of significant exporters, including China, do not release data on the financial value of their arms exports. The difference between the SIPRI and CRS estimates is a further demonstration of the difficulty of estimating the financial value of the international arms trade.

The SIPRI arms transfers database provides information on international arms transfers from 1950 to the most recent calendar year. Its coverage is narrower than that of the ACDA, CRS, and national control lists; for example, it does not include transfers of most small arms and light weapons (SALW). However, it provides information on the number of units transferred and employs a unique pricing system to measure the volume of arms transfers. The SIPRI trend indicator value allows researchers to track developments in transfers to and from different suppliers, recipients, and regions. SIPRI data form the basis for the discussion below.

Arms Trade Trends

The volume of international arms transfers in the post-World War II period peaked in 1982. Following the end of the Cold War, there was a steady decline in global arms transfers. They reached their lowest point in 2002, when transfers amounted to only 38 percent of their Cold War high. This decline has reversed, and the volume of international transfers of major conventional weapons during 2005-2009 was 22 percent higher than during 2000-2004.

One of the most marked aspects of the international arms trade has been its dominance by five suppliers. During 1980-1984, when global arms transfers were at the highest level, the Soviet Union (37 percent), the United States (29 percent), France (8 percent), the United Kingdom (5 percent), and the Federal Republic of Germany (5 percent) accounted for 84 percent of all exports. The five largest suppliers of major conventional weapons during 2005-2009 were the United States (30 percent), Russia (23 percent), Germany (11 percent), France (8 percent), and the United Kingdom (4 percent), collectively accounting for 76 percent of exports.

The governments of these major suppliers are actively engaged in assisting the export efforts of their domestic arms industries in the competitive international arms market. Some governments also provide military equipment to allies at beneficial rates as a key plank of their foreign and defence policies, something that often has clear benefits for commercial arms manufacturers based in these states.

Since 2001, the United States has increased foreign military aid for allies in regions of tension or conflict. President Barack Obama has maintained the Bush administration's pledge to increase foreign military financing aid for Israel, which is set to reach $3 billion in 2012. Egypt and the members of the Gulf Cooperation Council have been the recipients of increased assistance as well.

Russia has announced its willingness to develop and produce arms jointly with other countries to help strengthen ties, accept payments through barter, participate in joint economic projects, and offer credit and exchanges of debt for arms. In 2009, Russia extended a $2 billion line of credit to Venezuela for arms purchases. In addition, it agreed to cancel Vietnam's debt to Russia and help modernize its shipbuilding industry in exchange for Vietnam's commitment to purchase 20 Su-30MK combat aircraft and six Type-636 Kilo-class submarines and further expand the involvement of Russian companies in the exploration and extraction of Vietnamese oil.

In 2007 the French government simplified and modernized France's arms export licensing system and began taking a more active role in promoting exports abroad. It has demonstrated a willingness to engage in far-reaching technology transfer agreements in order to win contracts. In September 2009 French President Nicolas Sarkozy visited Brazil to conclude an almost $10 billion deal to supply four conventionally powered submarines and technology to assist in the development of Brazil's first nuclear-powered submarine.

Attempts by countries beyond the traditional major producers to develop their own arms industries and increase their share of global arms exports have typically had limited success, largely because of high technological barriers or an inadequate civilian industrial base. Yet, many countries still seek to increase their levels of autonomous capability in arms production, with some developing state-of-the-art products for particular niche items. For example, Israel is widely recognized as a leading producer and supplier of unmanned aerial vehicles (UAVs), supplying systems and licenses for production for more than 100 UAVs to 18 states, including all of the top five suppliers, during 2005-2009.

In addition, licensed production agreements have led to an increase in the number of states that are capable of manufacturing less-advanced weapons systems, particularly small arms and light weapons. Although licensed production agreements often include controls on who can receive the weapons produced, this is not always the case, or the agreements are not enforced. Soviet Avtomat Kalashnikov (AK) and German Heckler and Koch G3 assault rifles serve as classic examples of cases in which licensed production has led to exports being made without the express permission of those issuing the original license. Russia perceives the production of Kalashnikov rifles in a number of former Warsaw Pact countries to be unlicensed and illegal, claiming that arrangements concluded during the Soviet era have expired. The decision to give designs and information on product technology to Warsaw Pact states and clients during the Soviet era therefore remains a source of concern. Nonetheless, Russia continues to issue licensed production agreements for Kalashnikov rifles, revealing recently that 10 states had applied to build factories. The possibility remains that today's license holders could produce or export Kalashnikovs without the express permission of Russia in the future.

In contrast to the largest suppliers, the largest recipients of major conventional weapons have varied considerably over the years. During 1980-1984, the five largest recipients of military equipment—Iraq (7 percent), India (6 percent), Libya (5 percent), Syria (5 percent), and Egypt (4 percent)—accounted for 27 percent of total imports. The five largest recipients of major conventional weapons during 2005-2009 were China (9 percent), India (7 percent), South Korea (6 percent), the United Arab Emirates (6 percent), and Greece (4 percent), accounting for 32 percent of total imports. After the end of the Cold War, China imported a large volume of aircraft, ships, submarines, air defence systems, and missiles from Russia, but Chinese arms imports from Russia have declined dramatically in recent years. One explanation for this drop is that China appears to have overcome many of the problems that have dogged its arms industry and is now able to manufacture advanced weapons systems domestically. There are persistent allegations that many of China's "indigenous" weapons systems are actually copies of other countries' designs. It continues to rely on imports of components and subsystems for a number of its weapons systems, but is regarded as an example of a country in which arrangements for licensed production and technology transfers as part of arms import deals have helped with the development of an indigenous arms industry. India has sought to develop its own arms industry and decrease its reliance on arms imports but with limited success to date. It is expected to replace China as the largest arms importer in the coming years.

Recent acquisitions by states in Latin America, the Middle East, North Africa, and Southeast Asia indicate the possible emergence of reactive arms acquisition patterns that could develop into regional arms races. The volume of deliveries to Southeast Asia nearly doubled during 2005-2009 compared to 2000-2004. Deliveries were 722 percent higher to Malaysia, 146 percent higher to Singapore, and 84 percent higher to Indonesia. In 2009, Malaysia received six Su-30MKM combat aircraft with advanced missiles from Russia, two Scorpène submarines from France and Spain, two MEKO-100 frigates from Germany, and 21 PT-91 tanks from Poland. Singapore received eight F-15E combat aircraft with advanced air-to-air and air-to-ground missiles from the United States, two La Fayette frigates from France, and 40 Leopard-2A4 tanks from Germany.

There is limited empirical evidence to suggest a direct causal link between an increase in the volume of arms imported and the outbreak of conflict or an increase in the intensity of conflict. It has been suggested, however, that states that acquire significant quantities of military equipment may be more prone to use armed force to resolve disputes. For example, the recent conflicts in Sri Lanka and Georgia, both of which are relatively minor arms importers, were preceded by significant increases in transfers. In both cases, governments sought to restore what they perceived to be their state's territorial integrity against forces that were seeking independence and had established high levels of autonomy to some degree within clearly defined regions.

As the graph on this page demonstrates, the volume of Georgian imports of major conventional weapons in the years preceding the August 2008 conflict in South Ossetia increased significantly, with the largest volume of arms imports for Georgia, excluding acquisitions by forces in Abkhazia and South Ossetia, taking place in 2007. Significant increases in arms imports and military spending were perceived by some as indicating that the Georgian government was preparing to use force to restore Georgia's territorial integrity.

PRACTICAL ASPECTS OF ARMS TRADE TAXATION

Tax collection

An arms export tax would best be collected at the point of export. While in theory there is no difference whether the tax was collected at the point of production, export or import, practical considerations make it more plausible to focus on exports. One reason is that the number of exporting countries is considerably smaller than the number of importing countries (about half as many countries). A second reason is that exporting countries are predominantly industrialized countries which in general have more experience in collecting export taxes and more effective customs services.

Tax basis

While national definitions of weapons differ and international trade statistics do not cover weapons comprehensively (Brzoska, 1995), there exist a number of definitions of weapons which would be readily available for taxation purposes. Two definitions, for heavy weapons and for light weapons have been developed within the UN system. In addition, the Wassenaar Arrangement, an informal information mechanism which includes more then 30 countries responsible to close to 95 percent of all arms exports has developed a comprehensive munitions list. The European Union has adopted a list which is very similar to the Wassenaar munitions list.

Reexports

The implementation of an arms trade tax would face a number of specific issues that would need to be addressed. One such issue is reexports. It lies in the logic of an arms export tax that all exports of arms should be taxed, whether they are exports of new or old weapons. On the other hand, exports of parts (which are classified as weapons) within coproduction projects should not be taxed, rather the export of the completed should be taxed.

Principal issues

The idea of an arms trade tax has also been questioned from more fundamental points of view. Singling out the trade in weapons While several observers found it very attractive to tax specifically the trade in weapons, others have objected. Proponents of an arms trade tax have highlighted the detrimental effects that weapon imports can have. Thus Oscar Arias has argued that spending on weapons has been detrimental for development and that excessive transfers of arms have been a major factor in the escalation of conflict into wars, their prolongation and human costs (Arias, 1995). Opponents, on the other hand have argued that the links between arms transfers and wars are weak, and that it is a solemn right of governments to import arms, indirectly guaranteed through Article 51 of the UN Charter on the right to individual and collective selfdefense.

As usual, there is some truth in all these observations. Arms imports are reducing import capacities and growth prospects of developing countries. They have contributed to the escalation and prolongation of some, but not all, conflicts (Brzoska and Pearson, 1994). It is a solemn right of countries to import arms for their defence, but not for purposes of aggression. On balance, it seems that there are good reasons for singling out and demeritorizing weapons. In fact this is already done in several ways. For instance, as was mentioned above, the UN maintains the Register of Conventional Weapons, an instrument of early warning of excessive accumulation of arms put into place after Iraq's armaments programs of the late 1980s had help make it into an aggressive military power. Arms exports restrictions are also the major form of sanctions under Chapter VII of the UN Charter exercised by the UN Security Council in the 1990s (Brzoska, 2001). Finally, a UN conference has been organized to address specifically the trade in small arms.

An arms trade tax would be a further, though not radically new, step in differentiating arms from other goods. It would signal, similar to specific consumption taxes in many countries that there are social costs which are not covered in market prices.

CORRECTING MARKET DISTORTIONS THROUGH SUBSIDIES

Arms exports are heavily subsidized by exporter countries. Export subsidies include the following forms:

- Direct subsidies. A number of suppliers financially support buyer countries, or buy weapons from producers and sell them, below production costs, to allies. An example of such a subsidy is the grant portion of the United States' Foreign Military Financing program. The US government plans to spent US $3.7 billion under this program in Fiscal Year 2002, predominantly for arms transfers to Israel (US $2 billion) and Egypt (US $1.3 billion).
- Indirect subsidy. A form of indirect subsidy results from the transfer of partly fungible resources to buyer governments which than use these resources, or their own resources freed by these transfers, to purchase weapons. The US government for instance plans to provide, in Fiscal Year 2002, US $2.3 billion of foreign aid under the Economic Support Fund, which predominantly is used to help Egypt and Israel defray the costs of weapons bought from US companies. Another, form of indirect subsidy is the linking of military and civilian projects. The UK government, for instance, funded the Pergau Dam in Malaysia with the tacit understanding that the Malaysian government would buy British Hawk aircraft. A High Court ruled this an

illegal use of development aid money in October 1994.

- Export financing schemes. A number of countries maintain subsidized export credit schemes that regularly also cover arms sales. In addition, major supplier governments also give direct credit. The German government, for instance, is directly covering sales of submarines to Turkey at a concessional rate of interest. Military exports are explicitly exempted from the OECD's Guidelines for Officially Supported Export Credits as well as from the authority of the World Trade Organization.
- Marketing subsidies. Marketing or arms is often supported at government level, in the British case, for instance, by the Defence Export Services Organization. Centralized government marketing can be an instrument to ensure that the seller government receives a part of the proceeds from arms exports, such as in the case of Russia's Rosoboronexport, in other cases, however, the government subsidizes sales through government agencies.
- Operational support. In many cases, governments are willing to provide training support to purchaser of weapons, either in their own countries, as a form of military aid, or in the buyer country. Sweden, for instance, has trained Indian officers to use Bofors guns sold to the country.
- Payment of initial research and development. Exports of weapons are often calculated on the basis of variable unit costs, not total costs. Initial research and development costs, which often are a large chunk of total costs are predominantly borne by the original producer government and not charged to export customers.

There are a number of estimates of arms export subsidies for individual countries which range between a few percent of the total value to more than a third of the value. The global amount of dedicated aid for military exports has declined drastically since the Cold War (Brzoska, 1992) but it is still substantial. The United States alone is planning close to US $6 billion to support arms transfers. Not included in the data on arms trade subsidies are generally cases of defaults by customers. Arms trade debts are not separated from other forms of debt and are, if need be, rescheduled as part of general debt relief. However, it is known that around the time of the Gulf War the US and other industrialized countries canceled close to $10 billion of debt outstanding from arms imports by coalition countries. Iraq, on the other hand, continues to have a similar debt to France and Russia for arms deliveries prior to the Gulf War (Brzoska, 1992). An arm s trade tax could correct for the general market distortion brought about by these subsidies. However, as mentioned, subsidies vary considerably among suppliers. A flat tax rate would not eliminate the distortion among suppliers (and, to the extent that they buy predominantly from one supplier, recipients) but could reduce the effective demand for weapons.

7

Nuclear Proliferation

In addition to the United States and the Soviet Union, three other nations, the United Kingdom, People's Republic of China, and France also developed far smaller nuclear stockpiles. In 1952, the United Kingdom became the third nation to possess nuclear weapons when it detonated an atomic bomb in Operation Hurricane in Australia on October 3, 1952. During the Cold War, British nuclear deterrence came from submarines and nuclear-armed aircraft. The Resolution class ballistic missile submarines armed with the American-built Polaris missile provided the sea deterrent, while aircraft such as the Avro Vulcan, SEPECAT Jaguar, Panavia Tornado and several other Royal Air Force strike aircraft carrying WE.177 gravity bomb provided the air deterrent.

France became the fourth nation to possess nuclear weapons on February 13, 1960, when the atomic bomb Gerboise Bleue was detonated in Algeria, then still a French colony [Formally a part of the Metropolitan France.] During the Cold War, the French nuclear deterrent was centered around the Force de frappe, a nuclear triad consisting of Dassault Mirage IV bombers carrying such nuclear weapons as the AN-22 gravity bomb and the ASMP stand-off attack missile, Pluton and Hades ballistic missiles, and the Redoutable class submarine armed with strategic nuclear missiles.

The People's Republic of China became the fifth nuclear power on October 16, 1964, when it detonated a uranium-235 bomb in a test codenamed 596. Due to Soviet/Chinese tensions, the Chinese might have used nuclear weapons against either the United States or the Soviet Union in the event of a nuclear war between the United States and the Soviet Union. During the Cold War, the Chinese nuclear deterrent consisted of gravity bombs carried aboard H-6 bomber aircraft, missile systems such as the DF-2, DF-3, and DF-4, and in the later stages of the Cold War, the Type 092 ballistic missile submarine.

Richard Nixon's Program of Détente

Economic problems caused by the arms race in both powers, combined with China's new role and the ability to verify disarmament led to a number of arms control agreements beginning in the 1970s. This period known as détente allowed both states to reduce their spending on weapons systems. SALT I and SALT II limited the size of the states arsenals. Bans on nuclear testing, anti-ballistic missile systems, and weapons in space all attempted to limit the expansion of the arms race through the Partial Test Ban Treaty. These treaties were only partially successful. Both states continued building massive numbers of nuclear weapons, and new technologies such as *multiple independently targetable reentry vehicles* (also known as MIRVs) limited the effectiveness of the treaties. Both superpowers retained the ability to destroy each other many times over.

Reagan and the Strategic Defense Initiative

Towards the end of Jimmy Carter's presidency, and continued strongly through the subsequent presidency of Ronald Reagan, the United States rejected disarmament and tried to restart the arms race through the production of new weapons and anti-weapons systems. The central part of this strategy was the Strategic Defense Initiative, a space based anti-ballistic missile system derided as "Star Wars" by its critics. During the second part of 1980s, the Soviet economy was teetering towards collapse and was unable to match American arms spending. Numerous negotiations by Mikhail Gorbachev attempted to come to agreements on reducing nuclear stockpiles, but the most radical were rejected by Reagan as they would also prohibit his SDI program.

Post–Cold War

With the end of the Cold War the United States, and especially Russia, cut down on nuclear weapons spending. Fewer new systems were developed and both arsenals have shrunk. But both countries still maintain stocks of nuclear missiles numbering in the thousands. In the USA, stockpile stewardship programs have taken over the role of maintaining the aging arsenal. After the Cold War ended, a large amount of resources and money which was once spent on developing nuclear weapons in USSR was then spent on repairing the environmental damage produced by the nuclear arms race, and almost all former production sites are now major cleanup sites. In the USA, the plutonium production facility at Hanford, Washington and the plutonium pit fabrication facility at Rocky Flats, Colorado are among the most polluted sites.

United States policy and strategy regarding nuclear proliferation was outlined in 1995 in the document "Essentials of Post–Cold War Deterrence". Despite efforts made in cleaning up uranium sites, significant problems stemming from the legacy of uranium development still exist today on the Navajo Nation in the states of Utah, Colorado, New Mexico, and Arizona. Hundreds of abandoned mines have not been cleaned up and present environmental and health risks in many Navajo communities.

India and Pakistan

The South-Asian states of India and Pakistan have also engaged in a nuclear arms race. India detonated what it called a "peaceful nuclear device" in 1974 ("Smiling Buddha") much to the surprise and alarm of the world who had been giving India nuclear technology for civilian, energy producing and peaceful purposes. The test generated great concern in Pakistan, which feared that it would be at the mercy of its long-time arch rival and quickly responded by pursuing its own nuclear weapons program. In the last few decades of the 20th century, Pakistan and India began to develop nuclear-capable rockets, and Pakistan had its own covert bomb program with Chinese proliferation which extended over many years since the first Indian weapon was detonated. In 1998 India, under Atal Bihari Vajpayee government, test detonated 5 more nuclear weapons. While the international response to the detonation was muted, domestic pressure within Pakistan began to build steam and Prime Minister Mian Muhammad Nawaz Sharif ordered the test, detonated 6 nuclear war weapons in a tit-for-tat fashion and to act as a deterrent.

NUCLEAR PROLIFERATION POLICIES DURING THE COLD WAR

In the South Asian context, a conflictual bipolar security complex, India and Pakistan's transformational process of emerging as opaque nuclear powers was an example of different motivations, aspirations and ambitions for obtaining nuclear status. While the dominance of *realpolitik* trends over states' nuclear decision-making process is not an entirely surprising phenomena, the evolution of India's approach to the nuclear option is interesting from philosophical and strategic viewpoints. The genesis of the Indian nuclear policy from a categorical opposition to nuclear weapons in the Nehru era to Pokhran I, India's first so-called Peaceful Nuclear Explosion (PNE) in 1974, signified a discontinuity in New Delhi's post-1947 strategic thinking. What caused this discontinuity? What factor(s) led the country of Mohandas Gandhi, who once labelled nuclear weapons as 'diabolic', to obtaining potential nuclear power status under Indira Gandhi? Do the same factors suffice in explaining Pakistan's motives for developing its own nuclear capabilities in the mid-1980s? While some political scientists emphasised national security considerations in locating the roots of India and Pakistan proliferation policy, others have used an alternative theoretical approach with a greater level of structural balance between domestic, military security and symbolic motives. The latter multi-causal approach, summarised by Scott D. Sagan, is particularly useful in providing an inclusive analysis of nuclear proliferation causes. In this context and through the application of Sagan's explanatory models, the essay attempts to analyse the layers in India and Pakistan's 'nuclear thinking' leading to the development of military nuclear technology. The alternative multi-causal explanation constitutes a practically efficient theoretical framework for the comprehensive understanding of states' hybrid logic for nuclear proliferation.

Opposing the neorealist mono-causal security-oriented analysis (i.e. "the security model"), Sagan's approach considers the domestic and norms aspects as effective factors in triggering military nuclear proliferation, thus offering two additional explanations: "the domestic politics model" and "the norms model." According to Sagan, security model states (either weak or strong) perceive nuclear weapons as an enormously powerful means of deterrence to secure their national security in an anarchic international system, if their regional or trans-regional rival(s) acquire nuclear capability. Strong resourceful states develop their own bomb, while weak states, incapable of proliferation, are obliged to join a balancing alliance with a nuclear power to maintain their security and sovereignty with the promise of nuclear retaliation. In contrast, the domestic politics model reflects the influence of three main domestic actors on governments' nuclear proliferation policies: first, states' nuclear energy establishments (consisting of scientific institutions and civil companies); second, the military elites (especially in the Air Force branch) as domestic bureaucratic actors; and third, politicians who tend to profit from the nuclear weapons discourse for political parties or individual standing regarding pro-proliferation public opinion. Therefore, these pro-proliferation actors gain additional influence if nuclear weapons are a positive symbol in states' domestic debates – thus the states proliferate in accordance with the influence of one or more of the aforementioned actors. Finally, in the norms model, states' nuclear policies are pro-proliferation due to 'nuclear symbolism' and the 'nuclear myth': states observe military organisation and advanced weaponry as essential elements in their image as modern and sovereign states. The 'nuclear myth', or symbolic implications of nuclear proliferation (e.g. technological advancement, military might, projection of grandeur, etc), are perceived as a means of forming states' modern identity and enhancing their international prestige. While there seems to be an analytical overlap and theoretical interference between the domestic and symbolic models, Sagan's three models offer an efficient toolbox for examining the deciding factors in India and Pakistan's nuclear policies.

The security-model analysis of Indian nuclear policy prior to Pokhran I can be conducted by analysing India's threat perception at the regional and trans-regional levels. The trans-regional level analysis confirms the gravity of Sino-centrism in India's trans-regional threat perception sphere, and the validity of Sagan's security-model explanation. The dynamics of post-1962 Sino-Indian bilateral relations is the fundamental factor in India's horizontal proliferation policy in the security model. While the Sino-Indian protracted conflict began in 1953 over territorial claims, the 1962 Sino-Indian war and its disastrous consequences for the non-aligned India moved the Chinese threat factor from the periphery of New Delhi's threat perception circle to its centre, triggering incremental yet significant changes in Indian defence policy and military strategy. The subsequent Indian military reorientation towards re-equipment and operational reinforcement (e.g. the creation of ten mountain divisions designed for warfare in the Himalayas and increasing the Army's manpower ceiling to 825,000) confirms the demise of Nehru's *moralpolitik*-type policies regarding China. However, the fundamental shift in India's nuclear weapons position occurred when Beijing shocked New Delhi with the detonation of its first nuclear device in October 1964. New Delhi's subsequent reaction to China's nuclear capability demonstrated a paradigm shift in India's previously Nehruvian anti-proliferation policy towards what then Prime Minister Lal Bahadur Shastri reluctantly phrased as India considering "nuclear explosion for peaceful purposes". Compatible with the security-model's two policy scenarios, India's inability to develop its own nuclear weapons forced New Delhi to secure nuclear deterrence by joining a balancing alliance with a nuclear power. Accordingly, when India's request to the United States, the Soviet Union and the United Kingdom for nuclear guarantee was refused, India's only option for deterring a nuclear China and maintaining its national security was to obtain horizontal proliferation on its own, leading to the 1974 PNE.

Similarly, the regional-level analysis indicates the significance of nuclear weapons in India's quest for regional hegemony and security in the South Asian region, although against the much less significant threat of Pakistan. A quick glance at pro-Indian political scientists' analysis of the motivation of India's quest for regional security through nuclear weapons reveals New Delhi's mindset regarding Pakistani conventional threat as well as India's strategic policy manoeuvre to achieve several objectives at once. In the bipolar South Asian security complex, Pakistan was (and is) India's major regional security and strategic concern. In spite of its conventional inferiority to India, Pakistan attacked its greater and more militarily powerful neighbour in 1948, 1965 and 1971. While India's decisive military victory in the 1971 war, and the subsequent disintegration of Pakistan through the independence of Bangladesh, considerably weakened Pakistan, it managed to retain most of its military infrastructures. The series of Indo-Pakistani military conflicts convinced Indian strategists that Pakistan could use the period of Indian domestic political instability to launch other military attacks on India. In the light of alarming Sino-Pakistani cordial relations, and the presumption of Pakistani will to attack India, India's nuclear proliferation became instrumental in maintaining Indian regional security as well as establishing Indian regional hegemony through deterring Pakistan from future attacks. As Saira Khan formulates, the most efficient war-avoidance strategy for India in such conflictual regional settings was 'deterrence by possession of nuclear weapons.'

Similar to the Indian behavioural pattern for proliferation, but in contrast to India's multi-layered threat perception, the application of the security-model framework on Pakistan's nuclear policy produces a mono-causal explanation: Pakistan's nuclear proliferation was a linear reactionary policy to India's 1974 nuclear detonation. In addition to Indo-Pakistani territorial, ideological and ethnic elements of conflict that have formed the essentials of the South Asian security complex since 1947, the 1971 war and dismemberment of Pakistan reinforced Indo-centrism in Pakistan's threat perception. The war crippled Pakistan's economy and displayed the perceived unreliability of Pakistan's allies (i.e. the United States and China) in the time of crisis. Realising its conventional military inferiority to India, in 1972 President Zulfiquar Ali Bhutto initiated a nuclear policy in pursuit of nuclear weapons. Islamabad's nuclear program, however, gained a critical boost by India's 1974 PNE. Closely resembling the pattern of India's reaction to the 1964 Chinese nuclear test, Pakistan's nuclear policy was decisively directed towards inevitable nuclear proliferation after India's 1974 PNE. Against India's combined conventional military superiority and nuclear weapons capability, Pakistan had to obtain its own nuclear weapons as soon as possible to provide deterrence against the gravest threat to its national security. In this context, with Islamabad's failure to obtain security guarantees from the nuclear powers against a nuclear India, Pakistan had no other option other than to embark on its own nuclear proliferation program.

Applying the domestic-model of analysis on the Indian case clearly exhibits the decisive influence of two of the three domestic actors outlined by the model on India's nuclear decision for horizontal proliferation: nuclear energy establishments (consisting of pro-proliferation scientists and defence laboratories) and politicians eager to enhance their respective parties or/and individual standing in public opinion. Due to the pattern of the civil-military relationship in India where the former utterly dominates the latter, military elites as bureaucratic domestic actors had practically no influence over New Delhi's process of nuclear decision-making. After the Chinese 1964 nuclear test, Homi Bhabba, the head of India's Atomic Energy Commission (AEC), tenaciously lobbied for the allocation of required resources for developing nuclear weapons. Eventually, the AEC leadership's lobbying for proliferation along with pro-nuclear Congress party pressure on the government forced the reluctant Shastri to order the initiation of a classified project to develop technical ability to design and detonate a PNE within a certain timeframe. In spite of Bhabba's successor, Vikram Sarabhai's fierce opposition to any form of nuclear proliferation, the AEC developed an alliance with defence laboratories for lobbying the new Prime Minister Indira Gandhi. In a meaningful coincidence, the dynamics of Indian domestic politics in the early 1970s were defined in terms of economic recession, large-scale riots in various regions and the internal conflict in the ruling Congress party, thus an all-time low domestic support for Gandhi's government. In such dire circumstances, with the Prime Minister acknowledging that a theatrical nuclear explosion could have been a decisive 'political ace' for increasing her standing in public opinion, Gandhi's approval of 1974 PNE is hardly surprising. In a later interview, in spite of her initial denial, Gandhi admitted that the PNE "would have been useful for election". As the result, immediately after the detonation, public support for Gandhi's government and the ruling Congress party increased by one-third, both being "restored to the nation's confidence." Considering the pre-PNE Indian domestic politics dynamics, the influence of AEC, the Prime Minister and the ruling party on nuclear proliferation is evident.

Domestic-model Framework

In contrast, the application of the domestic-model framework on the Pakistani case constitutes the presence of non-political domestic dynamics and a higher level of military influence on the process of Pakistan's pursuit of nuclear weapons. As mentioned earlier, a year after the 1971 war and two years before Pokhran I, Pakistan's former leader Bhutto instructed the country's top scientists to concentrate on the development of nuclear weapons. Yet, such policies could not be pursued without the involvement of the military institution in the process.

Decades of military rule has promoted the Pakistani military as the strongest bureaucratic institution in the country, setting the pattern of the country's civil-military relationship in favour of military control. However, in spite of the military's vast influence in Pakistan's polity, nuclear decisions were made within a coordinated policy framework consisting of Prime Minister Bhutto, the chiefs of the armed forces, the Foreign Minister and the chief of joint services headquarters. The pro-bomb direction of Pakistani organic nuclear decision-making machinery was maintained even after the fall of Bhutto in 1977.

The policy momentum and continuity in the country's pursuit for nuclear weapons in the post-Bhutto era confirms the absence of a domestic politics perspective in favour of the strong presence of a national security perspective: all Pakistani political leaders with different attitudes and policy perspectives maintained the essentials of Bhutto's nuclear policy. As for the nuclear establishment agency's influence, however, a division in the scholarly literature is detectable: while Kapur introduces I. H. Usmani, chairman of Pakistan Atomic Energy Commission (PAEC) as the most important figure in Pakistan's nuclear decision-making during 1970s, Khan maintains that the scientific institutions' influence was largely barred by the institutionalised military, limiting their range of influence to the lobbying of politicians and military elites in favour of proliferation. Yet, in spite of Kapur's exaggerated emphasis on Usmani's influence, the dominance of the security discourse over Pakistan's nuclear policy process is to such a degree that the domestic model's dynamics echoes the trends of the security model.

Finally, analysis of India's Cold War period nuclear proliferation policy signifies the link between India's quest for obtaining international prestige as a mean of gaining 'great power' status and its pursuit of the absolute weapon. From India's perspective, a direct link between nuclear proliferation and international prestige existed: countries in possession of nuclear weapons enhanced their standing in the international system's power pyramid. Nuclear states, developed or underdeveloped, were (and continue to do so) taken seriously by other members of the international community because of the practical implications of possessing the ultimate weapon. India's perspective regarding nuclear symbolism was formed by observing the impact of China's 1964 nuclear explosion on Beijing's power status and international recognition of Chinese power which followed. In addition, China obtained its seat in the United Nations which had previously been denied. The United States' recognition of China's power demonstrated to India the symbolic importance of nuclear weapons in establishing a state's prestige. Remembering the existence of rivalry between the two states, the Chinese model of enhancing prestige propelled India to embark on a quest for horizontal nuclear proliferation to enhance its prestige, not only in the international context, but in regard to its territorial quarrel with China.

In contrast to India, and in spite of the 'Islamic bomb' rhetoric, Pakistan's nuclear proliferation program did not focus on enhancing the country's international prestige nor did it perceive nuclear weapons as a means of promoting a sense of Islamic nationalism. Reviewing the views of Pakistani scholars, strategists and officials regarding the country's motivations for nuclear proliferation clarifies the symbolic-model inefficiency for explaining the rubric of Pakistani proliferation policy. In an interview with Khan, former Pakistani Foreign Minister Agha Shahi rejected the existence of any considerations of symbolic type in Pakistan's military nuclear program. Similarly, the strategist Ross Masud, the Chairman and Director General of the Islamabad's Institute of Strategic Studies confirmed Shahi's view that the projection of Pakistani grandeur by nuclear weapons "has never been a factor in Pakistan's decision-makers' minds", contributing any enhancement in Pakistani prestige to an unintended "spillover effect". In this context, Pakistan's nuclear policy was fundamentally less concerned about the notion of prestige enhancement than national security. However, as mentioned by Masud, while the Pakistani horizontal nuclear proliferation could produce the prestige dimension, such an outcome could not be regarded as the cause of proliferation but as its secondary consequence. In addition, the much referred notion of the 'Islamic bomb' was in fact more of a rhetorical strategy to attract financial support from wealthy Arab states than a symbol of the Muslim states' international prestige. Therefore, the application of a symbolic-model framework on Pakistan's proliferation policy does not demonstrate the symbolic motive as a primary factor in the country's nuclear weapons development.

After outlining the general theoretical frameworks and their policy implication, the essay discussed India and Pakistan's motivations for horizontal nuclear proliferation according to the security model, the domestic politics model and the symbolic model, respectively. Analysing India's motivations through the security-model framework introduces nuclear China as primary incentive for India's nuclear proliferation and India's thrive for regional hegemony in the South Asia through deterring Pakistan as the secondary motivation. In contrast, the same model shows that Pakistan's sole concern for deterring India as its primary motivation for nuclear proliferation. In the domestic level, while India's nuclear policy was heavily influenced by leaders' political motivations and nuclear energy establishments lobbying – Pakistan's proliferation policy, witnessing a high level of military influence, lacked a domestic politics perspective and was mostly concerned with security perspective. Finally, while the application of symbolic model on India's nuclear policy confirms the significance of nuclear symbolism in India's quest for international prestige through nuclear proliferation, it demonstrates prestige angle as secondary to security-centric Pakistani proliferation policy.

NUCLEAR PROLIFERATION ISSUES

India (along with Pakistan and Israel) was originally a 'threshold' country in terms of the international non-proliferation regime, possessing, or quickly capable of assembling one or more nuclear weapons: Their nuclear weapons capability at the technological level was recognised (all have research reactors at least) along with their military ambitions. Then in 1998 India and Pakistan's military capability became more overt. All three remained remained outside the 1970 Nuclear Non-Proliferation Treaty (NPT), which 186 nations have now signed. This led to their being largely excluded from trade in nuclear plant or materials, except for safety-related devices for a few safeguarded facilities.

India is opposed to the NPT as it now stands, since it is excluded as a Nuclear Weapons State, and has consistently criticised this aspect of the Treaty since its inception in 1970.

Regional rivalry

Relations between India and Pakistan are tense and hostile, and the risks of nuclear conflict between them have long been considered quite high. In 1974 India exploded a "peaceful" nuclear device at Pokhran and then in May 1998 India and Pakistan each exploded several nuclear devices underground. This heightened concerns regarding an arms race between them.

Kashmir is a prime cause of bilateral tension, its sovereignty has been in dispute since 1948. There is persistent low level military conflict due to Pakistan backing a Muslim rebellion there. Both countries engaged in a conventional arms race in the 1980s, including sophisticated technology and equipment capable of delivering nuclear weapons. In the 1990s the arms race quickened. In 1994 India reversed a four-year trend of reduced allocations for defence, and despite its much smaller economy, Pakistan pushed its own expenditures yet higher. Both then lost their patrons: India, the former USSR; and Pakistan, the USA.

In 1997 India deployed a medium-range missile and is now developing a long-range missile capable of reaching targets in China's industrial heartland.

In 1995 the USA quietly intervened to head off a proposed nuclear test. The 1998 tests were unambiguously military, including one claimed to be of a sophisticated thermonuclear device. Their declared purpose was "to help in the design of nuclear weapons of different yields and different delivery systems".

It is the growth and modernisation of China's nuclear arsenal and its assistance with Pakistan's nuclear power program and, reportedly, with missile technology, which now exacerbates Indian concerns. In particular, China's People's Liberation Army operates somewhat autonomously within Pakistan as an exporter of military material.

Indian security policies are driven by:

- its desire to be recognised as the dominant power in the region;
- its increasing concern with China's expanding nuclear weapons and missile delivery programs; and
- its enduring concern about Pakistan, with its nuclear weapons capability and now the clear capability to deliver such weapons deep into India.

It perceives nuclear weapons as a cost-effective political counter to China's nuclear and conventional weaponry, and the effects of its nuclear weapons policy in provoking Pakistan is, by some accounts, considered incidental.

India has had an unhappy relationship with China. Soundly defeated by China in the 1962 war, relations were frozen until 1998. Since then a degree of high-level contact has been established and a few elementary confidence-building measures put in place. China still occupies some Indian territory. Its nuclear and missile support for Pakistan is however a major bone of contention.

India's weapons material initially came from the Canadian-designed 40 MWt CIRUS "research" reactor which started up in 1960 (well before the NPT), and the 100 MWt Dhruva indigenous unit in operation since 1985, using local uranium. CIRUS was supplied with heavy water from the USA and it was probably only after the 1962 war that it was employed largely to make weapons-grade plutonium.

Development of nuclear weapons apparently began in earnest in 1967. It is estimated that India may have built up enough weapons-grade plutonium for one hundred nuclear warheads.

In response to India's 1974 nuclear test explosion using plutonium from CIRUS, demonstrating that nuclear technology transferred to non-nuclear-weapons states for peaceful purposes could be misused, the Nuclear Suppliers Group was formed and began regulating nuclear trade, particularly with India. This is one reason why the closure of CIRUS is a condition of the NSG waiver in 2008.

Nuclear arms control in the region

The public stance of India and Pakistan on non-proliferation differs markedly. Pakistan has initiated a series of regional security proposals. It has repeatedly proposed a nuclear-free zone in South Asia and has proclaimed its willingness to engage in nuclear disarmament and to sign the NPT if India would do so. This would involve disarming and joining as non-weapon states. It has endorsed a US proposal for a regional five power conference to consider non-proliferation in South Asia.

India has taken the view that solutions to regional security issues should be found at the international rather than the regional level, since its chief concern is with China. It therefore rejects Pakistan's proposals. Instead, the 'Gandhi Plan', put forward in 1988, proposed the revision of the NPT, which it regards as inherently discriminatory in favour of the Nuclear-Weapons States, and a timetable for complete nuclear weapons disarmament. It endorsed early proposals for a Comprehensive Test Ban Treaty (CTBT) and for an international convention to ban the production of highly enriched uranium and plutonium for weapons purposes, known as the 'cut-off' convention.

The USA has, for some years pursued a variety of initiatives to persuade India and Pakistan to abandon their nuclear weapons programs and to accept comprehensive international safeguards on all their nuclear activities. To this end the Clinton administration proposed a conference of nine states, comprising the five established nuclear-weapon states, along with Japan, Germany, India and Pakistan. This and previous similar proposals have been rejected by India, which countered with demands that other potential weapons states, such as Iran and North Korea, should be invited, and that regional limitations would only be acceptable if they were accepted equally by China. The USA would not accept the participation of Iran and North Korea and such initiatives lapsed.

Another, more recent approach, centres on the concept of containment, designed to 'cap' the production of fissile material for weapons purposes, which would hopefully be followed by 'roll back'. To this end India and the USA jointly sponsored a UN General Assembly resolution in 1993 calling for negotiations for a 'cut-off' convention, the Fissile Material Cut-off Treaty (FMCT). Should India and Pakistan join such a convention, they would have to agree to halt the production of fissile materials for weapons and to accept international verification on their relevant nuclear facilities (enrichment and reprocessing). In short, their weapons programs would be thus 'capped'. It appeared that India was prepared to join negotiations regarding such a FMCT under the 1995 UN Conference on Disarmament (UNCD).

However, despite the widespread international support for a FMCT, formal negotiations on cut-off have yet to begin. The UNCD can only approve decisions by consensus and since the summer of 1995, the insistence of a few states to link FMCT negotiations to other nuclear disarmament issues has brought progress on the cut-off treaty there to a standstill. In connection with its 2006 agreement with the USA, India has reiterated its support for a FMCT.

Bilateral confidence-building measures between India and Pakistan to reduce the prospects of confrontation have been limited. In 1990 each side ratified a treaty not to attack the other's nuclear installations, and at the end of 1991 they provided one another with a list showing the location of all their nuclear plants, even though the respective lists were regarded as not being wholly accurate. Early in 1994 India proposed a bilateral agreement for a 'no first use' of nuclear weapons and an extension of the 'no attack' treaty to cover civilian and industrial targets as well as nuclear installations.

Having promoted the CTBT since 1954, India dropped its support in 1995 and in 1996 attempted to block the Treaty. Following the 1998 tests the question has been reopened and both Pakistan and India have indicated their intention to sign the CTBT. Indian ratification may be conditional upon the five weapons states agreeing to specific reductions in nuclear arsenals.

SOUTH ASIA AND THE MIDDLE EAST: PROLIFERATION LINKS

While an analysis of proliferation in the Middle East is outside the scope of this study, it is necessary to highlight existing and potential links between the Middle East and South Asia, apart from the A.Q. Khan network mentioned above. Khan's network provided significant know-how to Iran in the late eighties and early nineties (including centrifuge technology), though the full extent of these transfers has still not been confirmed. While nuclear links between Iran and Pakistan have ended for now, Islamabad's nuclear connection to the Middle East remains, such as through possible collaboration with Saudi Arabia.

From the South Asian proliferation perspective, the close ties between Saudi Arabia and the development of Pakistan's nuclear program is a crucial development. News reports as well as official U.S. government analyses have claimed that Riyadh provided considerable financing for Pakistan's nuclear and missile program in the past, but some reports now suggest a more proactive role by Saudi Arabia-in terms of nuclear energy development itself. This is in line with the announcement in November 2006 by six Arab states-Saudi Arabia, Morocco, Egypt, Algeria, Tunisia, and the United Arab Emirates-that they would develop civilian nuclear programs. Earlier, in 2005, Saudi Arabia applied for and was granted exemption from nuclear inspections through the IAEA's 'small quantities protocol.' Before that, a widely quoted 2003 report in The Guardian stated that Riyadh was considering three nuclear options: (a) building a nuclear deterrent, (b) allying with a nuclear power, or (c) working toward a nuclear weapon free zone in the Middle East. Recent developments suggest that a combination of the first two options might be adopted given that it is highly unlikely that Iran and Israel relinquish their nuclear programs in the near future.

This is where Pakistan's role could be significant. German news reports stated in early 2006 that Pakistani scientists assisted Saudi efforts to develop a nuclear program and that this was done under the guise of pilgrimages to Saudi Arabia between 2003 and 2005. Several high-ranking Saudi royals as well as government officials are among the few non-Pakistanis who have toured Islamabad's nuclear facilities.

These include defence minister Prince Sultan (now also crown prince) who visited the Kahuta uranium enrichment facility in 1999, and a son of the current Saudi ruler, King Abdullah, who attended a test of the nuclear-capable 950-mile range Ghauri missile in 1999. These developments suggest that if Riyadh decides to acquire nuclear weapons, the spotlight could be on Pakistan as one of the sources. A factor that could prompt Saudi Arabia to pursue nuclear weapons would be if Tehran unambiguously builds it own nuclear weapon, prompting Israel to shed the opacity over its arsenal.

While disincentives for Pakistan to go along this route are considerable (most notably, U.S. opposition), there are also incentives for Islamabad to aid the Saudis in their quest-cheap oil from Saudi Arabia, and a favorable endorsement for the Musharraf regime (or a successor regime) from powerful conservative Sunni religious and political groups within Pakistan. A 2003 news report quoted an anonymous Pakistani official who claimed that Riyadh and Islamabad had concluded a secret agreement under which Pakistan would receive subsidized oil in exchange for transferring nuclear technology. In 2004, Iranian government sources also claimed that they had information that confirmed this agreement, but there was no further corroboration of this from other sources. Therefore, even if there is no immediate possibility of such a transfer, Saudi Arabia could pursue this with Pakistan in the future to hedge against nuclear developments in the Middle East.

A key incentive for Pakistan could also be to use Saudi Arabia for strategic depth purposes. Islamabad's traditional geographic buffer against Indian military campaigns was Afghanistan, but that was lost after the fall of the Taliban in 2001. Ostensibly, Pakistan requires strategic depth to protect its forces (conventional and nuclear) from an armored offensive by the Indian military, which could cut off the country similar to the 1971 war. Saudi Arabia could provide a base for stationing Pakistani nuclear devices that would be safe from the reach of Indian missiles and give Islamabad a semblance of second-strike capability. This idea of looking towards the Middle East for strategic depth is not new. In the 1990s, former Prime Minister Benazir Bhutto, skeptical of the reliance on Afghanistan, recommended Iran as a more useful ally for purposes of strategic depth.

Apart from the Pakistan-Saudi Arabia link, concerns have also been expressed (especially in the U.S. Congress) over India's ties to Iran, at a time when the IAEA and western powers led by the United States are working toward controlling Tehran's uranium enrichment program. These concerns have arisen during the broader debate in Washington on the nuclear agreement with India. In particular, attention has focused on India's long-standing political and diplomatic relationship with Iran as well as the imposition of sanctions on two private Indian companies suspected of transferring chemicals meant for rocket fuel as well as chemical weapons. The Indian government claimed that both companies (Balaji Amines Ltd. & Prachi Poly Products) were doing legitimate business with Iranian firms. Balaji Amines insisted that they had been supplying products used for manufacturing life-saving drugs such as ampicillin and other antibiotics, but nevertheless, New Delhi ordered the company to stop all trade with Iran.

Both India and Pakistan have attempted to ensure that they are in compliance with the latest international regulations against Tehran's nuclear program. In February 2007, Pakistan froze assets of several individuals and other entities connected to Tehran's nuclear and missile projects in accordance with UN Security Council resolution 1737. In the same month, New Delhi banned exports of equipment and technologies to Iran that could be used in nuclear and missile development projects.

The Iran nuclear issue has been an important point of discussion in context of the Indo-U.S. nuclear agreement. The Hyde Act, passed by the U.S. Congress in December 2006, endorses nuclear cooperation between India and the United States, but it also states that New Delhi should assist the international community in clamping down on Iran's nuclear program. Furthermore, in May 2007, a group of U.S. senators sent a joint letter to Indian Prime Minister Manmohan Singh articulating their dissatisfaction over India's military ties with Iran, especially a 'joint defence working group' between the two countries. Nuclear ties between India and the United States are not limited to nuclear trade between the two, but also extends to discussions over restricting proliferation elsewhere.

Prime Minister Manmohan Singh has stated in the past that New Delhi does not favour another nuclear power in the neighborhood, and India voted against Iran at the IAEA in September 2005 and February 2006. However, two factors have restrained the Indian government from opposing Iran's nuclear weapons program more forcefully. First, the scramble for energy resources has made the Iran-Pakistan-India (IPI) natural gas pipeline a crucial economic issue for India. Stern Indian opposition to Iran's nuclear program would jeopardize the proposed IPI pipeline from Iran to India. The pipeline is considered to be of crucial importance to India in order to sustain high economic growth rates in the coming years. Thus, economic imperatives, specifically the need for energy sources, are an important factor in nonproliferation positions of countries such as India and China. In this context, New Delhi has reiterated that the construction of the pipeline will proceed in spite of pressures from Washington to cancel the project.

Second, for New Delhi, another variable is satisfying domestic political constituencies that are skeptical of the nuclear overtures from Washington that come at the cost of long-standing ties with Tehran. Since the Congress Party-led coalition government depends on parliamentary support from Communist parties, the government is obliged to periodically hold positions on contentious issues such as the Iranian nuclear program. The Manmohan Singh government has stated that it would be guided by India's national interest on the Iran nuclear issue, but this does not clarify to what extent India would be willing to go along with the United States on this issue. Some recent reports have also stated that New Delhi could play a more formal role in mediating the growing tensions over Iran's nuclear program in conjunction with the UN Security Council. However, it is unclear what form this would take.

In sum, nuclear issues in South Asia cannot be examined in isolation from developments elsewhere. Historically close political ties have existed between the South Asian subcontinent and the Middle East, and therefore, regional rivalries and bilateral relations play an important role in shaping decisions that impact broader nuclear issues, including horizontal proliferation.

Indo-U.S. Nuclear Cooperation

Since July 2005, when the U.S. and Indian governments unveiled their nuclear cooperation agreement, a debate has risen over its impact on the global nonproliferation regime. This agreement will allow India to acquire nuclear technology and materials from the United States and other suppliers. In return, New Delhi will designate which of its nuclear facilities are for civilian use and which are for military use. The former list would be opened up for international inspections. Prior to implementation, New Delhi will have to conclude a safeguards agreement with the IAEA, while the Nuclear Suppliers Group (NSG) will have to effect changes in its rules to enable nuclear cooperation between its member states and India.

The Hyde Act passed by the U.S. Congress in December 2006, authorized the Bush administration to bring into place a nuclear cooperation mechanism with India, after concluding a bilateral agreement under Section 123 of the U.S. Atomic Energy Act. Negotiations on the '123' agreement began in early 2007, but as of early June, talks were stalled on a few contentious issues. The disagreement is over five main items; (i) the right to reprocess spent fuel, (ii) the conversion of a voluntary moratorium on nuclear testing into a legal commitment by India, (iii) the assured supply of fuel by the United States, (iv) the return of all equipment to the

United States if India conducts a nuclear test, and (v) the level of inspections of Indian facilities.

The nuclear deal reflects an influential view in India that the nonproliferation regime embodied in the NPT is defective. According to Indian Prime Minister Manmohan Singh, the regime is ineffective and that the international community should introduce measures that restrict nuclear proliferation more effectively without suppressing peaceful uses of nuclear energy. At the same time, the contention is that India is a responsible nuclear state that has adhered to the guidelines of nonproliferation (without legally being part of the NPT regime) through strict export controls and denying nuclear assistance to other states, unlike the record of some nuclear weapon states.

A basic feature of this agreement is that by acquiring uranium from foreign sources (to free up domestic supplies) and by placing a set of nuclear facilities on the military list, India can increase its fissile material production for weaponization purposes. However, a different line of analysis examines the implications of increased uranium supplies in the context of India's fledgling nuclear submarine project. This perspective views that rather than increasing nuclear warhead production, New Delhi would use the expansion of its uranium supplies and enrichment capability to fuel its nuclear submarine project, a key element of India's desire to achieve a secure second strike capability under its credible minimum deterrence doctrine.

There are two separate lines of criticism of the deal; the first focuses on the nonproliferation objective, and the second on India's strategic needs. The first perspective is that the agreement will weaken the global nonproliferation regime by condoning India's nuclear weapons program. The argument is that by introducing India-specific changes to global as well as domestic U.S. nonproliferation laws, it will be more difficult to prevent nuclear transfers involving other countries such as China-Pakistan and Russia-Iran. A further objection is that even with 14 reactors under safeguards, 8 others will remain on the military list, free to manufacture plutonium for several nuclear weapons annually. Additionally, critics have stated that the agreement so far does not commit India to eschew nuclear testing formally, or to end fissile material production.

The second criticism comes most notably, from members of the nuclear scientific community in India, who contend that elements of the agreement would in effect cap India's nuclear program and constrain its thorium-based three stage nuclear project. They argue that while New Delhi has maintained a unilateral moratorium on nuclear testing, it does not want such a clause legalized in a bilateral treaty. The argument here is that India might have to reconsider its moratorium in the event that China or Pakistan conducts a nuclear test.

In addition, India's scientific community and government have insisted that it be explicitly granted the right to reprocess spent fuel for the three stage nuclear project that exploits the ample thorium reserves in the country (about 30% of the global supply). The Indian government wants to retain reprocessing rights as part of an advanced nuclear fuel cycle. This would involve recycling uranium oxide fuel while the consequent plutonium would be used with thorium in fast breeder reactors. However, some Indian scientific experts have stated that even if reprocessing rights and technology are not granted under the 123 agreement, it is likely that the initial reactors bought by New Delhi will come from Russia and France, rather than the United States. It is entirely possible that trade with these two countries, especially Russia, will involve reprocessing rights and sale of reactors and fuel. On the other hand, Indian analysts criticize the reported objective of the U.S. government of insuring that India's nuclear trade with other supplier states has equally rigorous conditions attached. Finally, Indian analysts have faulted the U.S. position of not allowing assurances of fuel supplies and of prohibiting India from stockpiling nuclear fuel.

Thus, the nuclear agreement between India and the United States has been criticized on the grounds of its potential impact on the global nonproliferation regime as well as its impact on India's strategic nuclear program. It must also be noted that since the bilateral 123 agreement between India and the United States is still under negotiation, it is too early to assume the eventual direction of the nuclear agreement framework. Even if the two countries conclude the 123 agreement satisfactorily (for both sides), India still must obtain approval for nuclear trade from the NSG and has to negotiate a safeguards agreement with the IAEA.

The China Issue

Several rationales have been offered as justification for the nuclear agreement (such as economics, strategic alliance, and nonproliferation benefits), but perhaps the most intriguing is one has been left largely unstated by the two governments-that of balancing China. Both India and the United States are concerned about the future direction of Chinese foreign and security policy. For the United States, aiding India through nuclear cooperation as well as a strategic partnership, Washington would be able to balance China more effectively in the region. In the process it would divert China from its main security issue-Taiwan. For India, the agreement is a significant diplomatic and strategic addition to its capabilities vis-à-vis China, with both the possible increase in fissile material production and a strengthened strategic partnership with the United States.

One argument supportive of the Indo-U.S. agreement stresses that China has built up Pakistan as a counter to India for several decades, a policy that involved transfers of nuclear and missile technology. It must also be noted that more than a year before the Indo-U.S. nuclear agreement was first announced in July 2005, there were reports in March 2004 that China was planning to provide Islamabad with a nuclear reactor. The implication is that that the Beijing-Islamabad nuclear partnership might have continued in any case. Nevertheless, it is important to consider the current pattern of nuclear cooperation between China and Pakistan in the light of the Indo-U.S. deal. Regardless of the pros and cons of the deal, it can be used by Beijing to lay the grounds for legitimizing continued nuclear collaboration with Pakistan. A sign of this has been China's argument that any changes in the NSG rules should be criteria-based rather than country specific.

In December 2005, China began construction of the 300 MW second phase of the Chashma Nuclear Power Plant (contracted in

May 2004), subsequent to the commissioning of the first phase in September 2000. Parallel to the Indo-U.S. deal, China and Pakistan also reportedly agreed to a nuclear cooperation arrangement under which as many as six nuclear reactors of at least 600 MW capacity would be provided to Islamabad. As of now, no other details are available so it is not clear what kind of safeguards will be installed, though some sources have stated that this initiative is being opposed by the NSG.

Reports of a possible Beijing-Islamabad nuclear agreement gained ground ahead of Chinese President Hu Jintao's visit to Pakistan in November 2006. However, no such deal was announced during the visit, leading to a conclusion that Beijing is possibly waiting to see the final shape of the Indo-U.S. agreement to gauge its impact on China. However, one influential Pakistani analyst stated that the lack of a public nuclear cooperation agreement between Beijing and Islamabad does not mean that such an arrangement will not come about; China can supply Pakistan with the required nuclear technology at a more politically convenient time.

Pakistan's desire for a stronger and more public nuclear relationship with China is in part because Islamabad failed to obtain a similar arrangement with the United States. Some Pakistani commentators have in fact argued that their country needs nuclear cooperation with the United States (and other suppliers, for that matter) more than India because the gap between existing energy supplies and future energy requirements is far more serious for Pakistan that it is for India.

A senior Pakistani official connected to the nuclear program, stated in October 2006 that Washington's nuclear policy should be guided by a "criteria-based" approach rather than one geared toward a single country. However, U.S. government officials have stated that they have no intention of considering a similar agreement with Pakistan.

It is likely that this refusal has much to do with the activities of the A.Q. Khan network as well as Islamabad's reluctance to allow a full interrogation of Khan by U.S. experts that would shed light on some unanswered questions related to the network.

Islamabad has cited the fact that Washington declined to offer Pakistan a nuclear cooperation agreement as a motivation for increased self-reliance on nuclear energy, through indigenous fuel manufacturing capabilities. In this context, government officials in Pakistan stated in April 2007 that the country would set up an installation for fuel testing for use in nuclear plants in a quest for "complete technological capability." As highlighted previously, Pakistan's overall agenda is to redress the perceived widening of the nuclear imbalance with India. Nevertheless, Pakistani experts have admitted that Islamabad's quest for increased nuclear capability is a result of the tacit rivalry between Beijing and New Delhi and the latter's desire to catch up with China. Apart from the impending nuclear technology transfers from Beijing, recent reports have also stated that the Musharraf regime has commenced construction of a 1,000 MW heavy water reactor that will potentially produce adequate plutonium for as many as 50 warheads per year. In addition, Islamabad is setting up a commercial scale nuclear reprocessing plant to allow production of weapons grade plutonium. Such activities would enable Islamabad to stockpile as much fissile material as possible before a future FMCT comes into force.

These developments suggest that Islamabad is attempting to diversify its nuclear weapons program through plutonium, as opposed to its traditional reliance on uranium as fissile material. Plutonium allows for more compact weapons and provides increased flexibility for the arsenal. For Islamabad, this is critical for developing a second strike capability against India. However, some Indian scientific experts have stated that even with the new Pakistani reactor, India will still be able to maintain an insurmountable lead in fissile material production through unsafeguarded reactors under the nuclear agreement.

Chinese support is key to Pakistan's quest for some strategic benefits vis-à-vis India, especially if the U.S.-India nuclear agreement reaches the implementation stage. In a possible attempt to reduce Chinese opposition to the nuclear deal with Washington, New Delhi has committed itself, in principle, to civilian nuclear cooperation with Beijing, a declaration announced during President

Hu's visit to New Delhi in November 2006. This could be viewed as an incentive from Beijing to dissuade India from a potential anti-China partnership with Washington. Nuclear trade between India and China is not necessarily an empty proposal; it has a precedent. In 1995, India acquired low enriched uranium from China for the Tarapur nuclear reactors. The official Chinese position is opposition to any NSG amendments that would adversely effect the non-proliferation regime, and that they would consider viable arrangements at the NSG, and not bilaterally. Beijing's response reiterates its view that any exceptions should not be India-specific and should include other states.

Interestingly, Indian Foreign Minister Pranab Mukherjee stated in November 2006 that New Delhi does not have any problem with a similar nuclear agreement between Pakistan and China. If this attitude is indeed the Indian government's position, the implication could be that New Delhi is confident that the benefits it will accrue from the agreement with the United States far outweigh the possible increase in nuclear cooperation between China and Pakistan.

Commercial Issues

The Indo-U.S. nuclear agreement also demonstrates that changes in the nuclear supplier regimes will not be restricted only to bilateral nuclear trade between the United States and India. Nuclear energy firms from several countries other than India are already lining up to negotiate commercial nuclear deals with India. NSG member states such as Australia are considering approval of changes in the group's rules to permit nuclear cooperation with New Delhi. Even though Australia (a major uranium producer) has not yet agreed to revoke the prohibition of supply to India, Australian companies such as BHP Billiton are anticipating lucrative sales. Other important members of the NSG have also supported civilian nuclear cooperation with India, within the appropriate IAEA safeguards framework. French and Canadian companies have also contacted the Nuclear Power Corporation of India (one of the main government nuclear energy entities), in connection with the supply of light-water nuclear power related equipment.

Thus, nuclear energy companies are important players in the future of this agreement as well as the broader nonproliferation regime. Firms such as General Electric and Bechtel have lobbied the Bush administration in favour of the agreement. Besides deals in the nuclear energy sector, the expectation is also that such cooperation will facilitate contracts in the conventional military sector, especially with respect to the impending deal for 126 fighter aircraft for the Indian Air Force, a deal worth about $9 billion. Aerospace giants such as Lockheed Martin and Boeing are among the contenders for the contract. Therefore, the implication is that the incentives go well beyond the nuclear energy sector.

Finally, it is instructive to consider the scenario if the nuclear agreement between India and the United States is scrapped, either because of insurmountable differences over the 123 agreement or later in the implementation stage. In India, several members of the influential atomic energy scientific community have expressed reservations over the agreement as have the communist parties and the opposition Bharatiya Janata Party (BJP). In the United States as well, there has been considerable opposition from nonproliferation experts as well as sections of the political establishment. It is not certain if the reservations expressed by the Indian government towards certain clauses of the December 2006 Hyde Act will be rectified in New Delhi's favour in the bilateral 123 agreement, which again has to be approved by the U.S. Congress. Given these complicating factors, the implications of scrapping the agreement are immense; affecting broader bilateral ties between India and the United States, the nonproliferation regime in general, and the global nuclear energy market.

SECURITY DISPUTES, NUCLEAR DOCTRINES, AND PROLIFERATION TRENDS

To begin with, proliferation issues in South Asia must be understood in context of vertical and horizontal proliferation. Vertical proliferation takes place as nuclear states modernize their nuclear arsenals with more reliable delivery systems and warheads. Countries including the United States, China, India, and Pakistan, are in the process of modernizing their arsenals through actions such as proposals for "a reliable replacement warhead" (as in the case of the United States). In the context of South Asia, nuclear modernization is mainly a function of prevailing threat perceptions arising from security dilemmas. Modernization of arsenals includes the development and testing of longer-range missiles-such as the tests of the Agni-III by India, and the Shaheen-II by Pakistan in the first half of 2007. Horizontal proliferation is the spread of nuclear weapons technology from nuclear states to other entities, including aspiring nuclear weapon states, as well as non-state actors such as terrorist groups. Horizontal proliferation generally involves a significant role for WMD supply networks that may or may not have a connection to official entities in a nuclear state. In the South Asian context, this variant of proliferation is especially pertinent, given the history of the A.Q. Khan network and its assistance to states such as North Korea and Iran. In addition, horizontal proliferation includes second-tier proliferation, where developing countries trade and barter nuclear technology with each other. While vertical and horizontal proliferation are variants of the proliferation dynamic, it is entirely possible that a nuclear state (such as Pakistan) could make use of non-state networks in the pursuit of nuclear modernization.

From the subcontinental perspective, one main question arises-given the lack of a comprehensive resolution of the disputes between India and Pakistan and India and China, how do nuclear doctrines in South Asia impact trends in the acquisition of nuclear and missile technology? The answer to this question links threat perceptions and nuclear doctrines with recent proliferation-related developments and requires a brief discussion of existing nuclear postures of India and Pakistan.

Subcontinental Rivalry

So what are the characteristics of the sub-continental rivalry that make nuclear proliferation in South Asia such a crucial security issue? Threat perceptions based on long-standing security disputes shape nuclear doctrines and proliferation dynamics. The intensity of disputes brings in security dilemmas that ensure continued dependence on nuclear weapons in South Asia.

South Asia is one of the most populated regions of the world, with India and Pakistan alone accounting for about 1.35 billion people. Both countries have been bitter rivals since partition of the subcontinent in 1947 that led to the creation of independent Pakistan and independence for India. The two countries have fought two wars over Kashmir (1947, 1965), one over East Pakistan/Bangladesh (1971), one limited war (Kargil, 1999) and the ongoing insurgency in Kashmir (since 1989). The 2001-2002 crisis further highlighted the dangers of terrorist violence provoking a conventional conflict that could lead to a nuclear crisis. Kashmir, which lies at the heart of the dispute, is more than a simple territorial problem. The province has a Muslim majority, and for India it is a symbol of its secular credentials as well as a repudiation of the partition, which was based on religion. For Pakistan, Kashmir is crucial because it is seen as an unfinished agenda of partition, which was supposed to provide a homeland for the subcontinent's Muslim community. Thus, Kashmir is an integral part of both countries' perceived self-identities. Since the 2001-2002 crisis, Islamabad and New Delhi have conducted several rounds of peace talks aimed at bringing a lasting settlement to the Kashmir issue. This peace process has involved several confidence-building measures such as strengthening of transport links between the two countries. The two sides also signed a crucial agreement on reducing the risk of nuclear accidents in February 2007. Nevertheless, the key dispute, Kashmir, is nowhere near resolution. This implies that both New Delhi and Islamabad are more inclined toward strengthening existing military capabilities, both conventional and non-conventional, to prevent an unfavorable scenario in a future standoff.

Apart from notions of sovereignty and nationhood, Kashmir is also of considerable strategic importance. Rivers originating in the Kashmir region provide crucial water supplies for food producing areas in the heartland. Furthermore, the Siachen glacier is also a region of military significance. The glacier, to the north of Kashmir, commands a strategic overlook of the small border between Pakistan and China and can potentially be used as a point of attack on India from northwest Kashmir. The glacier became a battle ground between the two armies in April 1984 and despite repeated talks, there has been no movement toward demilitarization. The complex rivalry between India and Pakistan involves territorial disputes based on notions of national identity as well as terrorist violence. Another integral element of the subcontinental security dyad is the role of China.

The China Factor

The role of China in South Asian security issues as well as in future conflict scenarios is crucial when considering two realities- (a) the historical animosity between India and China, and (b) the long standing 'all-weather' political and military alliance between Pakistan and China. Indian analysts often cite transfer of nuclear and missile technology from Beijing to Islamabad as evidence of an encircled threat to India. Through nuclear and missile technology transfers to Pakistan, Beijing restricts India to the South Asian strategic framework, and this constrains New Delhi's stated desire to seek a more global presence. From the Chinese political establishment's perspective, the concern is over India's defence expansion, its desire and movement toward a stronger regional and global role, and its increasing strategic connections with Washington.

Thus, any examination of the South Asian proliferation framework takes into account the Sino-Indian rivalry and dispute, the lowest point of which was the 1962 border war. In recent years, Indian and Chinese leaders and special representatives have met for regular talks on the border dispute issue; the most recent session (the 10th such round), took place in April 2007. In early rounds of these talks, China granted de facto recognition of Sikkim as a province of India, while India accepted Tibet as part of China. However, serious differences remain, and strategically important areas such as the state of Arunachal Pradesh have been claimed by China, while India has claimed Aksai Chin and certain parts of Kashmir handed over by Pakistan to China.

Despite periodic meetings, little progress has been made on these issues, and from time to time, controversial statements by each side threaten to derail talks. Whether a hardening of positions or a negotiating strategy, it demonstrates that the potential for friction is ever-present. Furthermore, there is also some dispute over an earlier agreement between the two sides to not insist on territorial exchanges of areas with settled populations, reflected in Beijing's recent demands that India cede Arunachal Pradesh, especially the Tawang tract. Therefore, in the absence of a permanent settlement, both India and China have adopted a hedging strategy to guard against any future strategic disadvantages.

A hedging strategy involves bolstering military-related capabilities in an ambiguous way that is not directly threatening to the adversary. At the same time, cooperative ties are encouraged without necessarily making any major concessions.

In part, such an approach is chosen due to uncertainty over the adversary's future intentions and capabilities and as a way to safeguard against a downturn in future ties or in the regional or global strategic environment. Therefore, modernization of nuclear arsenals in South Asia has to be considered in this context.

Similarly, in the case of India and Pakistan, despite sustained peace talks and CBMs, the two sides continue a hedging strategy to guard against future uncertainty, such as another crisis situation like Operation Parakram in 2001-2002. This is done by developing more reliable nuclear delivery systems (especially longer range ballistic missiles), perfecting and increasing fissile material stock, and acquiring conventional weaponry in line with contemporary war-fighting doctrines.

Thus, in South Asia, underlying security disputes, based on territorial rivalry and terrorist violence, combined with a need to expand the nation's global and regional position encourages future uncertainties that shape the actors' nuclear policy decision-making.

As mentioned earlier, apart from the Indo-Pakistan rivalry, strategic uncertainty, and suspicion in New Delhi is also generated by Pakistan's close military links with China. With China in the picture as a rival of India and a strategic ally of Pakistan, even if Delhi and Islamabad move towards a peaceful resolution of the Kashmir dispute, Beijing is likely to be the biggest factor in Indian threat calculations.

At the same time, the present threat perceptions between India and China are not the same as between India and Pakistan, which are more immediate and based on a 'hot' territorial dispute and state-sponsored terrorism. Nevertheless, analysts in New Delhi have long pointed to Chinese military modernization as a coercive threat to India. This modernization includes missile development, such as the current deployment of the DF-21 and DF-3 missiles in Qinghai and Yunnan provinces.

Furthermore, there is some suspicion among Indian analysts that though Beijing's stated policy is that of minimum deterrence, the stationing of missiles such as DF-3 and DF-21 reflects a posture of nuclear coercion, and under some conditions, does not preclude a first strike against its neighbors. It is also possible that since 1998, Beijing may have deployed nuclear weapons on the Tibetan plateau in response to a perceived Indian conventional military advantage and the May 1998 nuclear tests. Thus, despite growing trade between the two sides, there is some degree of unease in India over China's long-term intentions, more so in light of predictions of increased competition between the two countries for global energy resources. The concern in New Delhi is that if bilateral relations take a negative turn at some point in the future, China's current military modernization will give Beijing a significant advantage.

The Sino-Indian security dilemma is also a function of China's desire to establish close relationships with other countries in the Indian Ocean region (most notably Myanmar), a policy that is seen as a potential threat by India and termed as "strategic containment." For India and China, the security dilemma also arises from threat perceptions based on consequences of future nationalistic tendencies. Both sides fear that a rise in nationalism in the other could lead to more hostile attitudes.

China's concerns over future expansions of the U.S. nuclear arsenal, missile defence and space dominance plans also lessen the possibility of any immediate restraint with respect to Beijing's nuclear plans. Therefore a chain reaction exists in South Asia where New Delhi, at the very least, wants to maintain its current relative capabilities vis-à-vis Beijing, if not actually improve them.

The interconnected security dilemmas in the Asia-Pacific region shape defence policies and impact stability.

NON-STATE ACTORS AND SECURITY IN SOUTH ASIA

As aforementioned, nuclear weapons development and enhancement in South Asia are intricately related to long-standing rivalries between the concerned states. However, instability does not just stem from the risk of nuclear warfare between states in the region. Non-state actors also play a significant role in the nuclear security framework, aside from their role in facilitating nuclear proliferation. First, terrorist groups (such as Jaish-e-Mohammed and Lashkar-e-Toiba) that are connected to the Pakistani religious-political establishment can provoke tensions between India and Pakistan through mass casualty attacks. This was amply demonstrated following the December 2001 attack on the Indian Parliament by Jaish-e-Mohammed militants, which led to a ten-month stand-off between the two armies.

A second danger is through a Kargil-style episode in which militants, in cooperation with official Pakistani agencies and the military, occupy territory in Kashmir. As the July 2007 siege of the Lal Masjid (Red Mosque) complex in the heart of Islamabad showed, militant groups are steadily expanding their geographical area of influence, adversely affecting the stability of Pakistan. Although the nuclear weapon complex is under military control, there might be pockets within the military that are sympathetic to fundamentalist groups. At the very least, political and religious instability in Pakistan creates uncertainty in the minds of policymakers within and outside the region.

Finally, fears have been heightened since 9/11 over the possibility of nuclear weapons technology transfers from Pakistan to terrorist networks, especially after it was revealed that some senior Pakistani nuclear scientists met with the Al Qaeda leadership prior to 9/11. A related concern in the aftermath of 9/11 is that a fundamentalist Islamic group with Taliban/Al Qaeda links could take over Pakistan and with it, possession of the country's nuclear arsenal. Thus, Indian (as well as U.S.) threat perceptions include not just bilateral nuclear stability issues between India and Pakistan, but also the consequences of nuclear technology and materials falling into the hands of militant groups.

In general, the complex nuclear weapons scenario in South Asia is shaped by two main factors. First, the intense nature of the dispute between India and Pakistan strikes at the very core of their nationhood. It involves territorial disputes and terrorist violence, and is further complicated by the desire of some terrorist groups to acquire non-conventional technology. Second, South Asia is part of a broader nuclear weapons context that includes China and the United States. Military developments by either Washington or Beijing, which are perceived as a direct threat, also impact military policies (both conventional and non-conventional) in South Asia. At the same time, the continued strategic military collaboration between China and Pakistan (such as the joint development of the JF-17 fighter plane) is a factor that motivates India to continue nuclear and conventional modernization. Furthermore, while the territorial disputes between India and China are relatively dormant, there is no final resolution. As developments in 2006-2007 demonstrated, there is still a considerable gap between the two sides on the territorial issue. Due to this combination of factors, there are no clear incentives for either party to drastically reorient its nuclear policy.

Nuclear Policies in South Asia

Keeping the various security disputes and attitudes in mind, the next step is to consider the nuclear doctrines and policies of protagonists in the region. Both India and Pakistan strive for a minimum deterrent. The objective of India's nuclear strategy is credible minimum deterrence (CMD), meaning a secure and reliable second-strike capability after absorbing an adversary's first strike. The main potential targets of this projected deterrence capability are Pakistan and China. Pakistan's nuclear doctrine also seeks a credible deterrent, against India, and according to one senior nuclear weapons planner, its weapons are "aimed solely at India." In particular it seeks to deter New Delhi from launching a conventional military attack such as an offensive for limited war objectives, including destruction of terrorist training camps, as well as attacks on nuclear facilities.

For both India and Pakistan, key components of their attitudes in nuclear defence demonstrate the incompatibility between their mutual nuclear postures. India's offer of a no-first use pact has been rejected by Pakistan as nuclear weapons are an integral element of its (Islamabad's) defence doctrine. On the other hand, Islamabad has offered New Delhi a no-war pact, which ostensibly would reduce the prospect of full-scale conventional war and the risk of nuclear crises. However, such a proposal does not touch upon the proxy war waged by the Kashmiri militants and therefore has been rejected by New Delhi.

Thus, both India and Pakistan strive for a secure second-strike capability as an integral element of their credible minimum deterrent doctrines. Since neither side has constructed systems that are deemed completely satisfactory and reliable, nuclear modernization continues. For India, this means a survivable delivery mechanism that can conceivably strike major cities in China. At present the longest range deployed missile is believed to be the Agni-II with a range of 2,000-2,500 km, and can reach parts of western China. To have an increased range capability, the Indian Defence Research and Development Organization (DRDO) is developing the Agni III intermediate range ballistic missile, which was successfully tested for the first time in April 2007 and has a range of about 3,500 km. Nevertheless, reports have stated that the Indian military is not altogether satisfied with the nuclear capable missiles that are in its arsenal-Prithvi I (short range ballistic missiles) and the Agni I & II. Thus, India's nuclear delivery systems are deemed far from adequate and for the time being. In the opinion of the Indian Air Force, there will be considerable reliance on fighter bombers such as the Mig 27, Jaguar, and Mirage-2000 for a nuclear delivery role.

This implies that for the foreseeable future, the Indian scientific-military establishment will reinforce their commitment to adequate delivery systems, especially the Agni III and the nuclear submarine project (the Advanced Technology Vessel or ATV) that could carry a sea-based deterrent in the form of a submarine-launched cruise missile (the Sagarika-currently under development). Reports in May 2007 stated that the ATV will be commissioned in 2011-2012 and that two Russian nuclear submarines might be leased before that. As stated earlier, Pakistan's deployed missile systems can reach most parts of India. These deployed missiles include the Ghaznavi (Hatf-3, range 290 km), Shaheen-I (Hatf-4, range 600-800 km), and the Ghauri-I (Hatf-5, range 1,500 km). Development is also taking place on the Shaheen-II (Hatf-6, range 2,000-3,000 km), which was successfully tested in February 2007. These missile developments illustrate Pakistan's desire for a more secure deterrent, once the range issue had been dealt with. In addition, Pakistan is also seeking a more secure second-strike capability through the acquisition of the Agosta 90B class submarine in late 2007. This vessel, the second to be added to Pakistan's navy, can carry the nuclear capable Harpoon cruise missiles.

Both countries have also achieved considerable progress in manufacturing another delivery system-cruise missiles. India, in partnership with Russia, has developed the BrahMos, while Pakistan has the Babur. These missiles are meant to have land, sea, and air versions, and at least in the case of the BrahMos, will also have a variant for export. In the near future, Indian defence planners hope to introduce land attack cruise missiles with the capacity to carry a nuclear warhead over 1,500 km. In addition, submarine and air force versions of the BrahMos are due to be tested in 2007. The missile is also being installed on ships and IL-38D maritime reconnaissance aircraft to give "strategic relevance" to the Indian Navy. Similarly, Pakistan has successfully tested its nuclear capable Babur (Hatf VII) cruise missile (range 700 km), most recently in March 2007.

In sum, in order to strengthen their nuclear delivery capabilities both India and Pakistan are seeking to perfect their missile arsenals, both ballistic and cruise. The dynamic nature of the pursuit of more reliable deterrence capabilities is also affected by strategic developments involving extra-regional actors, especially China and the United States.

Fissile Material Accumulation

The final factor with an impact on nuclear acquisition dynamics is fissile material production. The renewed discussion on the Fissile

Material Cutoff Treaty (FMCT) in 2006 focused attention on the attitudes of India and Pakistan (among other concerned states). The argument put forward by some is that capping the production of fissile material in South Asia would be an important step toward nuclear stability in the subcontinent. However, issues arising from the South Asian security dilemma play a role in stalled FMCT negotiations.

As some analysts have stated, a key motivation for Washington's support of the FMCT is to limit China's nuclear arsenal. Beijing is unlikely to agree to the FMCT under the current circumstances without amelioration of its concerns. If Beijing does not accept the treaty, there is little chance that New Delhi would accept it either resulting in Islamabad's refusal as well. While the Chinese government considers the FMCT to be crucial, its concern also lies in progress on a framework for the Prevention of an Arms Race in Outer Space (PAROS). Beijing has effectively linked progress on the FMCT to that on PAROS. Further, while Beijing is supposed to have stopped fissile material production, there is no official confirmation of this. In addition, theoretically the Chinese government can restart production of fissile material.

The lack of progress on PAROS is said to have been one of the reasons behind China's anti-satellite test in January 2007. Certain policymakers and analysts in the United States perceived the tests as symbolic of the potential military threat from China, a view that reinforces their arguments for the need for dominance in space. In response, China needs to counter a future U.S. national missile defence (NMD), possibly by increasing its quantity of warheads through increased fissile production. China's concern is that U.S. policies under the Bush administration, such as the withdrawal from the ABM Treaty and the reinforced focus on NMD, degrade Beijing's deterrent, which relies on about two dozen intercontinental ballistic missiles (ICBMs). Also, Washington's reluctance to consider a "no first use" policy increases the threat perception of the U.S. use of nuclear weapons in a Taiwan crisis.

From the Indian perspective, Beijing's anti-satellite test refocused the attention of analysts on the considerable gap between Indian and Chinese aerospace capabilities and its consequences for the strategic balance. Indian defence scientists have stated that India would take appropriate measures to deal with this expansion of Beijing's offensive capabilities, possibly through collaboration between the Defence Research and Development Organization (DRDO) and the Indian Space Research Organization (ISRO). The test came at a time when both India and China are pushing ahead with space-based projects (especially lunar missions) and this would be the sign of a new rivalry. Thus, security perceptions in South Asia (including by extension China and the United States) contain a reinforced belief in the necessity of nuclear weapons and delivery systems development.

Even if China maintains its undeclared moratorium on fissile material production, it is unclear if India would consent to capping its fissile stock at a level much lower than that of China. This also strengthens the argument of Indian analysts who advocate more than just the minimum deterrent-related warheads stockpile and propose a thermonuclear arsenal. Furthermore, the Indian government also has a problem with the lack of verification measures in the existing FMCT proposals. Pakistan for its part has opposed any FMCT that would effectively perpetuate the fissile material asymmetry in the subcontinent, and wants negotiations to cover existing stocks as well. Pakistan's contention is that since its nuclear weapons program is a product of the threat from India, Islamabad would consent to a cap on fissile material production only as part of a bilateral moratorium.

However, since New Delhi's nuclear weapon expansion is driven by the need to construct a secure deterrent against Beijing, such a proposal is a non-starter in the present circumstances. Thus, while Pakistan may have reached the fissile material capacity to suit its credible minimum deterrent needs, this is not necessarily the case for India. Nevertheless, in the context of the proposed FMCT, some Indian analysts have stated that New Delhi has to decide whether its existing stocks are adequate for "strategic purposes," and if so, the FMCT could be beneficial for international stability.

In sum, from the South Asian perspective, there are no credible proliferation disincentives that would surmount security concerns driving India and Pakistan toward strengthening their nuclear capabilities. In essence, nuclear modernization, or vertical proliferation is likely to continue in South Asia. Next, we turn to the issue of horizontal proliferation in the South Asian context.

SOUTH ASIA AND HORIZONTAL PROLIFERATION

As a starting point, it is helpful to focus on cases of horizontal proliferation elsewhere that are connected to South Asia. This includes potential WMD supply routes as well as entities that might be involved, some of whom may be operating outside state control. In particular, the focus is on connections between entities in Pakistan and proliferation dynamics in other regions. Three major issues need to be addressed-(i) the North Korean nuclear program, and in particular the impact of the October 2006 nuclear test on South Asia; (ii) the current state of the A.Q. Khan network and its implications for WMD supply trends; and (iii) proliferation links between South Asia and the Middle East.

The North Korean Nuclear Test and South Asia

As expected, North Korea's nuclear test put renewed focus on the dangers of nuclear proliferation, and policymakers in India assumed it would lead to more stringent criticism of its nuclear agreement with the United States. Indian experts expected the North Korean test to impact especially on any nuclear test-related provisions of the nuclear agreement with the United States. Consequently, New Delhi swiftly condemned the test and indirectly highlighted Islamabad's contribution to Pyongyang's nuclear test. Some Indian officials even stated that Pyongyang's illegal acquisition of nuclear technology would actually spur reluctant supplier countries (such as Australia) to legitimately sell nuclear fuel to India, especially since it would be used for civilian purposes.

On the other hand, Islamabad refuted any suggestion that the activities of the A.Q. Khan network had contributed to Pyongyang's test, stating that North Korea's nuclear program is based on plutonium while Pakistan relies on uranium. In this manner, both India and Pakistan tried to ensure that proliferation in South Asia was not equated with proliferation in Northeast Asia. To a certain extent, the Bush administration obliged the subcontinental nuclear powers, as senior officials dismissed any parallels between North Korea's path to nuclear weapons to those of India and Pakistan. However, while Pakistan denied any links to the test, it did not help Islamabad's case when Japanese sources stated that days before Pyongyang's test, several Pakistani nuclear technicians arrived in North Korea through China. This augmented the suspicions that Pakistani agencies may have had some role in the test, perhaps through data sharing before or after the explosion.

The A.Q. Khan Network and Proliferation Dynamics

The A.Q. Khan network, which provided nuclear assistance to North Korea and Iran, has represented the most serious proliferation problem in recent years. Since Khan's public confession in February 2004, the Musharraf regime has consistently asserted that this network was the work of a rogue scientist and that the Pakistani government and its military leaders were not involved in these activities. However, it is not clear to what extent this assertion is accurate. Analysts and officials in Pakistan as well as in the United States have expressed skepticism over Khan's confession as well as the implicit professed innocence of the Pakistani political and military establishment. A highly publicized report released in April 2007 by the London-based International Institute for Strategic Studies, also stated that individuals and entities involved in the network could still be dormant and can conceivably be reactivated in the future.

So far, Islamabad has refused to allow foreign interrogators to question Khan even though the U.S. government has regularly expressed dissatisfaction over information released by Pakistan. > Furthermore, most individuals connected to the network are still at large, including important figures such as B.S.A. Tahir, while others, such as Henk Slebos, have been given light sentences. Moreover, the Khan claimed in a signed statement that successive army chiefs in the 1990s (Generals Mirza Aslam Beg and Jehangir Karamat) had authorized the sales of nuclear technology. While this could be taken as Khan's attempts to remove the burden of guilt, it is true that the military was closely associated with the nuclear and missile programs. In fact, in 1990, Gen. Beg warned U.S. government officials that Pakistan would be forced to provide nuclear technology to Tehran if Washington did not offer support to Pakistan.

Other circumstantial evidence, such as visits by the Pakistani military leadership to North Korea throughout the nineties, suggests that there was a barter deal between Pyongyang and Islamabad (uranium enrichment technology in exchange for missiles). Additionally, in August 2005, Gen. Musharraf conceded that Khan had transferred centrifuge machines to North Korea through which uranium hexafluoride (which was also transferred) can be enriched for eventual processing into civilian reactors fuel or for military purposes. Shipping out such large centrifuge machines without the military's knowledge would have been impossible. Therefore, it would have been highly unlikely that these activities were carried out without the military's acquiescence. On a side note, it is possible that Washington's attitude was colored by the need to retain Islamabad's support in the anti-Taliban/Al Qaeda campaign in Afghanistan.

Additionally, for a country to acquire a nuclear delivery system (such as the No Dong missiles transferred to Pakistan), the decision-making process incorporates several factors, as well as the opinions of numerous government agencies to ensure compatibility among the various systems. It is therefore not very plausible that a nuclear-missile barter deal with such serious and risky international consequences could have been approved without cooperation from senior levels of the political-military establishment in Pakistan. The issue of the Pakistani military-scientific establishment's involvement (or endorsement) in the Khan's network activities is crucial due to its implications for contemporary proliferation routes and processes. If these elements within and outside Pakistan (including non-Pakistani nationals) and their methods and routes remain undiscovered, it has two broad consequences for proliferation in South Asia.

First, it allows Islamabad to potentially procure missile and nuclear technology in the future, in an attempt to catch up with India. In this regard, a Pakistani national, Mohammed Aslam, working at the Tabani Corporation's Moscow office, was named by the Russian government in 2006 as having attempted to acquire dual-use technology and other materials for Pakistan's nuclear and missile development programs. This example demonstrates that elements of the network are still active, though it is unclear if they are directly connected to Pakistani nuclear and missile development programs. Given Islamabad's need to construct a secure deterrent against India (especially long-range missiles that can reach southern and eastern India), it is possible that the above case is an instance of continuing efforts to exploit non-state networks to procure prohibited equipment. As one analyst noted, due to Pakistan's apparent inability to acquire nuclear weapons components legally, it is encouraged to look toward illegal sources. Furthermore, according to some experts, apart from Pakistan, other countries can easily utilize the same supply networks. The Iranian government has made use of these networks for its nuclear and missile programs. As the previously mentioned IISS report states, Tehran controls a clandestine nuclear materials network comparable to the one run by Khan, and in the past has procured technology from some of the same suppliers used by Khan. In context of nuclear proliferation networks, a further concern is that if North Korea dismantles its nuclear weapons program, it will create a potential source of unwanted nuclear materials in the process. Such discarded, but nevertheless lethal technology, could be bought by illegal nuclear supply entities that may or may not have had any connection to the Khan network.

Second, the continued existence of the kind of middlemen that the network generated increases the possibility of nuclear technology leakage out of Pakistan in the event of a coup or widespread instability from radical groups. Since 9/11, there have been periodic fears of internal upheavals in Pakistan, especially from groups linked to the Taliban. Recent reports have also stated that two nuclear scientists from the Pakistan Atomic Energy Commission (PAEC) were kidnapped by the Taliban in late 2006, and as of March 2007 remained in captivity in the Waziristan area. > Soon after that kidnapping, there was an aborted attempt to capture six more PAEC officials in the North West Frontier Province of Pakistan in January 2007. While it is not clear if the officials and scientists were targeted specifically because of their links to Pakistan's nuclear program, these incidents demonstrate the potential danger of non-state actors' participation in the illegal market in nuclear technology. In order to demonstrate to the international community that it is a responsible nuclear power, Islamabad has decided to set up a "Strategic Export Control Division" in its foreign ministry that will ostensibly prevent prohibited WMD-related technology from being exported. However, this does not necessarily address the problem of possible involvement of government entities and officials that have remained under the radar even after the network was uncovered. In general, the proliferation-related fear for U.S. policymakers is twofold-first, that nuclear technology could be transferred to a terrorist organization; and second, that the Musharraf regime could be overthrown, resulting in uncertainty for the counter-terrorism as well as nonproliferation campaigns.

The case of Pakistan demonstrates the difficulty that arises when nonproliferation goals collide with other strategic imperatives such as counter-terrorism. While the Khan network problem is one of the reasons why Washington has refused to offer a nuclear cooperation agreement to Pakistan, the perceived tilt toward India (through the Indo-U.S. nuclear agreement) can also be a reason why Washington has not pressured Islamabad any further on the A.Q. Khan issue. Nevertheless, in January 2007, in a proactive step, the U.S. Congress under the Democratic leadership passed the Nuclear Black Market Counter Terrorism Act, which authorizes the administration to implement "punitive actions" against states condoning or cooperating with entities actively engaged in nuclear proliferation.

PAKISTAN-CHINA NUCLEAR DEAL AND NON-PROLIFERATION

Pakistan-China nuclear cooperation has always been under the certain obligations to non-proliferation concerns. It has been ensured from the very first day of cooperation between the two countries that mutual cooperation shall be only for peaceful purposes and will be subject to IAEA safeguards, which is evident by the *Article V(1&2)* of the Nuclear Cooperation agreement 1986 that *"The cooperation pursuant to this Agreement shall be solely for peaceful purposes and the two Governments agree that the recipient country shall request the International Atomic Energy Agency to apply its safeguards."* Moreover, all reactors provided by international community to Pakistan are safeguarded by IAEA. China has been a time-tested friend of Pakistan who has always been the sole supporter of Pakistan in any event of trouble. In spite of a huge criticism by international community, China has extended its cooperation with Pakistan, which is in line with the international obligations; therefore Pakistan would never create an awkward position for China before the international community by misusing any technology or equipment provided by China. Pakistan has also faced a lot of loss due to the so-called AQ Khan story and would not be able to face another incident like the earlier if happens; therefore, it has strengthened the security of its nuclear program according to international standards. Now, there is no chance of nuclear embezzlement in Pakistan.

The non-proliferation concerns of international community on Pakistan-China nuclear deal can be mitigated through the credible domestic legislation in both countries. According to NTI website, Chinese nuclear exports are governed by some certain principles, i.e. "(1) acceptance of IAEA safeguards; (2) peaceful use only; and (3) no re-transfers to a third country without China's prior consent. China has also promulgated domestic laws regulating nuclear and dual-use exports." (China's Nuclear Exports and Assistance to Pakistan 2003)

Pakistan has also adopted credible measures in this regard. Pakistan is member of multiple non-proliferation conventions at international level and it has sufficient controls on its nuclear related entities. Recently Pakistan has given its stance about the efforts to promote non-proliferation at Nuclear Security Summit in Washington DC held on 12-13 April 2010, and assured the world community about the establishment of effective Command & Control system, Strict Regulatory Regimes, Extensive Export Control Regime and International Cooperation consistent with its National Policies.

Pakistan government has also taken credible legislative measures domestically against proliferation including nuclear, chemical, and biological transactions, which can provide an assurance to international community about Pakistan's commitment to non-proliferation. Pakistan has taken multiple measures which are supported with rules regarding licensing, diversion and 'catch all clause' providing heavy penalties of imprisonment up to 14 years or Rs. 5 million fines, or both, or confiscating the property of the convict inside Pakistan or outside Pakistan, depending upon the nature of the crime. (IAEA 2004) A brief view of these measures is given below

- Pakistan Nuclear Safety and Radiation Protection (PNSRP) Ordinance, 1984 and PNSRP Regulation, 1990. Controls the transaction of radioactive materials and nuclear substances.
- Statutory Notification No. SRO-782 (1), 1998 provides controls over the export of fissionable material.
- Chemical Weapons Convention Implementation Ordinance, 2000 (Ordinance No.LIV of 2000). Regulates the transaction of chemicals under chemical weapons convention obligations.
- Pakistan Nuclear Regulatory Authority Ordinance, 2001. Ordinance. PNRA is established to regulate all kinds of imports and exports of radioactive materials and sources of radiation.

Berkeley Journal of Social Sciences Vol. 1, Issue 3, March 2011

- Export Control Act 2004, "The materials, equipment and services which could contribute to the designing, development, production, stockpiling, maintenance or use of nuclear and biological weapons and their delivery systems shall be subject to the provisions of this law." (Hussain 2006)
- Biological Weapon Bill 2010 (Proposed), It is proposed by the ministry of foreign affairs Pakistan to enact a law against the Biological weapon offenders, and suggests a death penalty for those who use or attempt to use Biological weapons, and suggests life imprisonment for those who

develop, manufacture, import, export, or possess them. (News 2010)

An evaluation of the elements of effective export control system and its presence in Pakistan has been evaluated by Nazir Hussain, According to an analysis of Pakistan India laws about prevention of proliferation at Stimson centre, "India's and Pakistan's export control legislation nearly mirror one another in substance and structure. Both pieces of legislation explicitly define relevant terms, and there is near symmetry in the layout and organization of the various provisions." (Saha, Ziad Haider and Souvik 2009)

Pakistan's nuclear posture also shows that it has adopted a strategy of 'minimum credible deterrence' with lower nuclear threshold. Following its MCD strategy, Pakistan does not need to have a huge number of nuclear weapons, therefore, Pakistan need not to clandestinely divert peaceful civilian nuclear technology to the military purposes. Moreover, Pakistan's nuclear program is Uranium based, which was developed purely through indigenous means. Pakistan has its own Uranium enrichment plants and sufficient natural Uranium reserves at its own soil; therefore, it does not need international resources for the development of its nuclear weapon program that may invite huge undue international concerns. The Khaleej Times editorial suggests that "the US needs to realize that it cannot control or dictate developments between third states no matter how distasteful they may be. It must not forget that China would not have done this if it was not comfortable with controls and security measures implemented by Pakistan. It is also a good opportunity for Pakistan to alleviate previous concerns about proliferation and prove it is a responsible nuclear state, one that deserves due respect." (Pakistan-China civilian nuclear deal 2010)

The so called allegations of nuclear terrorism regarding Pakistan's nuclear weapon, is also a part of international propaganda against Pakistan's nuclear arsenal. One should be aware that stealing, manufacturing, and launching a nuclear weapon is not a task that can be fulfilled by some terrorists. Nuclear weapons are high-tech weapons which involve a complex mechanism for explosion. Such kind of knowledge cannot be obtained or used without having an organized institutional support. Moreover, Nuclear weapons are useless in the absence of credible delivery system, which is also very complicated and impossible to be designed, manufactured, and launched. Nuclear weapons cannot be launched through simple rocket launchers. Without having the involved technical equipments and the knowledge about their complicated operations, it is impossible for any group to use those weapons. It takes a lot of time and efforts to become capable of acquiring and launching nuclear weapons, which is even more difficult for sovereign states to obtain despite having huge resources and capabilities. In this scenario, how it is possible that Pakistan's nuclear weapons can fall into the hands of terrorist. The whole debate in this regard is baseless and just meant for the purpose of creating fuss against Pakistan.

8

India's Nuclear Delivery Systems

Development continued on India's nuclear delivery systems - on 11 April 1999 India conducted a successful 14 minute test flight of the 2,500 kilometer Agni-II missile. "The entire process of achieving a minimum deterrent has been completed," Vajpayee announced following the test. "We are satisfied that we are now fully capable of defending our borders," he added. Pakistan responded with an eight-minute test flight of the Ghauri II three days later.

The promise of the Lahore Declaration proved to be stillborn. On 5 May 1999 two Indian army patrols in the snowy Yaldor area in Kargil, a border region next to Kashmir, were surprised to encounter a group of armed men, apparently from Pakistani Kashmir (known in India as "Pakistan-occupied Kashmir" or POK; in Pakistan they are called the Northern Areas or NA). This was the first contact with an infiltration operation from Pakistan to seize the mountain peaks inside India as an escalation of the long-standing Kashmir conflict, which would be become known as the Kargil War.

The "line of control", or LoC, between India and Pakistan runs across some of the harshest, most rugged, and highest territory in the world and consequently much of it consists of "unheld areas", territory so inhospitable that both sides abandon it during the brutal winters. It was because India had suspended patrol operations in the winter that made it possible for infiltrators to set up camp without being detected. The patrols that encountered them were the first of the season. Such areas had been opportunities for adventurousness in the past, as when the Siachen glacier was suddenly occupied by armed forces many years ago - becoming the highest and coldest battlefield on Earth. But this was the first time Pakistan had ever tried to exploit this particular region.It appears the infiltration operation was already underway during the signing of the Lahore Declaration The larger of the two patrol parties went to check on the strangers, and found itself in an ambush and lost four soldiers. Firing continued for nearly a week before aerial surveillance on 12 May revealed to the army realized that the incursion was far more serious than it had assumed. Around 500 heavily armed guerillas had occupied at least 35 well-fortified positions atop the ridges facing Dras, Kargil, Batalik and the Mushko valley. Cover fire was being provided by the Pakistani artillery, which had begun a systematic bombardment of National Highway 1A that connects Leh to Srinagar in the Dras-Kargil region.

Within days the Indian army moved nearly 30,000 troops into the Kargil-Dras area along with special forces dropped on the high ridges by helicopter, and the battle was on in earnest; "Operation Vijay" (victory) to recapture the heights was launched in late May. Pakistan initially claimed not to be involved with the infiltration effort, a remarkable attempt at dissociation considering that the infiltrators were very well equipped and supplied, came from territory controlled by the Pakistani military, and were clearly in direct contact with the Pakistanis from which they were receiving direct artillery fire support. Eventually the continued direct involvement of regular Pakistani forces made the pretense an embarrassment for Pakistan, which dropped the attempt at evasion.

Over the next several weeks India outmaneuvered Pakistan both on the battlefield and in international diplomacy. Heavy Pakistani fire directed by the infiltrators from their commanding positions made the situation very difficult for India, but Pakistani positions on the Indian side were progressively captured or cut off from support as the superior weight of Indian forces made itself felt. By promising not to cross the LoC itself, India garnered nearly universal international support - and especially active Amercian support - for its position, while at the same time by mobilizing its forces along the entire Pakistani border it signalled that India was prepared to escalate and use its full military strength if necessary to prevent a Pakistani victory. The objective of this operation seems to have been to try to obtain a limited gain on the ground - revising the LoC several kilometers in Pakistan's favour. The LoC has after all always been defined in de facto terms - it has no recognized status, it simply marks the effective zones of control of the two nations. The operation was calculated to circumvent India's military superiority - by picking the most difficult terrain possible for India's operations, and achieving the initial gain through stealth alone. Pakistan evidently hoped that international pressure would halt the conflict before India succeeded in driving the guerillas back.

By mid June the tide was turning, and by mid July the Kargil incursion had turned into a rout for Pakistan, both militarily and diplomatically. Pakistani forces retreated behind the LoC, and Pakistan suffered another severe blow to its international credibility, and in turn boosted India's prestige. After the end of the war Pakistani Prime Minister Nawaz Sharif asserted that the operation had been instigated without his knowledge - a claim, which whether true or not, was unfortunately all too plausible in Pakistan, with its tradition of the military operating free from civilian control.

The total depth of penetration across the LoC was no more than eight or nine kilometres at most. As intended by Pakistan, the operations for retaking the occupied areas were very difficult for India and this short, sharp war resulted in 474 killed and 1109 wounded on the Indian side (as of July 26, 1999).

A crucial but at the time unreported consequence of the Kargil War, tied in with the Indian mobilization along the Pakistani border, was the apparent deployment of at least five nuclear armed missiles. "Four nuclear armed Prithvis and one Agni were deployed for retaliatory strikes" according to Dr. Sanjay Badri-Maharaj, author of *The Armageddon Factor* (Indian Express, 18 June 2000). This would have been a preproduction model of the Agni-II, the first deployable Agni version. Sharif's demurral became even more plausible three months later when a showdown occurred between PM Sharif and army chief Gen. Pervez Musharraf on 13 October 1999. Acting while Musharraf was out of the country, Sharif fired him, but hours later Musharraf returned and overthrew Sharif in a coup (later to put Sharif on trial for his life).

Following the aggressive, destabilizing, and ill-conceived military operation of Kargil, the military coup in Pakistan did absolutely nothing to reassure India or the world regarding Pakistan's soundness and circumspection. The result was naturally even deeper isolation for Pakistan, on top of the sanctions that followed the 1998 tests, and the Kargil adventure.

Overt hostilities along the border continued to persist after the conclusion of the Kargil War. On 10 August 1999 an Indian fighter jet shot down a slow-moving Pakistani reconnaissance plane, killing all 16 aboard. The Indians said the plane had strayed across the border, though most of the wreckage landed in Pakistan. On 17 August 1999, India took the major - though belated step - toward formalizing its declared status as a nuclear power by issuing a six-page document detailing a proposed doctrine governing its nuclear arsenal, entitled the "Draft Report of National Security Advisory Board on Indian Nuclear Doctrine". The report, which was prepared by a government-appointed advisory board, was made public Tuesday by National Security Advisor Brajesh Mishra.

The essential points of this doctrine were that India asserted a right to possess nuclear weapons, and would pursue a policy of credible "minimum" nuclear deterrence and use nuclear weapons only to retaliate against a first strike. According to the draft, "Any nuclear attack on India and its forces shall result in punitive retaliation with nuclear weapons to inflict damage unacceptable to the aggressor." "India's peacetime posture aims at convincing any potential aggressor that any threat of use of nuclear weapons against India shall invoke measures to counter the threat," the draft said. It further stated that India would not use nuclear weapons against a state that does not have them or is not aligned with a nuclear-armed power, and that nuclear weapons would be tightly controlled and launched only with the authorization of the prime minister, or a designated successor.

The draft said the size, components, deployment and employment of nuclear forces would be decided in light of the strategic environment, economic imperatives and the needs of national security. But it took an expansive view of the concept of "minimum deterrence", recommending an arsenal that is able to deliver a nuclear blast from "a triad of aircraft, mobile land-based missiles and sea-based assets," one that can respond to an attack "in the shortest possible time" and employs a space-based early warning system. To raise the threshold for the outbreak of military conflict, India also would maintain highly effective conventional warfare capabilities, the draft document said.

The draft did not mention the Comprehensive Test Ban Treaty (CTBT) but it criticized the Nuclear Nonproliferation Treaty, saying it legitimized the possession of nuclear weapons by states that already had them. The official U.S. State Department reaction given by Spokesman James P. Rubin was that India was "moving in the wrong direction" by trying to create a credible nuclear deterrence. Rubin said "We think it would be unwise to move in the direction of developing a nuclear deterrent and encouraging the other country to develop a nuclear deterrent and thereby creating an action-reaction cycle that will increase the risks to both countries."

China also condemned the document; and Pakistan, which 15 months ago matched India's nuclear tests with its own, said it would soon be matching India's doctrine with a published doctrine of its own. Unlike from the U.S., the initial reaction from Europe was cautious. France welcomed the draft doctrine as a logical consequence of the decision to develop nuclear weapons.

The situation was cogently summarized by Tanvir Ahmad Khan in the Pakistani newspaper *The Dawn* on 24 August 1999: The present draft is a landmark for three major reasons.

- First, it gathers together in a forceful single document elements that had surfaced disparately and with a certain air of tentativeness since the tests.
- Secondly, it relegates to history half-way concepts like existential deterrence and recessed deterrence that had been debated in both India and Pakistan. In doing so, it

delivers a mighty blow to efforts aiming at freezing Indian and Pakistani capability at a non-weaponized level.

- Third, the nuclear doctrine as set forth in the text has hardly any meaning unless the weapons are manufactured and actually deployed in large numbers, and a sizable reserve of warheads and delivery vehicles is permanently maintained.

Tanvir Khan also observed that "the draft published at the moment does not add any transparency to the Indian targeting policy. Nor does it specify Pakistan or China as the principal zones of targeting." He also made some interesting assertions about Indian strategic literature: Some analysts define the objective as the destruction of Pakistan as a social and economic entity. The targets considered in the relevant Indian literature include six to ten Pakistani metropolitan centres, four hydroelectric and thermal power stations, flooding of Punjab, obliteration of Pakistani railway system with attacks on Gujrat, Bahawalpur, Hyderabad and Dera Ghazi Khan, and disruption of all sea communications with nuclear attacks on Karachi and Gwadar. It has been calculated that a total of seventeen nuclear strikes will achieve all the objectives. If Pakistan also draws up a similar list of countervalue targets, breakdown of deterrence and the ensuing nuclear exchange would mark the end of a civilization. Although a the time of its announcement, it was expected that the government in place following the elections in the autumn of 1999 would enact the draft doctrine formally, by early 2001 no action had been taken and the draft remained a proposal without official weight, except to the extent it reflected the thinking of Indian government officialdom.

In May 2000 the Atomic Energy Regulatory Board (AERB) which has been set up on 15 November 1983 by order of the President of India to exercise regulatory and safety functions for atomic energy in India was split off from the Bhabha Atomic Research Centre (BARC). According too an unnamed senior official of the Dept. of Atomic Energy (DAE) quoted by *Aviation Week & Space Technology* (19 June 2000), this split indicated that nuclear warheads for India's armed forces had entered series production. The separation "means the weaponization program at BARC is completed," explained the official. "It is a clear assertion that BARC does not want the AERB to look into its weaponization program." Instead, BARC will have an internal safety committee, which was set up by BARC Director, Anil Kakodkar.

The order for the split issued by Atomic Energy Commission (AEC) Chairman, Rajgopalan Chidambaram stated, "The regulatory and safety mechanism of BARC and its functions, hitherto exercised by the AERB, will henceforth be exercised through an internal safety committee structure to be constituted by the BARC director.... This is being done so as to ensure safety of the strategic nuclear program." Chidambaram added that the regulatory body is "always transparent" and has frequent interactions with the public. He said that BARC's internal committee will ensure compliance "wherever applicable" with the principles of good safety management as given in safety standards developed by the AERB. Despite the assertion of 'transparency' Chidambaram, speaking to a UNI reporter declined to give any details of the new committee saying that it was of strategic importance and details could not be revealed.

The DAE official said, "Most weapon laboratories have their internal checks systems, the Lawrence Livermore [Laboratories] in the U.S. being an example." However, he omitted to mention that in the U.S. the Department of Energy maintains independent oversight with the Defense Nuclear Facility Safety Board (DNFSB) which even includes reviewers outside of the DOE. S. Rajagopal, an expert on nuclear affairs and a professor of the Bangalore-based National Institute of Advanced Studies, observed that this decision effectively reclassified BARC as a nuclear weapons laboratory. "This in turn will eliminate the need to place it under the International Atomic Energy Agency (IAEA) safeguards programme," he said.

Chidambaram's eight years in office as Chairman of the Atomic Energy Commission ended on 30 November 2000 when he was replaced by Dr. Anil Kakodkar today took charge as AEC Chairman, and as Secretary to the Government of India, Department of Atomic Energy in a brief ceremony held at Anushakti Bhavan, CSM Marg, Mumbai. Kakodkar This continued the tradition since Vikram

Sarabhai's death in 1971 of having the top official in Atomic Energy be a leader of India's nuclear weapon program. As BARC director, Kakodkar had been the principal scientist involved in the May 1998 nuclear tests.

HISTORICAL SUMMARY OF ARSENAL DEVELOPMENT

Although India first tested a nuclear explosive in 1974 (euphemistically called the PNE, for "peaceful nuclear explosive") it did not become a nuclear weapons state - in the sense of having the ability to deliver nuclear weapons until 1986-88 when, according to Dr. Sanjay Badri-Maharaj author of *The Armageddon Factor*, a rudimentary delivery system was in place [Indian Express, 18 June 2000]. This presumably refers to a developmental delivery system based on the Mirage 2000 that began development in 1986, after an attempt to integrate a DRDO developed nuclear bomb with the Jaguar fighter-bomber failed. This system provided India with a usable but limited nuclear weapons capability, but the weapon system did not actually enter service until it passed a full field drop test in May 1994 at Balasore, though most observers thought that this milestone had been passed years before.

The US CIA testified before congress in 1993 that it did not believe that India maintains assembled or deployed nuclear weapons, although it believed India was producing weapon components. The CIA's HUMINT (human intelligence, as opposed to electronic intelligence) reggarding India's nuclear program is famously poor however (witness the U.S. intelligence communities surprise about the 1998 tests) so it cannot be accorded great weight; nonetheless it could be true that in 1993 India still had not taken the step of maintaining weapons in a ready-to-use state. There is a vague report though of "a few" weapons existing as early as the early 1980s. Chengappa relates that hardened concrete bunkers were built in the early 1980s at Mumbai to house India's weapons plutonium stocks, a few weapons. Gen Sundarji was shown these weapons in the mid-80s, an unusual step since the military chiefs of staff had not been briefed on India's nuclear capability even as late as 1990. These weapons may not have been kept fully assembled, but there is little doubt that India could have made them ready in a matter of hours (or days at the most).

India has several aircraft that are nominally considered "nuclear capable", the Mirage 2000, Mig-27, and the Jaguar. Due to the cost of integrating and qualifying an aircraft for nuclear delivery, and maintaining a cadre of specially trained pilots, it is unlikely that India would choose to deploy nuclear weapons on more than one or two aircraft types. Only the Mirage 2000 is known to have been qualified as a nuclear delivery platform, and the Jaguar is known to have been abandoned for nuclear weapons delivery due to technical problems. Thus it may be that the Mirage 2000 remains the sole air breathing nuclear weapon delivery system.

India has developed short and medium-range nuclear-capable missiles. These are the Prithvi (range 250 km, payload 500 kg), and the Agni-II (range 2500 km, payload 1000 kg). The first operational capability of a missile deliverable nuclear warhead was probably soon after the official deployment of the Prithvi SS-250 missiles in September 1997, which occurred after the successful completion of integration and testing of the warhead and missile during 1996-97. Reportedly four nuclear armed Prithvis were deployed during the Kargil War in June 1999. Also during this war was the first deployment of the medium range Agni-II, apparently consisting of a single preproduction model. The Agni-II was not qualified for full production and deployment until after the second Agni-II test occurred on 17 January 2001 at 10:01 a.m. IST (Indian Standard Time) when it was tested in its final deployment configuration. India reportedly is investigating development of an ICBM-class missile called Suriya.

Development of Current Arsenal in India

There are no official figures for weapon stockpiles at any stage of development of India's arsenal. The only figures that can be offered are either explicit estimates made from considerations of India's probable ability to produce critical raw materials and considerations of likely production plans; or are unofficial statements of uncertain provenance and authenticity. To show the problems with figures of the latter sort we have only to look at the statement by K. Subrahmanyam, a leading strategic theorist, that by 1990 India had stockpiled at least two dozen unassembled weapons, versus the May 1998 estimate by G. Balachandran, an

Indian nuclear researcher, that India had fewer than 10 weapons ready to be assembled and mounted on warplanes or missiles.

The types of weapons India is believed to have available for its arsenal include:

- a pure fission plutonium bomb with a yield of 12 kt;
- a fusion boosted fission bomb with a yield of 15-20 kt, made with weapon-grade ploutonium;
- a fusion boosted fission bomb design, made with reactor-grade plutonium;
- low yield pure fission plutonium bomb designs with yields from 0.1 kt to 1 kt;
- a thermonuclear bomb design with a yield of 200-300 kt.

All of these types should be available based on the tests conducted during Operation Shakti (Pokhran-II). It may be possible to extrapolate significantly from these device classes however without further testing. There is reasonable doubt about whether the thermonuclear device actually performed as designed. Even if this so, it does not rule out the possiblity that sufficent test data was collected to field a successful design with reasonable confidence of good performance. Interest has been expressed in the development of a neutron bomb (a very low yield tactical thermonuclear device), but this would probably require additional testing to perfect.

The most widely accepted estimates of India's plutonium production have been made by David Albright ([Albright et al 1997], [Albright 2000]). His most recent estimate (October 2000) was that by the end of 1999 India had available between 240 and 395 kg of weapon grade plutonium for weapons production, with a median value of 310 kg. He suggests that this is sufficient for 45 - 95 weapons (median estimate 65). The production of weapon grade plutonium has actually been greater, but about 130 kg of plutonium has been consumed - principally in fueling two plutonium reactors, but also in weapons tests. His estimate for India's holdings of less-than-weapons-grade plutonium (reactor or fuel grade plutonium) are 4200 kg of unsafeguarded plutonium (800 kg of this already separated) and 4100 kg of IAEA safeguarded plutonium (25 kg of this separated). This unsafeguarded quantity could be used to manufacture roughly 1000 nuclear weapons, if India so chose (which would give it the third largest arsenal in the world, behind only the U.S. and Russia).

Indian Nuclear Force Planning

Nothing is publicly known about official Indian nuclear force planning, but assessments made by opinion leaders provide a context for judging the prevailing attitude in Indian government circles

India's first effort to formulate a nuclear policy and the determine the means needed to implement it was an informal but authoritative study group that was set up in November 1985 to answer queries by Rajiv Gandhi regarding defense planning. It encompassed the three services (Navy Chief of Staff Adm. Tahliani, Army Vice Chief of Staff Gen. K. Sundarji, Deputy Cheif of Air Staff John Greene), leaders of BARC (Ramanna), the DRDO (Abdul Kalam), and the AEC (Chidambaram), and India's most prominent strategic analyst K. Subrahmanyam. The outcome of the group's deliberations was to recommend building a minimum deterrent force with a strict no first use policy. The arsenal envisioned was 70 to 100 warheads at a cost of about $5.6 billion.

In 1994 K. Subrahmanyam suggested that a force of 60 warheads carried on 20 Agnis, 20 Prithvis and the rest on aircraft would cost about Rs 10 billion over 10 years. In 1996 Sundarji suggested a cost of some Rs 27.5 billion — Rs 6 billion for 150 warheads, Rs 3.6 billion for 45 Prithvis and Rs 18 billion for 90 Agni missiles.

DELIVERY SYSTEMS

Agni-I

Thermonuclear warhead (200-300 kt)?, fission/boosted fission warhead (>15 kt)? "Agni" is Hindi for "fire" and is also the name of the Hindu deity of fire. There is some question as to the operational status of the Agni-I. For many years the Agni-I program has been described as a "technology demonstration", which was consistent with the design varaitions that were tried, and the employment of a solid/liquid fuel two stage design that would be undesirable for operational use. However in August 2000 the U.S. defense industry weekly *Defense News* quoted an unnamed senior scientist at DRDO as stating that India had 10 Agni-I missiles in service. He added that the unit cost of the Agni-I is about $5 million.

Agni-I awaiting launch (17 K)

Developed by the Defense Research and Development Laboratory (DRDL) of Hyderabad. The first member of the Agni family was successfully launched on 22 May 1989 from the Chandipur test facility about 250 km southwest of Calcutta at Balasore. The two-stage missile impacted 800 km downrange in the Bay of Bengal. The Agni-I has been tested at a maximum range of 1400 km.

The Agni-I first stage was based on the Indian Satellite Launch Vehicle (SLV-3) used in satellite launches since 1979. The first stage motor was 10 meters long and capable of delivering about 45 tons average thrust with a 50 second burn duration. The second stage was a shortened version of the two chamber liquid fuel motor from the Prithvi. Second stage control was achieved through engine gimballing by its hydraulic actuation system.

Agni-II

The medium range Agni-II system is the first true strategic missile (in the Indian context) deployed by India. The Agni-II is designed to be mobile. It was originally developed in a road-mobile configuration but its deployment is being conducted using a rail-mobile version. The strap-down (limited degree of freedom) inertial guidance system may be replaced in the future with a full inertial system. The RV is reported to have an optical terminal guidance, and speculation has been made about the possible use or future use of a external positioning reference system. The Agni-II is an indigenously developed system, descended from the SLV-3 space launch vehicle via the Agni-I technology demonstrator. A pre-production road mobile Agni-II (Agni-I?) is said to have been made operational during the 1999 Kargil War. The Agni-II costs approximately Rs.400 million per missile and is manufactured by a partnership of the DRDO and Bharat Dynamics Limited (BDL) in Hyderabad. It is expected that BDL will be manufacturing 10-12 missiles every year.

The Agni-II was test fired in April 1999 with a range of 2300 km; on its second test on 17 January 2001 it travelled 2200 km. When the missile system is inducted, India will have the capability to strike at targets at least 2500 km away (up to 3000 km using specific payloads, according to some estimates).

Although the government has on several occasions stated that nuclear weaponization was now complete, the fact remains that the second Agni-II test occurred almost two years after the first and by all accounts more must take place before a true deployable arsenal is available.

In August 2000 Defence Minister George Fernandes stated that the Agni-II had "reached the point of operationalization". A DRDO scientist quoted in *Defense Weekly* reported in August 2000 at that time two pre-production Agni-II missiles were fully operational. He added that the unit cost of the Agni-II about $8 million and that, if required, DRDO's missile research laboratory could produce, in collaboration with Bharat Dynamics Limited, up to 18 Agni-IIs a year. Following the second successful test of Agni-II, on 17 January 2001, Scientific Advisor to the Defence Minister V.K. Aatre said that the Agni-II missile would be inducted into the Indian Air Force by year's end. This test was the first time the Agni-II was test-fired in its final operational configuration.

The Agni-II can be launched in 15 minutes, as opposed to half a day for the Agni-I. It uses far more accurate navigational and guidance systems and is designed to operate on a highly mobile platform which lends flexibility and reduces vulnerability to strikes.

Given its range and India's geopolitical situation, most observers say that the Agni-II was developed as a deterrent against China (it has far more range than is required to cover Pakistan). If that is the case, India has some way to go since with its current range, the Agni-II can at best cover Chinese territory as far as the western cities of Chengdu and Kunming, if based in the central plateau of Bihar. Even if based in Assam, a somewhat improbable scenario, the missile would not be able to reach either Shanghai or Beijing. For this purpose, India is developing the Agni-III, a longer-range missile capable of reaching targets out to 3500 km and beyond. The first test of this vehicle, which will feature entirely new first and second stages, is likely to take place in 2001. Speaking to the Lok Sabha in February 2001 Defence Minister George Fernandes gave the time frame for induction as 2001-2002.

Agni-III

A follow on version to the Agni-II, to be called Agni-III, with a range of 3500 to 5000 km and a 1000 kg payload, is under development. This is expected to be the final variant in the Agni family. According to DRDO sources two approaches are under consideration - an enlarged solid fuel first stage with a 1.8 meter diameter and 36 tonnes of propellant, or an added third stage to the existing Agni-II. The principal objective of the Agni-III would be to develop a missile capable of reaching China's capital of Beijing. The *Deccan Chronicle* reported on 23 September 2000 that Defence Minster George Fernandes had disclosed that the Agni-III had almost completed the development stage and was ready to be test fired soon. *Yahoo India News* reported a senior defence department official as saying India plans to build the third version of the Agni IRBM, but is yet to set a deadline for the project (8 February 2001). "Agni-III will obviously be of a higher range and better capabilities than its predecessor," said the official, who did not want to be identified. "But we have not set a date to test it," the official said on the sidelines of an aerospace conference in Bangalore.

Suriya

A higher performance missile in the ICBM class (the Suriya or Surya) with a range of over 6000 km has been discussed. It would be an entirely new development effort. Dr. APJ Abdul Kalam, Principal Scientific Adviser to the Prime Minister, was quoted in the *Hindustan Times* on 18 September 2000 as saying that "All technologies and industrial complexes are available for an ICBM. It'll not take much time, should India decide on it." He discounted speculation that the ICBM will be the derivative of the GSLV, India's latest space launch vehicle. "Cryogenic engines (used for the GSLV) are good for satellite launch vehicles, not missiles.

They require huge fuelling facilities, which can be detected by satellite."

Prithvi

Prithvi (Hindi for "Earth") is a single stage, road-mobile, short-range ballistic missile (SRBM). The missile's corrosive liquid fuel must be loaded immediately prior to launch, which is a serious disadvantage in the field. On the other hand the ability to control the liquid fuel motor, including throttling it or shutting it down (difficult or impossible with solid fuel) gives it great flexibility in range and trajectory, including in-flight maneuvering. The liquid propellant also has higher performance than solid propellants, giving the Prithvi an unusually high payload for its size and range. The inertial navigation system has been reported to have a CEP (Circular Error Probability) equal to.01% of its range, or 15 m for the Army version and 25 m for the Air Force version at maximum range (this is roughly comparable to an ICBM having a 1.5 km accuracy). The missile uses its maneuvering capability to follow up to six different trajectories so as to avoid ABM interception, and confuse launch system counter targeting. Another defense measure the Prithvi has is the use of radar absorbing paint to reduce its radar signature.

The fact that both the Indian Army and the IAF operate versions of the Prithvi is the result of a turf war over control of ballistic missile systems, a scenario that has played out in many other nations. The outcome of this struggle was that the Army controls land based missiles with a range of 150 km or less (a limit that was set by the initial range of the Prithvi) while longer range missiles belong to the Air Force. The DRDO is attempting to increase the payload of the IAF version to 1000 kg, by using higher performance liquid propellants to generate more thrust-to-weight ratio. The missile carries both nuclear warheads and a variety of conventional payloads. A family of warheads have been developed, including high-explosive (HE), pre-fragmented unitary HE, incendiary, cluster munitions (bomblets), sub-munitions, and fuel-air explosives (FAE).

For field operations, Prithvi is transported on an all-terrain, eight wheel Kolos Tatra 4x4 truck. The missile is deployed off this vehicle and fired from a simple launcher. Each battery of four Prithvi carrier vehicles is accompanied by a missile re-supply and loading vehicle, a propellant tanker and a command post vehicle to provide target data to the missile's guidance system before launch. In addition, a variety of other support support vehicles and equipment are used to support the batteries in the field.

Prithvi SS-150 which has been in serial production by Bharat Dynamics Limited in Hyderabad since 1997, following a development program that included 12 test flights.

Due to the limited strategic space of Pakistan (the Indus river valley where most major Pakistani cities are located runs close to the Indian frontier) the Prithvi has significant strategic value despite its short range. If it is deployed in states like Kashmir, Punjab and Gujrat which border Pakistan, it would place the capital of Islamabad, as well as the principal cities of Lahore and Karachi in range, as wells as many of Pakistan's strategic military installations.

In September 2000 *Defense News* reported that India would go ahead with full production of about 300 Prithvis for all three branches of the Indian defense forces. The decision, taken by Defence Minister George Fernandes on 25 August, was prompted by Pakistan's test-firing of its Ghauri-III IRBM 10 days earlier, on Independence Day, a senior Indian ministry official, who was not named, was quoted as saying. The production of 300 Prithvis was estimated to cost $200 million. The state-owned Bharat Dynamics in Hyderabad would invest $100 million to ready itself for production. According to company sources, the Army required 150 Prithvis with a range of 150 km while the Navy needed 100 missiles of equal range. 50 Prithvi missiles with a longer range of 250 km, known as Prithvi-II, have to be produced to meet the requirement of the Air Force, the company said.

The Prithvi is a descendant of an earlier program called "Project Devil", an attempt to reverse engineer the Soviet SA-2 liquid fuel surface-to-air missile by the Defense Research and Development Laboratory (DRDL) at Hyderabad. This latter project, initiated under the leadership of Dr. Basanti Dulal Nag Chaudhuri, was a failure and was cancelled in 1978; nonetheless valuable experience and technical skill was obtained which provided the basis for Prithvi.

Development was initiated in 1983 as part of the Integrated Guided Missile Development Programme (IGMDP) under the leadership of Dr. Avil Pakir Jainulabdeen Abdul Kalam, the project manager for the successful SLV-3 program. The Prithvi was intended to be a 150 km tactical missile and was first tested at Sriharikota on 22 February 1988..

In October 1995, 20 pre-production models of the initial Prithvi SS-150 (with a 150 km range) were secretly delivered to the Army to form the 333rd Missile Regiment based in Secunderabad. At this time the Prithvi was not yet equipped with a nuclear warhead. The first deployment of Prithvi missiles (numbering less than a dozen) was at Jalandhar, about 200 km from the Pakistani border in May 1997 prior to its formal operational adoption. Integration and testing of a nuclear warhead was completed in 1997 on the Prithvi SS-150 before these were formally deployed in September 1997. Significantly in December 1998, the Army deployed the Prithvi in a major military exercise code named Shiv-Shakti for the first time since its induction. According to Dr. Sanjay Badri-Maharaj during the 1999 Kargil War four nuclear armed Prithvis were actually deployed for retaliatory strikes. Some units are reported to have been moved to at least two northern locations close to the Pakistani border.

The fourth test flight of the extended range SS-250 was launched on 16 June 2000 at the Interim Test Range (ITR) at Chandipur-on-Sea on the east coast of India. The liquid-propellant weapon carried multiple warheads over a range of 250 km. At this point the SS-250 had not yet been inducted into service.

There is some question whether the Dhanush is really a Prithvi variant, or simply a new missile design in the same size class.

Jane's Missiles and Rockets reported on 9 August 2000 that John Pike of the Federation of American Scientists (FAS) has detected what it believes is the storage site for Indian's Prithvi missiles. An image of the Research Centre Imarat complex taken earlier this year by the Ikonos imaging satellite revealed an installation which Pike says "is probably the primary Prithvi garrison". The Imarat centre is associated with research and development of technologies for missiles and other advanced weapons. "Although it is reported that the 333rd Missile Group is headquartered in Secunderabad, it is evident that the military cantonment would be an inappropriate location for the actual missiles, given the urban congestion of the area," said Pike. The facility at the Imarat centre consists of three pairs of garages, each of which the FAS estimates to be large enough to house four vehicles, which suggests that each pair is used to house a battery of four launchers plus four support vehicles. The facility is surrounded by a security perimeter which incorporates a series of objects which may be guard houses. A nearby complex of buildings could be an administrative support facility for the Prithvi missiles, but "this complex is devoid of functional signatures that would support this interpretation, and is enclosed within a separate security perimeter that is suggestive of institutional associations unrelated to the Prithvi complex."

Dhanush

The Dhanush (Bow, as in "bow and arrow") is a derivative of the Prithvi program, adapted to naval use and given extended range. The first test firing was conducted on 10 April 2000 from the modified Sukanya class off-shore patrol vessel (OPV), INS *Subhadra* in the Bay of Bengal 20 km off Orissa state. It was a only partially successful with, the missile splashing down 25-30 km from its launch point. The launch platform used was a hydraulically-stabilized, rail-mounted platform built on the helicopter deck of the *Subhadra*. Dhanush is probably intended for deployment on a specialized ballistic missile submarine, either conventionally powered or the nuclear powered Advanced Technology Vessel (ATV). Neither is likely in the near future due to technical and financial constraints.

Sagarika

There have been conflicting reports about this program since Clinton administration officials in the United States reported on 27 April 1998 that India was developing a sea-launched ballistic missile with a 200 mile range intended for submarine deployment. More recent reports describe Sagarika as submarine-launched cruise missile (SLCM) intended for the nuclear-powered submarine known as the Advanced Technology Vessel (ATV). The initial description of Sagarika as a ballistic missile may have been due to confusion with the Dhanush. Sagarika had been expected to enter service by 2002, but the program has been troubled as has the ATV submarine itself. Work on an Indian nuclear powered submarine has proceeded fitfully and unsuccessfully for nearly 25 years.

Nuclear Facilities

The centre piece of India's nuclear weapons program is the Bhabha Atomic Research Centre (BARC) in Trombay near Mumbai (Bombay) which is the centre for nuclear weapons associated work. BARC was founded as the Atomic Energy Establishment, Trombay (AEET) on 3 January 1954 by Dr. Homi Jehangir Bhabha. Bhabha was the also the founder India's entire nuclear industry and infrastructure, and India's first Secretary of the Department of Atomic Energy (DAE) when it was created on 3 August 1954. In its early years BARC was already a very large, but primarily civilian-oriented nuclear research laboratory. When India's first nuclear device was designed and fabricated at there, the work was conducted surreptitiously (often at night) to hide it from the rest of the laboratory. But in May 2000 a watershed was reached in this tension between civilian and military work when the civilian Atomic Energy Regulatory Board (AERB) which had been exercising regulatory oversight was split off from BARC. As S. Rajagopal oberved, an expert on nuclear affairs and a professor of the Bangalore-based National Institute of Advanced Studies, this decision effectively reclassified BARC as a nuclear weapons laboratory - a laboratory with a primarily military function though also conducting civilian oriented work in a model similar to the U.S. weapons labs. But without much of the civilian oversight and management that the U.S. labs have.

BARC is the site of the two reactors used for weapons-grade plutonium production: the 40 MW CIRUS (Canadian-Indian-U.S.) reactor, and the 100 MW reactor named R-5, but usually called "Dhruva". Both of these are heavy water moderated and cooled natural uranium reactors.

CIRUS was supplied by Canada in 1954, but uses heavy water supplied by the U.S. (hence its name). The reactor is not under IAEA safeguards (which did not exist when the reactor was sold), although Canada stipulated, and the U.S. supply contract for the heavy water explicitly specified, that it only be used for peaceful purposes. Nonetheless CIRUS has produced much of India's weapon plutonium stockpile, as well as the plutonium for India's 1974 Pokhran-I nuclear test. India argued in 1974 that the contract allows its use in producing peaceful nuclear explosives, which is how it characterized this explosion, though in recent years the project director Raja Ramanna has conceded that this was a sham. CIRUS reactor achieved criticality on 10 July 1960. It can produce 6.6-10.5 kg of plutonium a year (at a capacity factor of 50-80%).

In 1977 work began on the larger Dhruva plutonium production reactor, which was developed indigenous but based on the Canadian supplied technology. It was commissioned on 8 August 1985 but startup problems caused by resonance vibrations from the cooling system damaged fuel assemblies soon required shutdown. After modifications were made (spring clips to damp fuel rod vibration) it began operating at one-quarter power in December 1986 and reached full operation in mid-January 1988. It operates at 100 MW and is capable of producing 16-26 kg of plutonium annually (at a capacity factor of 50-80%).

An additional possible source of plutonium are a number of unsafeguarded CANDU power reactors, including Madras Atomic Power Stations (MAPS, known as Madras I and II, or MAPS-I and MAPS-II); the Narora Atomic Power Stations (NAPS, known as NAPS-I and NAPS-II), and the Kakrapar Atomic Power Station (KAPS). Like CIRUS and Dhruva, the CANDU reactors are heavy-water moderated natural uranium reactors that can be used effectively for weapon-grade plutonium production.

The possible production by MAPS is much larger than CIR and Dhruva combined, although the fuel burnup in power reactors of this type normally produces lower grade plutonium that is less desirable for weapons. Each power station reactor could produce up to 160 kg/yr (at a 60% capacity factor). It is uncertain how practical it is to operate MAPS for weapons grade plutonium production, although even the reactor-grade output has weapons potential. If supergrade plutonium were produced at BARC by short irradiation periods, it could be mixed with MAPS plutonium to extend the plutonium supply. As of November 1998 India had a total of 10 small power reactors operating, with 4 under construction and due to begin operation in 1999, but with 12 more planned or under construction that would boost electrical output by another 5100 MW. Nuclear power supplied 2.65 percent of India's electricity in 1999 and this is expected to reach 10 per cent by 2005. Expectations for nuclear power growth have consistently fallen far short of goals for over 30 years, so this percentage is likely to continue to grow slowly. India's nuclear power program proceeds almost entirely without fuel or technological assistance from other countries.

Partly as a result its power reactors have been among the worst-performing in the world (with regard to capacity factors), reflecting the technical difficulties of the country's isolation, but are apparently now improving significantly. Its industry is largely without IAEA safeguards, though a few plants are under facility-specific safeguards.

In February 2001 India had 14 small nuclear power reactors in commercial operation, two larger ones under construction and ten more planned. The 14 operating ones comprise:

- two 150 MWe BWRs from USA, started up in 1969, now using locally-enriched uranium and are under safeguards,
- two small Canadian PHWRs (1972 & 1980), also under safeguards; and
- ten local PHWRs based on Canadian designs, two of 150 and eight 200 MWe.

The separated plutonium for the 1974 test was produced at the separation plant in Trombay, near to Bombay, capable of processing 50 tonnes of heavy metal fuel/yr. Construction on the first facility there began in the 1950s, and began operating in 1964. In 1974 it was shut down for repair and expansion and reopened in 1983 or 1984. Trombay handles the fuel from both the Cirus and Dhruva reactors. India also can separate plutonium in the Power Reactor Fuel Reprocessing (PREFRE) facility. This plutonium separation plant was built at Tarapur, north of Bombay, and began operating in 1979. The plant has encountered operating problems, but India reports having overcome these by 1990. The nominal annual capacity is given as 100-150 tonnes of CANDU fuel. A much larger plant is now under construction at Kalpakkam sufficient to handle all existing reactors.

Given its immense thorium resources, India is actively interested in developing the thorium/U-233 fuel cycle. India is known to have produced kilogram quantities of U-233 by irradiating thorium in CIR, Dhruva, and MAPS reactors. Substantial production of U-233 is not practical though with natural uranium fueled reactors. The thorium cycle requires more highly enriched fuel to have an acceptable breeding ratio with the non-fissile thorium blanket. Reactor-grade plutonium from MAPS could serve as start-up fuel for U-233 plants in the future. If available U-233 is as effective a weapon material as plutonium.

India has been developing the capability to produce heavy water domestically to provide the moderator load for future reactors. The heavy water for almost all existing reactors was imported however. The 110 tonnes of unsafeguarded moderator for Dhruva and Madras I and II were ironically provided by China.

India has acquired and developed centrifuge technology and built centrifuge enrichment plants in Trombay and Mysore in the 1980s. The larger Rare Metals Plant (RMP), as it is called, at Mysore has a cascade capable of producing 30% enriched uranium in kilogram quantities, beginning in 1992-93, although reliability has been a problem. These enrichment plants appear to have no role in India's power reactor development plans, so they may be intended to offset the prestige of Pakistan's enrichment capability, or to provide additional standby weapons production capability. India has reported that it plans to build an enriched uranium reactor, and a domestically fueled nuclear submarine.

India's interest in light weight weapon design can be surmised from BARC's acquisition in the 1980s of a vacuum hot pressing machine, suitable for forming large high-quality beryllium forgings, as well as large amounts of high purity beryllium metal. India is known to manufacture tritium, and may have developed designs for fusion-boosted weapons.

India is not a signatory to NPT and has opposed the treaty as discriminatory to non-weapons states. India has previously taken the position that a worldwide ban on nuclear testing, and the production of fissionable material for weapons is called for. Except for China, which continues testing, there is now a de facto halt to testing worldwide, as well as the production of weapons grade plutonium and uranium by the US and Russia. India has shown no interest so far in restricting its own activities despite these changes in the world situation. India has also rejected offers at bilateral negotiation with Pakistan, but in December 1988 the two nations signed an agreement prohibiting attacks on each other's nuclear installations and informing each other of their locations (though not their purposes).

NUCLEAR FACILITIES

The center piece of India's nuclear weapons program is the Bhabha Atomic Research Center (BARC) in Trombay near Mumbai (Bombay) which is the center for nuclear weapons associated work. BARC was founded as the Atomic Energy Establishment, Trombay (AEET) on 3 January 1954 by Dr. Homi Jehangir Bhabha. Bhabha was the also the founder India's entire nuclear industry and infrastructure, and India's first Secretary of the Department of Atomic Energy (DAE) when it was created on 3 August 1954. In its early years BARC was already a very large, but primarily civilian-oriented nuclear research laboratory. When India's first nuclear device was designed and fabricated at there, the work was conducted surreptitiously (often at night) to hide it from the rest of the laboratory. But in May 2000 a watershed was reached in this tension between civilian and military work when the civilian Atomic Energy Regulatory Board (AERB) which had been exercising regulatory oversight was split off from BARC. As S. Rajagopal oberved, an expert on nuclear affairs and a professor of the Bangalore-based National Institute of Advanced Studies, this decision effectively reclassified BARC as a nuclear weapons laboratory - a laboratory with a primarily military function though also conducting civilian oriented work in a model similar to the

U.S. weapons labs. But without much of the civilian oversight and management that the U.S. labs have. BARC is the site of the two reactors used for weapons-grade plutonium production: the 40 MW CIRUS (Canadian-Indian-U.S.) reactor, and the 100 MW reactor named R-5, but usually called "Dhruva". Both of these are heavy water moderated and cooled natural uranium reactors.

CIRUS was supplied by Canada in 1954, but uses heavy water supplied by the U.S. (hence its name). The reactor is not under IAEA safeguards (which did not exist when the reactor was sold), although Canada stipulated, and the U.S. supply contract for the heavy water explicitly specified, that it only be used for peaceful purposes. Nonetheless CIRUS has produced much of India's weapon plutonium stockpile, as well as the plutonium for India's 1974 Pokhran-I nuclear test. India argued in 1974 that the contract allows its use in producing peaceful nuclear explosives, which is how it characterized this explosion, though in recent years the project director Raja Ramanna has conceded that this was a sham. CIRUS reactor achieved criticality on 10 July 1960. It can produce 6.6-10.5 kg of plutonium a year (at a capacity factor of 50-80%).

In 1977 work began on the larger Dhruva plutonium production reactor, which was developed indigenous but based on the Canadian supplied technology. It was commissioned on 8 August 1985 but startup problems caused by resonance vibrations from the cooling system damaged fuel assemblies soon required shutdown. After modifications were made (spring clips to damp fuel rod vibration) it began operating at one-quarter power in December 1986 and reached full operation in mid-January 1988. It operates at 100 MW and is capable of producing 16-26 kg of plutonium annually (at a capacity factor of 50-80%).

An additional possible source of plutonium are a number of unsafeguarded CANDU power reactors, including Madras Atomic Power Stations (MAPS, known as Madras I and II, or MAPS-I and MAPS-II); the Narora Atomic Power Stations (NAPS, known as NAPS-I and NAPS-II), and the Kakrapar Atomic Power Station (KAPS). Like CIRUS and Dhruva, the CANDU reactors are heavy-water moderated natural uranium reactors that can be used effectively for weapon-grade plutonium production. The possible production by MAPS is much larger than CIR and Dhruva combined, although the fuel burnup in power reactors of this type normally produces lower grade plutonium that is less desirable for weapons. Each power station reactor could produce up to 160 kg/yr (at a 60% capacity factor). It is uncertain how practical it is to operate MAPS for weapons grade plutonium production, although even the reactor-grade output has weapons potential. If supergrade plutonium were produced at BARC by short irradiation periods, it could be mixed with MAPS plutonium to extend the plutonium supply. As of November 1998 India had a total of 10 small power reactors operating, with 4 under construction and due to begin operation in 1999, but with 12 more planned or under construction that would boost electrical output by another 5100 MW.

Nuclear power supplied 2.65 percent of India's electricity in 1999 and this is expected to reach 10 per cent by 2005. Expectations for nuclear power growth have consistently fallen far short of goals for over 30 years, so this percentage is likely to continue to grow slowly. India's nuclear power program proceeds almost entirely without fuel or technological assistance from other countries. Partly as a result its power reactors have been among the worst-performing in the world (with regard to capacity factors), reflecting the technical difficulties of the country's isolation, but are apparently now improving significantly. Its industry is largely without IAEA safeguards, though a few plants are under facility-specific safeguards.

Bibliography

Allison, Graham: *Nuclear Terrorism: The Ultimate Preventable Catastrophe*, New York: Times Books, 2004.

Bhatia, Shyam: *India's Nuclear Bomb*, Ghaziabad: Vikas Publishing House, 1979.

Dunne, J. P. and Brauer, J.: *Arms Trade and Economic Development: Theory, Policy*, Routledge, London, 2004.

Grimmett, Richard F.: *Conventional Arms Transfers to Developing Nations, 1993–2000*. Congressional Research Service Report to Congress. Washington, D.C., 2001.

Harkavy, Robert E. *The Arms Trade and International Systems*. Cambridge, Mass., 1975.

Kapur, Ashok: *Pakistan's Nuclear Development*, New York: Croom Helm, 1987.

Krause, Keith. *Arms and the State: Patterns of Military Production and Trade*. Cambridge, U.K., 1992.

Nininger, Robert D. *Minerals for Atomic Energy*. New York: D. Van Nostrand Company, Inc., 1954.

Pierre, Andrew J. *The Global Politics of Arms Sales*. Princeton, N.J., 1982.

Rhodes, Richard, *The Making of the Atomic Bomb*, New York: Simon and Schuster, 1988.

Robert E. Harkavy, eds. *Arms Transfers in the Modern World*. New York, 1979.

Schroeer, Dietrich, *Science, Technology, and the Nuclear Arms Race*, Ontario: John Wiley & Sons, 1984.

Sherwin, Martin J. A World Destroyed: *The Atomic Bomb and the Grand Alliance*. New York: Vintage Books, 1977.

Smith, C.: *The Diffusion of Small Arms and Light Weapons in Pakistan and Northern India*, Centre for Defence Studies, Brassey's, London, 1993.

Index

P

S

❑❑❑